"SIR, WE WOULD SEE JESUS"

A STUDY OF THE LIFE OF CHRIST

by
Bob and Sandra Waldron

GUARDIAN
OF TRUTH

ISBN 1-58427-113-2

Guardian of Truth Foundation
P.O. Box 9670
Bowling Green, Kentucky 42102

During the last week of Jesus' life, some Greeks were among those who had come for the Passover. They approached Philip and said, "Sir, we would see Jesus" (John 12:20-21).

What a wonderful thing it would be if all men wished to see Jesus. Though we cannot see Him personally in this life, we can see Him through the word-pictures left of Him by His disciples. Our desire in this work is to help men "see" Jesus in His moral and spiritual glory, in His gracious deity, and in His perfect humanity.

The reader will be able to detect from some statements in the book that this work is part of a greater whole. It is part of a series of books covering the entire Bible story from Genesis to Revelation. Each book can stand alone as a study source for a particular period of history, or it can be used in combination with the others. The entire series was written as a help to teachers in their preparation to teach Bible classes. If this book is used as part of the series of studies through the whole Bible, plan to spend at least two quarters on the life of Christ. You might even choose to spend a third quarter covering the last week and the resurrection and continue into the first part of Acts as the great commission begins to be carried out.

Sir, We Would See Jesus was written as a resource for teachers, to help them learn how to put the Bible in story form, to present the life of Jesus as a coherent, unified whole, and to provide notes which would be helpful to any student. The book will be of great value to anyone who wishes to read an easily understood, yet thorough study of the life of Christ. We hope it is the kind of book anyone could sit down and just read for the sheer pleasure of it.

It must be clearly understood that this work is *not* a translation. It does not adhere to the Greek New Testament closely enough for that; yet every effort has been made to bring out the sense of the text. The book is a retelling of the story of Jesus.

A second caution we would like to give is that our desire is to help people learn to read and study their Bibles. We do not want any of our writings to ever become a substitute for the Bible. Use this work as a key to open the door to understanding your Bible, not as something to replace it.

Our hope is that through this work, the "light of the gospel of the glory of Christ, who is the image of God" may dawn upon men (2 Cor. 4:4).

Table of Contents

Outline of Jesus' Life

Basic Outline

Years of Preparation
Beginning Ministry
Great Galilean Ministry
Period of Retirement
Closing Ministry
The Last Week
Resurrection
Exaltation

I. **The Years of Preparation** (the first thirty years)

A. The birth of John

1. Gabriel announces the birth of John to Zacharias (Luke 1:5-25)
2. Gabriel announces the birth of Jesus to Mary (Luke 1:26-38)
3. Mary visits Elizabeth (Luke 1:39-56)
4. The birth of John the Baptist (Luke 1:57-80)

B. The birth of Jesus

1. The angel announces the birth of Jesus to Joseph (Matt. 1:18-25)
2. The birth of Jesus (Matt. 2:1a; Luke 2:1-7)
3. The angel announces the birth of Jesus to shepherds (Luke 2:8-20)
4. Circumcision and naming of Jesus (Luke 2:21)
5. Presentation of Jesus at the temple (Luke 2:22-24)
6. Simeon's words about the baby (Luke 2:25-35)
7. Anna the prophetess (Luke 2:36-38)
8. The visit of the wise men (Matt. 2:1-12)
9. Flight into Egypt (Matt. 2:13-15)
10. Herod commands the slaughter of the babes of Bethlehem (Matt. 2:16-18)
11. Joseph takes his family back to Nazareth (Matt. 2:19-23)
12. Why worship this baby? Who is He? (John 1:1-18; Matt. 1:1-17; Luke 3:23-38)
13. Jesus grows up

        a.   Jesus in the temple at 12 years of age (Luke 2:41-51)

        b.   Jesus finishes growing up (Luke 2:52)

  C.   The beginning of John's ministry

      1.   Why John came (Matt. 3:1-3; Mark 1:2-3; Luke 3:1-6; John 1:6-18)

      2.   John's work (Matt. 3:4-12; Mark 1:4-8; Luke 3:7-18)

II. **The Beginning of Jesus' Ministry** (3 to 6 months)

  A.   The baptism of Jesus (Matt. 3:13-17; Mark 1:9-11; Luke 3:21-22; John 1:32-34)

  B.   Temptation of Jesus (Matt. 4:1-11; Mark 1:12-13; Luke 4:1-13)

  C.   John's testimony

      1.   John's testimony of himself (John 1:19-28)

      2.   John's testimony regarding Jesus' baptism (John 1:29-34)

      3.   John directs his disciples to Jesus (John 1:35-42)

  D.   Jesus meets Philip and Nathanael (John 1:43-51)

  E.   First miracle in Cana of Galilee (John 2:1-11)

  F.   Jesus visits Capernaum for a few days (John 2:12)

  G.   Jesus attends the first Passover in His ministry

      1.   Cleansing of the temple (John 2:13-22)

      2.   Many believe on Jesus during the feast (John 2:23-25)

      3.   Nicodemus visits with Jesus (John 3:1-21)

  H.   Jesus remains in Judea for a time

      1.   Jesus preaches in the countryside of Judea (John 3:22-24)

      2.   John's testimony regarding Jesus (John 3:25-36)

      3.   John rebukes Herod Antipas and is put in prison (Matt. 14:1-5; Luke 3:19-20)

  I.   Jesus leaves Judea

      1.   Jesus' reasons for leaving Judea (Matt. 4:12; Mark 1:14; Luke 4:14; John 4:1-4)

      2.   On His way through Samaria, Jesus talks to the woman of Samaria and then to others of the city (John 4:4-42)

      3.   Jesus arrives in Galilee (Matt. 4:12-17; Mark 1:14-15; Luke 4:14-15; John 4:43-45)

III. **The Great Galilean Ministry** (From this point on, we will use Mark's account for the order of the stories told. As we go along, we will also include stories that fit into the period that are told in other accounts but not in Mark.) (about 18 to 21 months)

  A.   The healing of the nobleman's son (John 4:46-54)

  B.   The first rejection at Nazareth (Luke 4:16-36)

  C.   Jesus moves to Capernaum (Matt. 4:13-16)

1. Jesus calls four disciples to follow Him (Mark 1:16-20; Matt. 4:18-22; Luke 5:1-11)
2. Jesus teaches in a synagogue and heals a demoniac (Mark 1:21-28; Luke 4:31-37)
3. Jesus heals Peter's mother-in-law (Mark 1:29-34; Matt. 8:14-17; Luke 4:38-41)

D. Jesus tours Galilee, preaching and healing (Mark 1:35-39; Matt. 4:23-25; Luke 4:42-44)
E. Healing of a leper (Mark 1:40-45; Matt. 8:2-4; Luke 5:12-16)
F. Jesus heals a paralytic in Capernaum (Mark 2:1-12; Matt. 9:2-8; Luke 5:17-26)
G. The call of Matthew (Levi) and his feast in honor of Jesus (Mark 2:13-17; Matt. 9:9-13; Luke 5:27-32)

   1. Jesus defends His disciples for their feasting instead of fasting (Mark 2:18-22; Matt. 9:14-17; Luke 5:33-39)

H. Conflicts about the sabbath

   1. Jesus attends a feast of the Jews and heals a lame man (John 5:1-47)
   2. The disciples pluck grain on the sabbath (Mark 2:23-28; Matt. 12:1-8; Luke 6:1-5)
   3. Jesus heals a man with a withered hand on the sabbath (Mark 3:1-6; Matt. 12:9-14; Luke 6:6-11)

I. Jesus teaches and heals great multitudes by the Sea of Galilee (Mark 3:7-12; Matt.12:15-21)
J. After a night of prayer, Jesus selects twelve apostles (Mark 3:13-19; Luke 6:12-16)
K. The sermon on the mount (Matt. 5-7; Luke 6:17-49)

   1. Matthew 5; Luke 6:17-36
   2. Matthew 6
   3. Matthew 7; Luke 6:37-49

L. Stories from Matthew and Luke that fit this period

   1. Jesus heals a centurion's servant at Capernaum (Matt. 8:5-13; Luke 7:1-10)
   2. Jesus raises the widow's son at Nain (Luke 7:11-17)
   3. Message from John the Baptist; Jesus praises John (Matt. 11:2-19; Luke 7:8-35)
   4. Woes upon the cities of Galilee (Matt. 11:20-30)
   5. Jesus attends a feast given by Simon the Pharisee; a sinful woman anoints His feet (Luke 7:36-50)
   6. Second tour of Galilee (Luke 8:1-3)

M. Jesus' busy day

   1. Jesus is accused of casting out demons by Beelzebub (Mark 3:20-30; Matt. 12:22-37)

2. Scribes and Pharisees ask for a sign (Matt. 12:38-45)
3. Jesus' mother and brethren come to see Him (Mark 3:31-35; Matt. 12:46-50; Luke 8:19-21)
4. Jesus teaches in parables

    a. Parable of the sower (Mark 4:3-25; Matt. 13:3-23; Luke 8:5-18)
    b. Parable of seed growing in the ground (Mark 4:26-29)
    c. Parable of the tares (Matt. 13:24-30, 36-43)
    d. Parable of the mustard seed (Mark 4:30-32; Matt. 13:31-32)
    e. Parable of the leaven (Mark 4:33-34; Matt. 13:33-35)
    f. Parable of the hidden treasure (Matt. 13:44)
    g. Parable of the pearl of great price (Matt. 13:45-46)
    h. Parable of the net (Matt. 13:47-50)
    i. Parable of the householder (Matt. 13:51-53)

N. Jesus stills the storm at sea (Mark 4:35-41; Matt. 8:18,23-27; Luke 8:22-25)

    1. Jesus heals the Gerasene demoniac (Mark 5:1-20; Matt. 8:28-34; Luke 8:26-39)

O. Healing of Jairus' daughter and the healing of the woman with an issue of blood (Mark 5:21-43; Matt. 9:18-26; Luke 8:40-56)
P. Jesus heals two blind men and a mute demoniac (Matt. 9:27-34)
Q. The last visit to Nazareth (Mark 6:1-6; Matt. 13:54-58)
R. Jesus' third tour of Galilee; The Twelve are sent on the limited commission (Mark 6:6-13; Matt. 9:35-11:1; Luke 9:1-6)
S. Herod Antipas hears of Jesus' work; Story of how Herod killed John (Mark 6:14-29; Matt. 14:1-12; Luke 9:7-9)

IV. **The Period of Retirement** (about 6 months; period begins at about the time of the Passover — one year before His death)

A. The first retirement from the crowds

    1. The twelve return from their mission; Jesus seeks rest across the Sea of Galilee; the multitudes follow and He feeds the 5,000 (Mark 6:30-44; Matt. 14:13-21; Luke 9:10-17; John 6:1-15)
    2. Jesus withdraws to a mountain to escape being made king (Mark 6:45-46; Matt. 14:22-23; John 6:14-15)
    3. Jesus walks on the water (Mark 6:47-52; Matt. 14:24-33; John 6:16-21)
    4. The reception of Jesus at Gennesaret (Mark 6:53-56; Matt. 14:34-36)
    5. The crowds begin to turn back; collapse of the work in Galilee (John 6:22-71)
    6. The Pharisees from Jerusalem criticize Jesus concerning the ceremonial washings (Mark 7:1-23; Matt. 15:1-20; John 7:1)

B. The second retirement

    1. Jesus and His apostles go to the region of Tyre and Sidon; He heals the daughter of a Syro-Phoenician woman (Mark 7:24-30; Matt. 15:21-28)

C.   The third withdrawal - through Decapolis

    1.   Feeding of the 4,000 (Mark 7:31-8:9; Matt. 15:29-38)
    2.   A brief visit to Dalmanutha (Magadan); Argument with the Pharisees and Sadducees (first public confrontation with the Sadducees) (Mark 8:10-12; Matt. 15:39-16:4)

D.   The fourth retirement — back to Bethsaida Julias and on to Caesarea Philippi

    1.   Jesus rebukes the spiritual dullness of the disciples (Mark 8:13-21; Matt. 16:5-12)
    2.   Jesus heals a blind man at Bethsaida (Mark 8:22-26)
    3.   Caesarea Philippi

        a.   Peter's confession of Christ as the Son of God (Mark 8:27-30; Matt. 16:13-20; Luke 9:18-21)
        b.   Jesus foretells His death and resurrection (for the first time to speak of it beyond the "riddles" such as "destroying the temple" and the "sign of Jonah;" time is barely over six months before His death) (Mark 8:31-37; Matt. 16:21-26; Luke 9:22-25)
        c.   Prediction of the coming of the Son of Man in His kingdom and in His glory within that generation (Mark 8:38-9:1; Matt. 16:27-28; Luke 9:26-27)

    4.   The transfiguration (Mark 9:2-8; Matt. 17:1-8; Luke 9:28-36)

        a.   The disciples question Jesus about Elijah as they come down the mountain (Mark 9:9-13; Matt. 17:9-13; Luke 9:36)
        b.   Jesus heals a demoniac boy whom His disciples could not heal (Mark 9:14-29; Matt. 17:14-20; Luke 9:37-43)

    5.   Jesus again foretells His death and resurrection (Mark 9:30-32; Matt. 17:22-23; Luke 9:43-45)
    6.   Jesus pays the half-shekel for the temple tax (Matt. 17:24-27)
    7.   The Twelve dispute over who would be the greatest in the kingdom of heaven; Jesus uses a child to teach lesson (Mark 9:33-37; Matt. 18:1-14; Luke 9:46-48)
    8.   Lesson on how to deal with a brother who has sinned against another brother; duty of forgiving the penitent (Matt. 18:15-35)
    9.   Christ's followers must be willing to give up everything to follow Him (Matt. 8:19-22; Luke 9:57-62)
    10.   Jesus' brothers tell Him to show Himself to the world (John 7:2-9)
    11.   Jesus goes privately to Jerusalem through Samaria (Luke 9:51-56; John 7:10)

V.   **The Close of Jesus' Ministry** (about 6 months; it is now fall; He will die in the spring)

A.   Jesus arrives in Jerusalem for the Feast of Tabernacles

    1.   He causes great excitement concerning the Messiah (John 7:1-8:1)

2. An adulteress is brought to Jesus (John 8:2-11)
3. Jesus claims to be the light of the world (John 8:12-20)
4. Jesus compares His Father and the Jews' father (John 8:21-59)
5. Jesus heals a man born blind (John 9:1-41)
6. Jesus is the good shepherd (John 10:1-21)

B. The stories in Luke that occur at this time (location uncertain)

1. Mission of the seventy (Luke 10:1-24)
2. Parable of the good Samaritan (Luke 10:25-37)
3. Jesus visits Mary and Martha (Luke 10:38-42)
4. Jesus encourages His disciples to pray (Luke 11:1-13)
5. Blasphemous accusations against Jesus (Luke 11:14-36)
6. While eating with a Pharisee, Jesus condemns the Pharisees and stirs up their wrath (Luke 11:37-54)
7. Jesus preaches to great multitudes (Luke 12:1-59)

   a. Warnings and encouragements (Luke 12:1-12)
   b. Parable of the rich fool (Luke 12:13-21)
   c. Lessons on attitudes toward material things (Luke 12:22-34)
   d. Parables about the waiting servants and the wise steward (Luke 12:35-48)
   e. Jesus said He came to bring division, not peace; Signs of the times (Luke 12:49-59)

8. The necessity of repentance for all; parable of the fig tree (Luke 13:1-9)
9. Jesus heals a crippled woman on the sabbath; repetition of the parables of the mustard seed and of the leaven (Luke 13:10-21)
10. Jesus teaches as He journeys toward Jerusalem; He is warned about Herod Antipas (Luke 13:22-35)

C. Feast of Dedication (by now it is winter; about three months before His death) (John 10:22-39)
D. Jesus withdraws to Perea (John 10:40-42)

1. Jesus eats with a ruler of the Pharisees on a sabbath day (Luke 14:1-24)
   a. He is being watched to see if He will heal a man; He does so and then defends His action (Luke 14:1-6)
   b. He rebukes the Pharisees for trying to sit in chief seats at feasts (Luke 14:7-14)
   c. Parable of wedding feast (Luke 14:15-24)

2. Jesus warns the multitudes about the cost of discipleship (Luke 14:25-35)
3. Three great parables reproving the Pharisees for their attitude toward sinners (Luke 15:1-32)

   a. The lost sheep (Luke 15:1-7)
   b. The lost coin (Luke 15:8-10)
   c. The lost boy (Luke 15:11-32)

4. Three parables on stewardship (Luke 16:1-17:10)

    a. The unjust steward (Luke 16:1-18)
    b. The rich man and Lazarus (Luke 16:19-31)
    c. The unprofitable servant (Luke 17:1-10)

5. Jesus raises Lazarus from the dead (John 11:1-44)
6. The effect of raising Lazarus (John 11:45-54)

E. Jesus starts His last journey to Jerusalem (Luke 17:11)

1. Ten lepers are healed (Luke 17:12-19)
2. Jesus explains the nature of the kingdom and predicts judgment (Luke 17:20-37)
3. Two parables on prayer: the unrighteous judge and the Pharisee and the publican (Luke 18:1-14)
4. As He travels through Perea, Jesus teaches concerning divorce and remarriage (Mark 10:1-12; Matt. 19:1-12)
5. Jesus receives little children (Mark 10:13-16; Matt. 19:13-15; Luke 18:15-17)
6. The rich young ruler (Mark 10:17-31; Matt. 19:16-20:16; Luke 18:18-30)

    a. The young ruler comes and Jesus speaks of the perils of riches (Mark 10:17-27; Matt. 19:16-26; Luke 18:18-27)
    b. Reward for following the Lord (Mark 10:28-31; Matt. 19:21-20:16; Luke 18:28-30)

        (1) Parable of the landowner who hired men for his vineyard (Matt. 20:1-16)

7. Jesus again foretells His death and resurrection (Mark 10:32-34; Matt. 20:17-19)
8. Jesus rebukes the selfish request of James and John (Mark 10:35-45; Matt. 20:20-28)
9. Jesus arrives in Jericho (Mark 10:46; Matt. 20:29; Luke 18:35)

    a. He heals blind Bartimaeus and his companion (Mark 10;47-52; Matt. 20:30-34; Luke 18:36-43)
    b. He meets Zacchaeus and tells the parable of the pounds at his home (Luke 19:1-28)

VI. **The Last Week**

A. Jesus arrives in Bethany (He probably reached there late Friday evening)

1. Multitudes gathering in Jerusalem for the Passover wonder about Jesus; officials have given orders to report it if anyone sees Jesus so they can arrest Him (John 11:55-57)
2. On Saturday evening, there is a feast given in Jesus' honor; Mary anoints His

feet (John 12:1-11; Mark 14:1-11; Matt. 26:6-13)

B.   On Sunday: the triumphal entry to Jerusalem (Mark 11:1-11; Matt. 21:1-11,14-17; Luke 19:29-44; John 12:12-19)

    1.   Returns to Bethany for the evening (Mark 11:11)

C.   On Monday:

    1.   Barren fig tree cursed (Mark 11:12-14; Matt. 21:18-19a)
    2.   Second cleansing of the temple (Mark 11:15-18; Matt. 21:12-13; Luke 19:45-48)
    3.   Certain Greeks desire to see Jesus; a sermon follows (John 12:20-50)

D.   On Tuesday: The day of conflict

    1.   The barren fig tree found to be withered (Mark 11:19-25; Matt. 21:19b-22; Luke 21:37-38)
    2.   The chief priests, scribes, and Sanhedrin come to challenge Jesus' authority (Mark 11:27-12:12; Matt. 21:23-22:14; Luke 20:1-19)

        a.   Jesus asks them about John's baptism (Mark 11:27-33; Matt. 21:23-27; Luke 20:1-8)
        b.   Parable of two sons (Matt. 21:28-31)
        c.   Parable of the wicked husbandmen (Mark 12:1-12; Matt. 21:33-46; Luke 20:9-19)
        d.   Parable of the wedding feast (Matt. 22:1-14)

    3.   The Pharisees and Herodians seek to trap Jesus with a question about paying tribute to Caesar (Mark 12:13-17; Matt. 22:15-22; Luke 20:20-26)
    4.   The Sadducees question Jesus about the resurrection (Mark 12:18-27; Matt. 22:23-33; Luke 20:27-40)
    5.   A scribe questions Jesus: What is the greatest commandment? (Mark 12:28-34; Matt. 22:34-40)
    6.   Jesus poses a question to the scribes and Pharisees: Whose son is the Christ? (Mark 12:35-37; Matt. 22:41-46; Luke 20:41-44)
    7.   Jesus denounces the scribes and Pharisees (Mark 12:38-40; Matt. 23:1-39; Luke 20:45-47)
    8.   The widow's mite (Mark 12:41-44; Luke 21:1-4)
    9.   Jesus speaks of the destruction of Jerusalem and of His coming (Mark 13; Matt. 24; Luke 21:5-36)
    10.   Three judgment parables (Matt. 25)

        a.   Ten virgins (Matt. 25:1-13)
        b.   The talents (Matt. 25:14-30)
        c.   Separation of the sheep and the goats (Matt. 25:31-46)

    11.   Jesus again predicts His crucifixion which would take place only two days later (Matt. 26:1-2)

12. The chief priests and elders plot to kill Him, but plan to wait until after the feast is over lest there be a riot (Mark 14:1-2; Matt. 26:3-5; Luke 22:1-2)

E. On Wednesday: a day of retirement with His disciples

1. Judas bargains with the rulers to betray Jesus (either late Tuesday evening or on Wednesday) (Mark 14:10-11; Matt. 26:14-16; Luke 22:3-6)

F. On Thursday: The Passover

1. Preparation for the last Passover (Mark 13:12-16; Matt. 26:17-19; Luke 22:7-13)
2. The last supper

   a. Strife among the apostles; Jesus washes their feet (Mark 14:17; Matt. 26:20; Luke 22:14-16; John 13:1-17)
   b. Jesus points out Judas as the betrayer (Mark 14:18-21; Matt. 26:21-25; Luke 22:21-23; John 13:18-30)
   c. Jesus warns all the disciples (Peter in particular) against desertion (Mark 14:27-31; Matt.26:31-35; Luke 22:31-38; John 13:31-38)
   d. Jesus institutes the Lord's Supper (Mark 14:22-25; Matt.26:26-29; Luke 22:17-20; cf. 1 Cor. 11:23-26)
   e. The farewell discourse in the upper room (John 14)
   f. Jesus and the disciples leave the upper room to go to the Mount of Olives (Mark 14:26; Matt. 26:30)

      (1) Discourse on the way to Gethsemane (John 15-16)
      (2) Jesus' prayer to the Father (John 17)

   g. Jesus enters Gethsemane and prays in agony (Mark 14:32-42; Matt. 26:36-46; Luke 22:39-46; John 18:1)
   h. Jesus is arrested (Mark 14:43-52; Matt. 26:47-56; Luke 22:47-53; John 18:2-12)

G. The trial of Jesus (late Thursday night and early Friday morning)

1. Jesus before Annas (John 18:12-14, 19-23)
2. At the house of Caiaphas; He is condemned and mistreated by the Sanhedrin (Mark 14:53,55-65; Matt. 26:59-68; Luke 22:54,63-65; John 18:24)
3. Peter denies Jesus three times (Mark 14:54,66-72; Matt. 26:58,69-75; Luke 22:54-62; John 18:15-18,25-27)
4. After dawn, Jesus is formally condemned by the Sanhedrin (Mark 15:1; Matt. 27:1; Luke 22:66-71)
5. Judas Iscariot commits suicide (Matt. 27:3-10; Acts 1:18-19)
6. Jesus is brought before Pilate the first time (Mark 15:1-5; Matt. 27:2,11-14; Luke 23:1-7; John 18:28-38)
7. Jesus before Herod Antipas (Luke 23:6-12)
8. Jesus before Pilate the second time (Mark 15:6-14; Matt. 27:15-23; Luke 23:13-

22; John 18:39-40)

9.   Jesus is scourged and mocked by the Roman soldiers (Mark 15:16-19; Matt. 27:27-31; John 19:1-3)

10.   Pilate gives in to the Jews and sentences Jesus to be crucified (Mark 15:12-15; Matt. 27:22-26; Luke 23:20-25; John 19:4-16)

11.   Jesus is led away to be crucified (Mark 15:20-23; Matt. 27:31-34; Luke 23:26-32; John 19:16-17)

H.   During the day on Friday: Jesus on the cross

1.   From nine o'clock until twelve noon (Mark 15:24-32; Matt. 27:35-44; Luke 23:33-43; John 19:18-27)

2.   From twelve noon until three o'clock in the afternoon (Mark 15:33-37; Matt. 27:45-50; Luke 23:44-46; John 19:28-30)

3.   Miracles accompanying the death of Christ (Mark 15:38-41; Matt. 27:51-56; Luke 23:45,47-49)

4.   The burial of Jesus' body in the tomb of Joseph of Arimathea (late Friday evening) (Mark 15:42-46; Matt. 27:57-60; Luke 23:50-54; John 19:31-42)

I.   On Saturday: The watch over the sabbath day (Mark 15:47; Matt. 27:61-66; Luke 23:55-56)

VII. The Resurrection and Exaltation

A.   On Sunday: The resurrection (Matt. 28:2-4)

1.   Visit of the women to the tomb to finish burying Jesus (Mark 16:2-8; Matt. 28:1-8; Luke 24:1-8; John 20:1)

2.   Mary Magdalene tells Peter and John about the empty tomb (John 20:2-10; Luke 24:12)

3.   Appearance of Jesus to Mary Magdalene (Mark 16:9-11; John 20:11-18)

4.   Appearance of Jesus to the other women (Matt. 28:9-10)

5.   The women report their findings to the other disciples (Luke 24:9-12)

6.   The guards report to the Jewish rulers (Matt. 28:11-15)

7.   Jesus appears to two disciples on the road to Emmaus (Mark 16:12-13; Luke 24:13-32)

8.   Appearance of Jesus to Peter (Mark 16:13; Luke 24:33-35; 1 Cor. 15:5)

9.   The appearance of Jesus to the disciples who were gathered together (Mark 16:14; Luke 24:36-43; John 20:19-23)

10.   Thomas was absent (John 20:24-25)

B.   The appearances of Jesus during the remainder of the forty days

1.   To the apostles one week later and the convincing of Thomas (John 20:26-31)

2.   To seven disciples by the Sea of Galilee; miraculous catch of fish (John 21)

3.   To five hundred brethren at once and to James (1 Cor. 15:6-7)

4.   The occasions of the great commission:

God's Plan for Salvation Now Complete
Go Tell the Good News

Introduction to the Life of Christ

We have come to the climax of our study of the Bible. We know that in the beginning God promised that the seed of the woman would come to bruise the head of Satan (Gen. 3:15). God told Abraham that all families of the earth would be blessed through his seed (Gen. 12:1-3). The Son of David was coming, and through Him the throne of David would be established forever (2 Sam. 7:11-14). This One would be born at Bethlehem of Judah (Mic. 5:2). His name would be Immanuel, which means "God with us" (Isa. 7:14). He would redeem His people from sin, not the Jews only, but also the Gentiles (Isa. 49:6). In the days of the Roman Empire the God of heaven would set up a kingdom which would never be destroyed (Dan. 2:44).

"In the fullness of the times God sent forth His Son born of a woman, born under the law, that He might redeem them that were under the law" (Gal. 4:4).

The day of the Lord was at hand. It was time for the messenger of the covenant to come (Mal. 3:1). In the day in which Jesus came there was an air of expectant waiting. Many anticipated the coming of the Lord's Christ. God had made His preparations; promise and prophecy had been given; the signs of the Messiah had been appointed. God had prepared for Himself a nation of people who refused to worship idols. Their holy scriptures, the Old Testament, had been translated into Greek, the most widely spoken language of the day. The sons of Israel were scattered throughout the world; scarcely a city knew not their presence. Their example had moved many of the Gentiles to accept Jehovah the true God.

Most of God's people themselves had grown lax, however. It was necessary that the forerunner of the Christ come and prepare His way. It was time for "Elijah" to come and "turn the heart of the fathers to the children and the heart of the children to their fathers" (Mal. 4:5-6).

As you approach the study of the life of Christ, help your students realize that the coming and the work of Christ are

1

the climax of the whole Bible story. Mankind had needed a savior since the day the first sin was committed in the Garden of Eden. From that moment until now in the Bible story we have watched how God has dealt with wicked mankind and how He has continually promised a day of redemption. That time has come in our story. Make it rich; show its glory in your presentation. It is the greatest story of all history.

The gospel writers were not historians in the normal sense. They did not try to present the story of Jesus in a strict historical, chronological order. Instead, they were presenting pictures of this man, this Divine-Man, in order to help us realize what He was like, what it would have been like to be there with Him. They were proving to their own generation and to all generations since that He was indeed all He claimed to be — "God with us," Deity come to earth in human form. Therefore, it is difficult for us to learn an exact chronology of the life of Christ. The broad outline is easy, but the details of which miracle was done on which day or which sermon was preached next is impossible to know exactly. We will be organizing this material into a chronlogical order, and we will emphasize the broad periods of Jesus' life, but do not be surprised if you see another chronological account which gives some of the stories in another order. Let us look at the broad outline of His life. Take time to memorize it and to note as we move from one period into the next.

     I. The Years of Preparation
    II. Beginning of Jesus' Ministry
   III. The Great Galilean Ministry
   IV. The Period of Retirement
    V. The Close of Jesus' Ministry
   VI. The Last Week
  VII. The Resurrection and Exaltation

A complete outline is provided immediately after the table of contents. Take time to look at it often and see how the stories fit together into this broad outline of His life.

There are many, many lessons that can be gleaned from the stories about Jesus, but no matter which points you emphasize, remember that your first priority is to *tell* each story so as to make it come alive. Help your students feel the awe and wonder that accompanied the miracles. Help them marvel at the lessons that were taught. Help them grow in their own ability to visualize and copy the example Christ left us.

As you begin, let your students experience the anticipation. The time is at hand. After a silence of over 400 years, events of great consequence are about to begin. The first of these marvelous stories, the birth of Christ, is associated with Christmas in the popular mind of today. Too often we as Christians spend our time trying to destroy all the false ideas associated with Christmas and fail to present the stories with the awe and beauty they deserve. Deal with the facts given; briefly correct misconceptions as you come to them; but primarily concentrate on telling the story beautifully. To do less is to rob ourselves of the heritage God has given.

Notice that on the next two pages there are two maps, one filled in and the other blank. As you proceed through the study, find each mentioned place on your map and fill it in on your blank map. You have our full permission to copy the maps for use in your classroom.

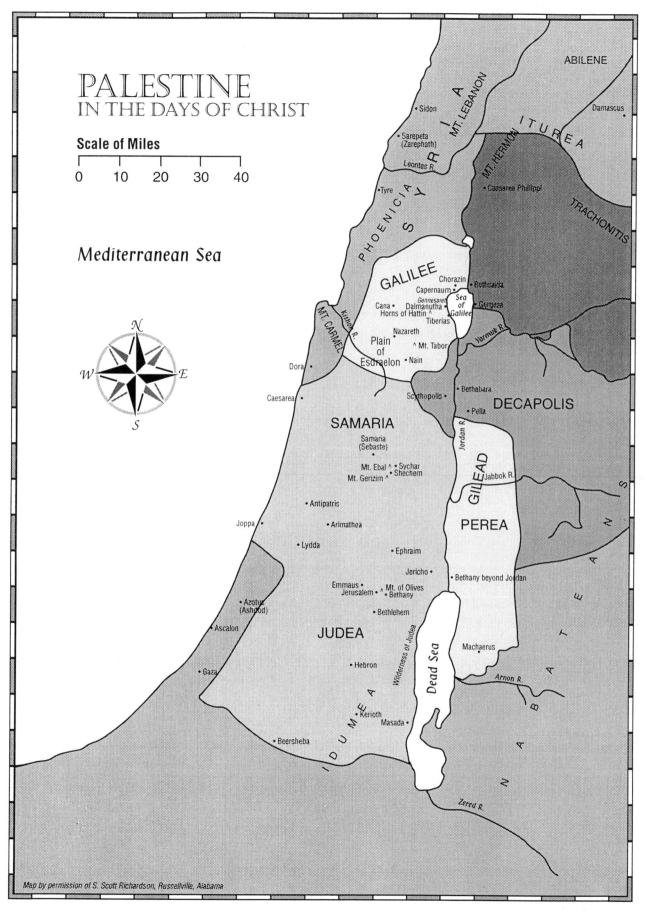

PALESTINE
IN THE DAYS OF CHRIST

Scale of Miles

0   10   20   30   40

Mediterranean Sea

N
W   E
S

ABILENE

MT. LEBANON

ITUREA

Damascus

Sidon

Sarepeta
(Zarephath)

Leontes R.

MT. HERMON

Caesarea Phillippi

TRACHONITIS

Tyre

PHOENICIA

SYRIA

MT. CARMEL

Kishon R.

GALILEE

Chorazin

Bethsaida

Capernaum

Gennesaret

Gergesa

Cana
Dalmanutha
Horns of Hattin ^

Sea
of
Galilee

Tiberias

Nazareth

Yarmuk R.

Plain
of
Esdraelon

^ Mt. Tabor

Nain

Dora

Caesarea

Scythopolis

Bethabara

DECAPOLIS

Pella

SAMARIA

Samaria
(Sebaste)

Jordan R.

Mt. Ebal ^ • Sychar
Mt. Gerizim ^ • Shechem

GILEAD

PEREA

Antipatris

Jabbok R.

Joppa

Arimathea

Lydda

Ephraim

Jericho

Bethany beyond Jordan

Emmaus
Jerusalem

^ Mt. of Olives
• Bethany

Azotus
(Ashdod)

Bethlehem

Ascalon

JUDEA

Wilderness of Judea

Dead Sea

Machaerus

Hebron

Gaza

Arnon R.

Kerioth

Masada

IDUMEA

NABATEANS

Beersheba

Zered R.

Map by permission of S. Scott Richardson, Russellville, Alabama

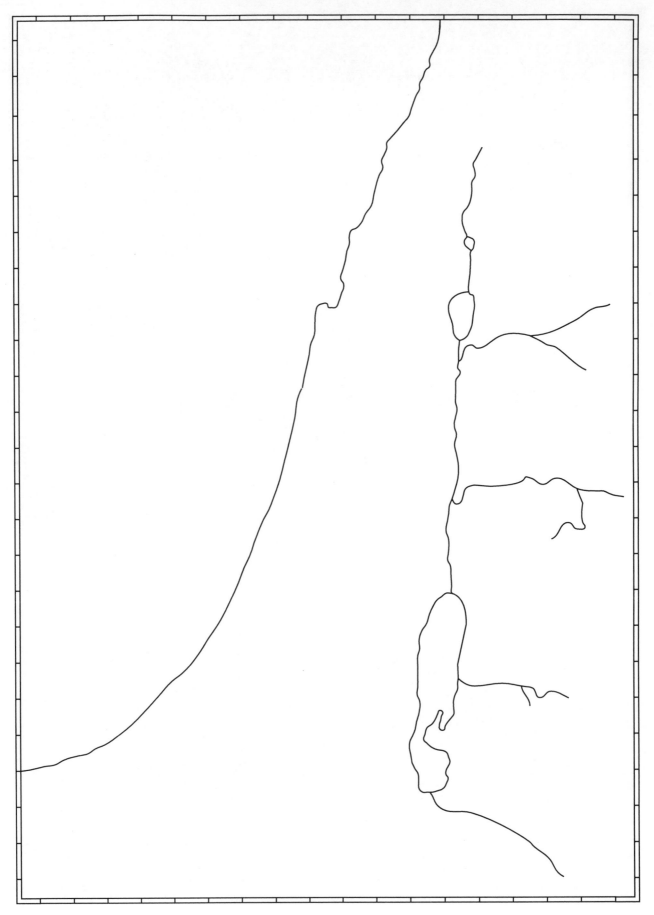

The Years of Preparation
(Matt. 1:1-3:12; Luke 1:1-3:38; John 1:1-18)

Life of Christ

*Preparation

 *Birth of John
 *Birth of Jesus
 *Work of John

Beginning Ministry
Galilean Ministry
Retirement
Close of Ministry
Last Week
Resurrection
Exaltation

The Birth of John

Gabriel announces the birth of John to Zacharias (Luke 1:5-25):

At long last, the silence of God was broken. An aged priest named Zacharias had entered the temple of the Lord to offer incense while a multitude of people were outside praying. Suddenly an angel appeared on the right side of the altar of incense.

Zacharias was frightened but the angel said, "Don't be afraid, Zacharias. Your request has been heard, and your wife Elisabeth is going to bear you a son. You will call him John. You will have joy and gladness, and many others will rejoice at his birth."

The angel continued: "He will be great in the sight of God. He is not to drink any wine or strong drink, and he will be filled with the Holy Spirit even from his mother's womb. His task is to turn the children of Israel back to God. He will go before the Lord in the spirit and power of Elijah, to turn the hearts of the fathers to the children, and to prepare the people for the Lord's coming."

> NOTE:
> Remember that Malachi had foretold the coming of "Elijah" (Mal. 4:5-6). "Elijah" would not be literal Elijah, but John the Baptist who came in the spirit of Elijah (see Matt. 17:9-13). This was the forerunner, the one to prepare the way for the coming of the Savior.

Zacharias asked, "My wife and I are old; how can I know that this thing is going to happen?" Not only were Zacharias and Elisabeth too old to have a son, Elisabeth was barren. It would take a miracle for her to have a baby.

The angel replied, "I am Gabriel. I have come from God Himself to tell you this news. Now you will be unable to speak until it comes to pass because you did not believe my words."

All these things delayed Zacharias, and the people outside wondered why he was staying so long in the temple. When he came out, he could not talk, and somehow, probably by his signals, they perceived that he had seen a vision.

When Zacharias finished his shift of work at the temple, he went home. After a time, Elisabeth was expecting a baby just as the angel had predicted.

> NOTE:
>
> Note that John was not to drink any wine or strong drink during his life, and he was to be filled with the Holy Spirit from his mother's womb. This means John was to live his whole life as a Nazarite, that is, as one who had a Nazarite vow (see Num. 6). So far as we know, there are only three men in the Bible who had a Nazarite vow all their lives. They were Samson (Judg. 13:3-5); Samuel (1 Sam. 1:11); and now John. These men were set apart to serve God in unique ways during their whole life spans. The Nazarite vow seems to have been a common one among the Jews, but it was normally taken for only a short time.

Gabriel announces the birth of Jesus to Mary (Luke 1:26-38):

Six months passed, and the angel appeared again. This time he came to a virgin named Mary who lived in Nazareth. She was engaged to be married to a man named Joseph of the family of David.

The angel said, "Hello, you who are highly regarded by God. The Lord is with you." Mary was very troubled at the angel's words and wondered what this was all about.

Gabriel said, "Do not be afraid, Mary. You have been found very pleasing to God. You are going to have a son, and you are to call Him Jesus. He will be great and will be called the Son of the Most High. Jehovah God is going to give Him the throne of His father David, and His kingdom will never end."

> NOTE:
>
> In this child would be fulfilled the promise of God to David that, through his son, his throne and kingdom would be established forever (2 Sam. 7:11-14). This is the child which Isaiah had foretold would be born to sit upon the throne of David and to rule his kingdom (Isa. 9:6-7). Even in the announcement of these events, we see the light of prophecy beginning to converge upon one person as He prepares to step out onto the stage of the divine play.

Mary asked, "How will this be, since I am a virgin?" Unlike Zacharias' question, Mary's question did not indicate doubt. She wanted to know what she was to do. Was this child to be her husband's, or what?

Gabriel answered, "The Holy Spirit will come upon you and the power of the Most High will overshadow you. Therefore that Holy One who is thus conceived will be called the Son of God." The Holy One to be born was to have no human father. He would be the only begotten Son of God.

The angel then gave Mary more exciting news: "Your kinswoman Elisabeth has conceived a son in her old age. It is now the sixth month of her that was barren, because no word of God will be empty of power."

Mary said, "I am the Lord's servant. Let it happen unto me as you have spoken."

NOTE:

Mary's baby was to be called Jesus. That is the New Testament equivalent to the name Joshua. He would be called Jesus which means "Savior" because He would save His people from their sins (Matt. 1:21). But the name Jesus was a relatively common name among Jews. Even though it had a meaning that would make it unique in the case of this baby, the name Jesus would serve as His personal name to identify Him just as our names identify us.

In addition, this baby would have many other names. The angel told Mary He would be called the "Son of God," because He would literally be conceived by the power of God. There would be no earthly father. Jesus was God's Son in a way that no other person can ever be. He was the "only begotten Son of God," the only one ever conceived in such a way. We will discuss the other names for this One as we come to them.

Mary visits Elisabeth (Luke 1:39-56):

Who could be honored more than Mary and Elisabeth, chosen to bear the Christ and His forerunner? Mary hurried to the hill country of Judea to visit her kinswoman in order to share the joy and ecstasy of being privileged to play such a part in God's plan.

When Mary arrived at the house of Zacharias and Elisabeth, Elisabeth heard Mary's greeting. At that moment, Elisabeth felt her babe leap within her. The Holy Spirit filled her heart and she said, "Blessed are you among women and blessed is the child you will bear! And why should I be so favored that the mother of my Lord should come unto me? When the sound of your greeting came to my ears, the babe leaped in my womb for joy."

NOTE:

Even the babe, six months along in his mother's womb, was moved to celebrate the moment. Do you remember that Zacharias was told that the baby John would be filled with the Holy Spirit even from his mother's womb?

By the Spirit, Elisabeth was led to forget her baby in her praise of Mary's baby. Normally any woman in Elisabeth's position would have felt that her baby was the greatest blessing ever given to the human family. Elisabeth, however, is led to realize that it is Mary's baby who will be Lord of all.

Mary responded with a song in which she magnified and praised God: "My soul praises the Lord because He has noticed the humble place of His servant. Now all generations will call me blessed because the Almighty has done great things to me. He is able to put down the mighty and to lift up the lowly. He can do great things even through those who amount to nothing. He has now helped His servant Israel because He has remembered to show mercy to Abraham and to his descendants forever, just as He promised to our fathers."

After three months of visiting with Elisabeth, Mary returned home.

NOTE:

There is nothing accidental or haphazard about God's fulfillment of His promises. Though men may take long years to see God's plan for man's redemption, from the beginning God carefully and continually unfolded His will. He gave promises and then fulfilled them. Every divine utterance during the months preceding the Lord's birth shows that God was doing these things in specific fulfillment of the promises He had made many, many centuries before.

The birth of John the Baptist (Luke 1:57-80):

When John was born it was an occasion of great joy. On the eighth day, when he was circumcised and named, the neighbors and relatives came. They wanted to name the child Zacharias after his father, but Elisabeth said, "No, his name will be John."

Everyone marveled, "Why? None of your relatives is named John." They went to Zacharias and wanted to know what he would have the baby called.

Signaling for a tablet to be brought, Zacharias wrote: "His name is John." When he had written those words, his tongue was loosed. He was filled with the Spirit and began to praise God, saying: "Praise be to the Lord, the God of Israel, who has raised up a horn of salvation for us in the house of David as He spoke beforehand through His holy prophets."

NOTE:

Notice that Zacharias praises one who is of the *house of David*. Both Zacharias and Elisabeth were of the family of Aaron, of the tribe of Levi. John, his *own* son, was therefore of Levi, not of the house of David. Zacharias' highest praise was not for his own son, contrary to human nature, but was for another, the Christ, who would be born of David's lineage.

As He did in the announcements of Gabriel, in Mary's song, and now in Zacharias' song, the Holy Spirit reminds us of the promises God made in the past and shows that the present events were in direct fulfillment of those promises.

Zacharias continued:

God has remembered His holy covenant from of old, the oath He swore unto our father Abraham to rescue us from the hand of our enemies and to enable us to serve Him without fear in holiness and righteousness all our days.

Then Zacharias spoke to his own beloved son:

And you, my child, will be called the prophet of the Most High, because you will go before the Lord to prepare His way, to give His people the knowledge of salvation through the forgiveness of their sins.

When the people round about heard these things they wondered what the child would accomplish in his life because, obviously, the Lord was with him.

NOTE:

Nothing more is said of John's youth except that he grew and became strong in spirit and was in the rugged hill country of Judea until he began his public work.

The Birth of Jesus

The angel announces the birth of Jesus to Joseph (Matt. 1:18-25):

When Mary arrived back in Nazareth, she was already three months along in her pregnancy. Joseph, the one to whom she was betrothed, was very upset and heartbroken because the only explanation he could think of was that Mary had been unfaithful to him. Since he was a righteous man, he had nearly decided to put her away. But since he did not want to make her a public example, he was going to put her away privately.

At this point, an angel of God appeared unto Joseph in a dream, saying, "Joseph, son of David, do not be afraid to take unto you Mary your wife, because what is conceived in her is from the Holy Spirit. She will give birth to a son, and you will call His name Jesus because He will save His people from their sins."

This great event thus fulfilled another ancient prophecy: "Behold, the virgin will be with child, and will give birth to a son, and they will call His name Immanuel which means 'God with us'" (Isa. 7:14).

Joseph awoke and did as the angel of the Lord had commanded him. He took Mary home with him to be his wife, but he had no sexual union with her until the child was born.

The birth of Jesus (Matt. 2:1a; Luke 2:1-7):

The prophet Micah had predicted that the Christ would be born in Bethlehem (Mic. 5:2). Yet Joseph and Mary lived in Nazareth, at the other end of the country from Bethlehem. Was Micah wrong in his prophecy?

Octavian, the nephew and heir of Julius Caesar, was ruling the Roman Empire. He had been given the title Augustus. Just at this time, Caesar Augustus made a decree that everyone in the Roman empire should be enrolled for taxation purposes. Everyone in Palestine was required to go to his home town to be listed in the census. Since Joseph was of the house of David, his ancestral home was Bethlehem. It is possible that Joseph himself had come from Bethlehem. Therefore he and Mary had to travel there.

The journey must have been difficult for Mary since the time for the birth of her baby was near. When she and Joseph arrived in Bethlehem, they could find no room in the inn. They found a place to stay in a stable where animals were kept. That night the baby Jesus was born. He was wrapped in strips of cloth as newborns of that day were and was laid in a manger.

NOTE:

It is strange to our thinking that at this great event, when the Ruler and Creator of the universe became flesh, none of the princes and nobles of the world were there. Yet it was part of the plan that Jesus should live in the humblest of circumstances. He did not come to be served but to serve others. He came to save all men, but it was the common people that heard Jesus gladly. It was primarily the lowly of the world who would respond to His gospel. Besides, two of the most noble people who ever lived were there when He was born — his foster father Joseph and His mother Mary.

There was more than one decree for enrollment for the purpose of taxation during this period of history, so there is no way to look into the history books and pinpoint the exact year nor the exact time of year from this fact.

Angels announce the birth of Jesus to Shepherds (Luke 2:8-20):

Certainly not all was ordinary at the birth of Jesus. There were shepherds in a field watching over their flocks by night. The calm of their vigil was broken when an angel appeared near them and said, "Do not be afraid for I am bringing you good news of great joy which will be for all the people. Today in the city of David, a savior for you has been born, Christ the Lord. This will be a sign to you: you will find the baby wrapped in swaddling clothes and lying in a manger."

Suddenly a great company of angels appeared, praising God and saying, "Glory to God in the highest, and on earth peace to men upon whom His favor rests."

After the angels were gone, the shepherds said, "Let's go to Bethlehem and see this thing which the Lord has told us about."

They hurried into the city and found Mary, Joseph, and the baby, who was lying in the manger. After they had seen these things, they went out and told everyone they saw about what had happened. All those who heard were amazed.

The shepherds returned to their place, praising God. Meanwhile, Mary treasured all these things in her heart.

Circumcision and naming of Jesus (Luke 2:21):

The covenant of circumcision was given to Abraham. According to it, every male child born into an Israelite household was to be circumcised on the eighth day (Gen. 17:12). A commandment to this effect is also found in the law of Moses (Lev. 12:3).

In keeping with the law, and with the ancient covenant, Jesus was circumcised and named when He was eight days old. He was given the name commanded by the angel — Jesus, which means Savior.

Presentation of Jesus at the Temple (Luke 2:22-24):

When a child was born, the mother was ceremonially unclean for a period of time. For a boy, the time was a total of forty days (Lev. 12:1-4). These days amount to almost exactly the time usually allotted today by a physician for a woman to be pretty well recovered from childbirth — about six weeks. After the days of purification, sacrifices were to be offered: a year old lamb for a burnt offering and a pigeon or dove for a sin offering (Lev. 12:6). If the couple were poor, and could not afford the lamb, they were permitted to offer two doves or two pigeons, one for a burnt offering, the other for a sin offering (Lev. 12:8).

At the proper time, therefore, in obedience to the law, Mary and Joseph took the baby to Jerusalem to offer the purification sacrifices and to present Him to God as their firstborn son (see

Exod. 13:1-16). Their poverty is shown in the fact they offered two birds.

Simeon's words about the baby (Luke 2:25-35):

While they were there, a man named Simeon came into the temple to meet them. His age is not given, but the implication is that he was an old man. He was righteous and very dedicated to God. He was one of those Israelites who realized that the Old Testament and its provisions were not the ultimate thing which they could expect from God. Simeon knew and believed the promises of God regarding redemption. He was looking for and counting on their fulfillment. God had given Simeon some very precious news: he would not die until he had seen the Lord's Christ. He was waiting with the greatest anticipation for this event.

On this certain day, the Spirit moved Simeon to go to the temple. There he saw the couple who had brought their baby for the purification sacrifices. He went to them and took the infant in his arms. It must have been an emotionally charged moment — even though the baby was perhaps oblivious to His surroundings.

Simeon felt bursting joy in his heart as he said, "O Lord, now let your servant depart in peace because, as you promised, my eyes have seen your salvation, the salvation you have prepared before all people, a light for revelation to the Gentiles and for the glory of your people Israel."

Joseph and Mary stood quietly, marvelling at the words of Simeon. Then Simeon spoke to Mary, saying, "This One is appointed for the falling and rising of many in Israel. He will be a sign spoken against." Then he added, "And a sword will pierce your own soul, so that the disposition of men's hearts will be revealed."

> NOTE:
>
> Simeon saw the ultimate fate of this infant which he held in his arms. The thing which would cause His mother her greatest heartache — His death on the cross — would not only be the redemption of the world, but would also be the dividing line between those who would accept His salvation and those who would not.

Anna the Prophetess (Luke 2:36-38):

There was a woman named Anna at the temple also. She was very old. She had been married seven years, and had been widowed for 84 years. That would be a total of 91 years. Add to that the age she was when she married, say 16, and you have 107 years of age. She never left the temple area, but was there worshiping day and night.

Coming up to the little group at this moment, she gave thanks to God. She, as Simeon had done, spoke concerning the child — words of interest to all those who were looking for the redemption of Jerusalem.

The visit of the Wise Men (Matt. 2:1-12):

Some time has passed since the birth of Jesus, because there has been time for His circumcision to take place and for the purification sacrifices to be offered. Some time after this, wise men came from the east to see Him. They came to Jerusalem asking the question: "Where is the one who has been born king of the Jews? We saw His star in the east and have come to worship Him."

When Herod heard of their questioning about one born to be king of the Jews, he was very disturbed, and all Jerusalem with him. He gathered all the chief priests and scribes and asked them where the Christ was supposed to be born.

The scribes replied, "In Bethlehem of Judea, because it is written in the prophets: 'And you, Bethlehem, land of Judah, are by no means least among the princes of Judah, because out of you shall come forth a governor, who will be shepherd of my people Israel'" (Mic. 5:2).

Herod called the wise men to him in secret and questioned carefully about when the star appeared. Then he sent them to Bethlehem saying, "Go and find out exactly where the child is, and then come and tell me so that I can go and worship Him."

When the wise men left Herod, they rejoiced that the star which they had seen in the east went before them until it stood over the place where the young child was. They went in and saw Him with Mary. Then they worshiped the child and gave Him gifts of gold, frankincense, and myrrh.

When they were ready to depart, God warned them in a dream not to go back to Herod. They returned home another way.

NOTE:

Wise men, such as these, were usually highly intelligent men. Most of them studied the stars, believing them to be indicative of the future. Often they served as advisers to kings because of their wisdom. Daniel was numbered among such men hundreds of years before.

We do not know exactly where these wise men came from because "the east" includes a lot of territory. It could have been Arabia, Babylon, Persia, India, or somewhere else. Nor do we know how many wise men there were. The three gifts they gave to Jesus have been taken as proof that there were three. Men have made up all sorts of legends about them, even their names and backgrounds, but nothing is known of them except this brief record in Matthew. We have no objection to there being three of them, but we do object to teaching there were three when the Bible does not say.

Atheists attempt to explain the appearance of the star in this story by saying it was some purely natural celestial event. Many Bible teachers accept this explanation without question, thinking they are shedding light on how this story "really" happened. Instead they are destroying faith. The language of the Bible account simply does not permit such an explanation. Note these reasons:

1. These men were familiar with all sorts of celestial phenomena from eclipses to conjunctions of planets and stars. They spent their lives studying the skies.
2. There would be nothing to connect a purely natural event with the birth of the king of the Jews.
3. The star experienced a radical change in its location in the sky to "lead" them on their journey. They saw the star in the east which means it was obviously to the west of them since it led them in that direction. They came to Jerusalem where they talked with Herod. Then that same star went before them again until it "stood over the place where Jesus was." From Jerusalem, the star would have had to be due south to lead them to Bethlehem. No known phenomenon of nature follows such a pattern.

4. Therefore, the only logical explanation is that this star was a miraculous sign in the sky, and that God communicated with these men to let them know it would lead them to the newborn king of the Jews.

Flight into Egypt (Matt. 2:13-15):

God knew what Herod would try to do, so an angel appeared to Joseph in a dream. He said, "Get up, take the little one and His mother and flee into Egypt because Herod will try to kill Him. Remain there until I call you."

Joseph promptly arose and took Jesus and His mother into Egypt, about 200 miles away. They remained there until the death of Herod. This sojourn in Egypt made it possible to apply the statement, "Out of Egypt did I call my Son" (Hos. 11:1), to Jesus.

Herod commands the slaughter of the babes of Bethlehem (Matt. 2:16-18):

When Herod found that he had been tricked by the wise men, he was enraged. He commanded his soldiers to go to Bethlehem and kill all babies (the original Greek word specifies male children) up to two years old both in and around the city. He figured the age estimate from the information gained from the wise men.

Six hundred years earlier, the Israelites were in captivity when Jeremiah wrote: "A voice was heard in Ramah, weeping and great mourning, Rachel weeping for her children; and she would not be comforted for they were gone" (Jere. 31:15). Of course, Jeremiah used figurative language because, at the time of Israel's captivity in Jeremiah's day, Rachel had been dead over a thousand years. If she had been alive, her tears would surely have fallen for her offspring and for their suffering.

No doubt this poignant memory was stirred in the case of the killing of the babes of Bethlehem because Rachel's tomb was at Bethlehem. The wailing of the mothers of the slain children were the wailing of Rachel for her dead babies.

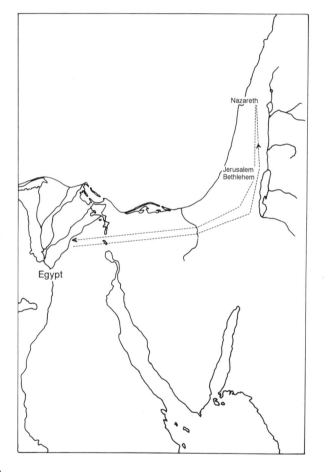

But Jesus, the baby Herod wanted killed, was not there. Jesus came to earth to die, but not at this time; not as a helpless infant, as a tragic victim, but as a willing sacrifice *after* He had done the work He came to do.

NOTE:

The prominence of the Herodian family began with a father and son, both named Antipater, who were governors of the Idumean people (O.T. Edomites) who moved into the southern portion of Judah during the time of the Babylonian captivity. Antipater, the father of Herod the Great, had a genius at choosing the right side in a conflict, and managed to be such a help to the Romans that they rewarded him by giving him power. Likewise, his son Herod won the favor of both Octavian and Mark Anthony to such an extent that they made him king of Judea. His kingdom included most of the land of Palestine.

During his long rule (37-4 B.C.) Herod the Great built a great many structures in the land, such as the great city and port of Caesarea on the old location of Strato's Tower (25-13 B.C.); an aqueduct thirteen miles long which brought water to that city; Masada which was a fortress city west of the Dead Sea; and in Jerusalem, the Tower of Antonia and many other buildings. His most famous project was the temple in Jerusalem. Herod wished to build a truly splendid temple consistent with other magnificent structures which he had built. The Jews did not trust him, but the lure of such a magnificent temple persuaded them to allow him to remove the temple which had been built upon their return from Babylon and build a new one. The building began about 20 B.C., and the finishing touches were completed just shortly before the final destruction of the temple in A.D. 70.

Herod became practically insane in his later years. He slew, or had slain, his senile father-in-law, his most adored wife, Mariamne, two sons, Aristobulus and Alexander, and others. It is no wonder that when Jesus was born, and Herod heard of it, he sought to kill him. It is ironic that this particular event is not referred to in any contemporary history, yet it is the best known of all Herod's deeds.

Prior to his death, Herod knew that there would be rejoicing when he died. To prevent this, he had a number of prominent Jews imprisoned with orders that when he died, they should be slain so there would be no joy at his death. Fortunately this order was not carried out.

During the rest of the New Testament we will read of the activities of Herod's sons: Philip, Herod Antipas, and Archelaus; and of his grandson, Herod Agrippa I (Acts 12); and his great grandson, Herod Agrippa II (Acts 26).

Joseph takes his family back to Nazareth (Matt. 2:19-23):

When Herod was dead, an angel of God spoke to Joseph and said, "Get up and take the little One and His mother and go back to the land of Israel because those who were trying to kill Him are dead."

Joseph did as the angel commanded. His first plan was to go back to Judea, to Bethlehem. In fact, the book of Matthew has not even mentioned Nazareth before this point. It is in Luke that we learn where they had lived before the birth of the baby. When the family arrived back in the land of Israel, however, Joseph learned that Archelaus, the son of Herod, was ruling in his father's stead. He therefore took his family back to Nazareth.

This move caused another prophetic statement to apply to Jesus: "He shall be called a Nazarene." No such statement is found in those exact words, but "Nazarene" probably comes from

Nazar which means a shoot or bud. Both Isaiah and Jeremiah referred to the predicted one to come as a shoot or a branch which would arise from the house of David (see Isa. 11:1; Jere. 23:5).

Why worship this baby? Who is He? (John 1:1-18; Matt. 1:1-17; Luke 3:23-38):

Angels announced the birth of this baby; shepherds came to see Him; wise men later worshiped Him. He looked like any ordinary baby, but He was very different. It is a stupendous thing to realize who this child really was, and why He was worthy of worship.

John describes Him this way (John 1:1-18): He *was* in the beginning. Always was! In eternity He was. He existed with God, separate in personality, but one in essence and purpose. He was divine. Through Him all things were created. Therefore, this was the Creator of the universe lying asleep in the manger. What an amazing thought! As the Eternal Word, He was the communication of God to man. The Word became flesh and dwelt among men. As the Son of God, He declared God to men.

This baby was also the legal heir to David's throne (Matt. 1:1-17). The genealogy of Jesus given in Matthew's account was to satisfy Jews that Jesus was the legal heir of David. Matthew gives the genealogy of Christ from Abraham through David, down through the royal line of the kings, through Joseph His legal father.

But Jesus was unique. He was the legal son of Joseph, but Joseph was not His real father. Yet the Bible says Christ was born of the seed of David *according to the flesh* (Rom. 1:3). The genealogy given by Luke proves this claim (Luke 3:23-38). It is the genealogy of Mary. She also was of the house of David. She came through David's son Nathan, a brother of Solomon, whereas Joseph came through King Solomon. If Luke's account is *not* of Mary's descent then there is no account of her genealogy and no way to prove the statement of Romans 1:3. Even though the genealogy names Joseph, that does not mean it has to be literally his own genealogy. Lineage was reckoned through fathers, therefore through husbands. Matthew says Joseph's father was Jacob, a descendant of Solomon. Luke says it was Heli, a descendant of Nathan. The most logical explanation is that the genealogies of both Mary and Joseph are given in the two passages, proving that both legally and physically, Jesus was fully qualified to take His place upon David's throne, fulfilling the promise of God to David (2 Sam. 7:11-14; Psa. 132:11-12; Acts 2:30-36).

NOTE:

Let us notice some more names applied to this baby. The term "Immanuel" that was told to Joseph emphasizes Christ's deity. This baby would be "*God* with us." This is God, Deity, come to earth in human form to dwell among men. The term Immanuel joins with the terms Son of God and the Word to describe His Deity.

In announcing the birth to the shepherds, the angels called Him "Christ the Lord." The term "Christ" is a title meaning "Anointed One." It is the New Testament equivalent to the Old Testament term "Messiah." To be anointed for a particular position was to be "chosen" and officially appointed. Therefore, this One was God's Anointed, chosen by Him for the particular work He came into the world to perform.

The word "Lord" was a term of respect. It literally meant "ruler," and could be used to refer to any ruler. Naturally Jesus is the ruler or Lord over all men in a unique way.

Jesus in the temple at 12 years of age (Luke 2:41-51):

Three times each year the Jewish men were supposed to go to Jerusalem to keep feast days. The Passover feast in the spring was one of these occasions. On this particular year, Jesus was twelve years old. He and His family made the trip with many others from Galilee.

NOTE:

At twelve years of age Jewish boys became "Bar Mizvah," a son of the commandment. In other words, according to Jewish tradition (the law did not specify an exact age) they became accountable to keep the law of Moses. There was, therefore, an added excitement and joy about this trip to Jerusalem for the Passover. Before this, whether Jesus went or not, He was not required to do so. This time He goes as a young man who has accepted the responsibility to keep the law of God.

The Passover was like a family reunion, a big dinner, and a religious service rolled into one. Figures exist dating to the reign of Nero from which it is calculated that as many as 2,565,000 people attended the Passover that given year. Josephus put it as 2,700,200, while at an earlier Passover, he estimated there were 3,000,000. Many of these people would have stayed in outlying areas such as Bethany and Bethphage. Nevertheless, Jerusalem would have been incredibly crowded during these feastdays.

After the feast was over, Joseph and Mary started back to Nazareth with a crowd of travelers. They supposed Jesus was with some of their kinfolks and friends from Nazareth. That evening, when they tried to find Him, He was missing. No one had seen Him all day.

In great fear they made their way back to Jerusalem. After three days they found Him in the temple. He was sitting in the midst of the learned teachers of the law both responding to their questions and asking questions of His own. Everyone who heard Him was amazed at His understanding.

Joseph and Mary were astonished. They said, "Son, why have you done this to us? Look, your father and I have been frantically searching for you."

In complete honesty Jesus replied that He was perplexed. "Why did you have to search? Didn't you know that I would be in my Father's house?" Jesus wondered why they did not know to look at the temple first. Of course, it had been an accident that He was left behind, but He could not understand why they would not immediately guess where He would go when He was alone.

His parents did not understand His remark. He went back home with them. It was not time for His great work to begin. Though He was a "son of the commandment," He was still a boy. So He went home and was subject to His parents until He was grown.

Mary kept this experience in her heart along with all the other remarkable things she knew about Jesus. How rich those memories must have grown to be as her own understanding of her Son's identity grew.

Jesus finishes growing up (Luke 2:52):

The next eighteen years pass in silence. During those years Jesus learned the trade of a carpenter (Mark 6:3) from Joseph who was a carpenter (Matt. 13:55). Jesus matured in all the ways He should have — mentally, physically, spiritually, and socially.

It seems that Joseph died during these years because he is never mentioned during the ministry of Jesus as being alive or with the family. Notice that he was not at the foot of the cross with Mary. At that time Jesus placed His mother in the care of John the apostle, indicating she no longer had a husband to care for her (John 19:25-27).

The Beginning of John's Ministry

Why John came (Matt. 3:1-3; Mark 1:2-3; Luke 3:1-6; John 1:6-18):

Two Old Testament passages are quoted in the gospels to set forth the reason why John came. Malachi recorded God's words: "Behold, I send my messenger before thy face, who shall prepare thy way" (Mark 1:2, quoting Mal. 3:1). Isaiah describes John as "The voice of one crying in the wilderness, 'Make ready the way of the Lord, make His paths straight'" (Mark 1:3, quoting Isa. 40:3). According to the gospel of John, John the Baptist used this verse to identify himself when the Jews from Jerusalem demanded to know who he was (John 1:19-23). John, therefore, came to get things ready for the Christ to do His work.

John's work (Matt. 3:4-12; Mark 1:4-8; Luke 3:7-18):

The theme of John's preaching was: "Repent ye, for the kingdom of heaven is near." The need of the Jews was to repent. Those Jews truly devoted to God would be receptive to His Son. John came, therefore, to call as many Jews to repentance as he could.

John also baptized. It was from this practice that he received his title "the Baptizer." John was the first man in Bible history to baptize. That is why he was given the title "the Baptist," while those who came after him were not.

The baptism of John was motivated by repentance and was an expression of penitence. Belief in Jesus as the Christ was not required, because Jesus had not yet begun His work. No one knew about Him at this point. Therefore the confession made at the time of being baptized by John was not one of faith in Jesus, but a confession of sins.

John was quick to point out that his baptism by itself was not enough to demonstrate penitence. He told the Pharisees and Sadducees who came to be baptized to "bring forth fruit worthy of repentance."

John did not just go around saying, "Repent." He told the multitudes specific changes they were to make in their lives. He said, "Share your possessions with those who are in need." To the publicans he said, "Require no more money for taxes than that which is appointed for you." To the soldiers (probably temple guards, or Jewish soldiers of Herod Antipas, or of one of the other local rulers, because it seems Gentiles were not in the crowds who gathered to hear John preach), John said, "Do not take things away from others by violence, neither make false accusations, and be satisfied with your wages."

The greatest role for John to play was announcing to Israel that Jesus was the Christ, but we will see how he did this shortly. During the days before this announcement was made, John told all the people, "There is One coming after me who is greater than I, so much greater that I am not worthy to take His shoes off. I baptize you in water. He will baptize you in the Holy Spirit and in fire. Even now He is ready to come to separate the wheat from the chaff. He will gather His wheat into the barn, but the chaff He will burn up with unquenchable fire."

John was very successful in his work. People went out from Jerusalem, all Judea, and the whole

17

region of the Jordan. Many, many of those in the multitudes heard his message gladly and were baptized. His message increased the feeling of expectation of the arrival of the Messiah.

NOTE:

John's baptism was unto the remission of sins (Mark 1:4; Luke 3:3). "Unto" or "for" the remission of sins is exactly the same expression found in Acts 2:38. Sins *were* removed by John's baptism. The question is how were they removed, since Jesus had not yet died on the cross.

All sins forgiven before the death of Christ and the new covenant were forgiven on the same basis. From the days of Adam, sacrifices were offered and sins were forgiven provisionally. That is, the sins were forgiven with the understanding that Christ would come and offer the ultimate redemption for the sins "done aforetime" (Rom. 3:25; see also Heb. 9:15). The Bible refers to the guilt of sins forgiven as being held under a note, a promissory note, which was the law. Jesus came and nailed that bond or promissory note (the "handwriting of ordinances") to the cross (Col. 2:14).

Therefore the people who lived before the cross repented of their sins and offered the sacrifices commanded, or obeyed whatever other commandments were given (such as John's baptism), in order to please God. Then it was as if God held a note bearing all the sins that had been forgiven. When Jesus died He paid that note in full as well as providing the means by which all future sins could be forgiven also.

Study your map:

Before we go further in our study, go back and look at the map on page 3 of this material. It shows the land as it was in Jesus' day. Notice it is very different to the last map we had at the close of the Old Testament. It is a prosperous region now, under the control of the Romans, rather than a poverty stricken dependency under the Persians.

Divide your blank map on page 4 into the major regions: Galilee, Samaria, Judea, Perea, and the Decapolis. Now mark the various places we have already come to in our study:

Jerusalem
Hill Country of Judea
Nazareth
Bethlehem
Jordan River

Put an arrow pointing off your map toward Egypt.

Put an arrow showing how the wise men would have entered the land "from the east."

Label each new place as it is mentioned in the story.

The Beginning of Jesus' Ministry
(Matt. 3:13-4:12; Mark 1:9-14; Luke 3:21-4:14; John 1:19-4:54)

Life of Christ

Preparation

*Beginning Ministry

 *Baptism
 *Temptation
 *First Disciples
 *First Miracle
 *First Passover
 *In Judea
 *John Imprisoned
 *Woman at Well

Galilean Ministry
Retirement
Close of Ministry
Last Week
Resurrection
Exaltation

Look at the short outline of Jesus' life again. We have covered the stories in the first heading of the outline and are now ready to start the second period. Be sure you know this outline by now. Look often to the more complete outline in the front of the book. Learn the main stories that fit under each main heading.

    I. The Years of Preparation
  *II. The Beginning of Jesus' Ministry
  III. The Great Galilean Ministry
  IV. The Period of Retirement
   V. The Close of Jesus' Ministry
  VI. The Last Week
 VII. The Resurrection and Exaltation

The baptism of Jesus (Matt. 3:13-17; Mark 1:9-11; Luke 3:21-22; John 1:32-34):

One day, when Jesus was about thirty years old, He knew it was time to begin His work. For thirty years He had lived the life of a private individual. It was time to leave the city of His youth behind, to go forth and fulfill the purpose for which He came to the earth. He knew His kinsman John was already preaching his message of repentance, and baptizing people in the Jordan. It was to John He had to go first.

John had a special mission in his baptizing people that no one but he knew. God had told him that some day someone would come to be baptized and that the Holy Spirit would descend and remain upon that person. By that sign, John would know that person was the Lord's Christ (the Lord's Chosen One). John must have been eagerly awaiting the arrival of that One.

As John was baptizing one day, One came whom John knew — it was his kinsman Jesus. John did not know that Jesus was the Christ (John 1:31), but he knew that Jesus was more righteous than he was himself. So John said, "I need *you* to baptize *me*. Why are you wanting me to baptize you?"

Jesus replied, "Permit it to be done the way I have asked

so that we may fulfill all righteousness."

John baptized Jesus in the Jordan, and when Jesus had emerged from the water, while He was praying, the heavens were opened, and the Holy Spirit came down in the form of a dove and sat upon Him. At the same time, a voice spoke from the heavens saying, "This is my beloved Son in whom I am well pleased."

Temptation of Jesus (Matt. 4:1-11; Mark 1:12-13; Luke 4:1-13):

Immediately after His baptism, the Holy Spirit led Jesus out into the wilderness to be tempted by Satan. He was there for forty days, during which He did without food, and was tempted by Satan. From the record, it seems the three temptations recorded were by no means the only temptations there were.

After the forty days of fasting, Jesus was very hungry, so hungry that death was on its way. Famished and weak, Jesus faced the three temptations recorded in Matthew and Luke.

The tempter said, "If you are the Son of God, command these stones to turn into bread." The thought of bread to a starving man would be almost irresistible, but there was more to the temptation than that. Satan was also trying to get Jesus to misuse the power God had given Him through the Spirit.

Though Jesus needed food very badly, there was something He needed more, and that was to obey the Father's will. Therefore He replied, "It is written: 'Man does not live by bread alone but by every word that comes from the mouth of God'" (quoted from Deut. 8:3). It was not the Father's will that He use His power merely to supply His physical needs. So Jesus refused the devil's suggestion.

Next the devil took Jesus into Jerusalem and set Him on the highest point of the temple. He said, "If you are the Son of God, throw yourself down, because it is written: 'He will command His angels concerning you, and they will lift you up on their hands, so that you will not strike your foot against a stone'" (quoted from Psa. 91:11-12).

Jesus replied, "It is also written: 'Do not test the Lord your God'" (quoted from Deut. 6:16). Jesus had no need to "try out" God, to see if He would do as He promised. For Him to have done so would have indicated a lack of faith on His part and would have destroyed any basis for our trusting God.

Finally the devil took Jesus to the top of a very high mountain and showed Him the splendor of all the kingdoms of the world. He told Jesus, "All these things will I give you if you will bow down and worship me."

In the strongest language yet, Jesus said, "Get out of here, Satan! Because it is written: 'Worship the Lord your God, and serve Him alone'" (quoted from Deut. 6:13).

After this, Satan left Jesus and God sent angels to attend to His needs.

NOTE:

The Bible says that Jesus was tempted in all points like as we are but without sin (Heb. 4:15). He had most certainly already been tempted many times as all men are, and would be many times again, but this temptation was special because He had now entered in upon His ministry. The Holy Spirit had descended upon Him, and the first thing the Spirit did was to lead (the book of Mark says "drive") Jesus into the wilderness to be tempted.

When Satan tempted Eve in the distant past, Satan triumphed. That was when God gave the promise that someday the seed of woman would come and smash the head of the serpent who was Satan (Gen. 3:15; Rev. 12:9; 20:2; 2 Cor. 11:3). One way in which Jesus had to defeat Satan was by refusing to sin. If ever He sinned, He could not possibly redeem men from their sins — because His death would have paid for only His own sin, not the sins of others.

John's testimony of himself (John 1:19-28):

NOTE:

Mark's account of the temptation stresses that immediately after Jesus was baptized, He was led away to be tempted. The testimony of John the Baptist about himself was given the day before he saw Jesus and pointed Him out to others as the Lamb of God (John 1:29). The gospel of John carefully describes what happened each day following until Jesus left for Galilee. Therefore, the temptation of Jesus had to take place before John 1:19.

The Jews of Jerusalem sent priests and Levites to ask John to identify himself. He said, "I am *not* the Christ."

They asked, "Who are you then? Are you Elijah?"

He said, "No, I am not." Now John *was* the figurative Elijah prophesied in Malachi 4:5, but he knew that the Jews believed that the original Elijah was to return. Their question was really, "Are you the original prophet Elijah?" John, therefore, said, "No."

Then they asked, "Well, are you the Prophet?" By this question they meant: "Are you the prophet Moses foretold?" Moses had foretold the coming of a prophet like unto himself (Deut. 18:15). He referred to the Messiah.

John answered, "No."

The Jews then demanded, "Who are you? Give us an answer we can take back to those who sent us. What do you say of yourself?"

John answered in the words of Isaiah the prophet, "I am the voice of one calling in the desert, 'Make straight the way of the Lord'" (quoted from Isa. 40:3).

This answer did not explain one big difficulty the Jews had with John's answer. "Why then are you baptizing people if you are not the Christ, nor Elijah, nor the prophet?"

"I baptize with water," John answered, "but there stands One among you whom you do not know. He is the one who is to follow me. I am not worthy to untie the thongs of His sandals."

John's testimony regarding Jesus' baptism (John 1:29-34):

The next day after the Jews questioned John, he saw Jesus coming toward him. He said, "Look, the Lamb of God, who takes away the sin of the world! This is the one I referred to when I said, 'A man who is coming after me is preferred before me because He existed before me.'

"I myself did not know Him as the Christ," continued John, "but the reason I came baptizing in water was so that He could be revealed to Israel. I saw the Spirit come down from heaven as a dove and remain on Him. I would not have known Him, except that the One who sent me to baptize with water told me: 'The man on whom you see the Spirit come down and remain is He who will baptize with the Holy Spirit.' I have seen this happen and do testify that this is the Son of God."

John directs his disciples to Jesus (John 1:35-42):

The next day John was with two of his disciples when Jesus passed by. John told them, "Look, the Lamb of God!"

When the disciples heard this, they followed Jesus. Turning around, Jesus saw them following and asked, "What do you want?"

"Rabbi" (which means, Teacher), they said, "where are you staying?"

Jesus replied, "Come and find out."

They followed Jesus to the place where He was staying and spent that day with Him. They joined Jesus at about ten o'clock in the morning.

One of these two disciples was Andrew. The first thing Andrew did after leaving Jesus was to find his brother Simon to tell him, "We have found the Messiah." Then he took Simon to Jesus.

Jesus looked at Simon and said, "You are Simon, the son of Jonah (or John). You will be called Cephas." The name Cephas was an Aramaic name meaning "rock." We know the name better by its Greek translation, "Peter."

> NOTE:
>
> The Romans used two methods of reckoning time: 1) They reckoned legal time from midnight. 2) On a practical level, they sometimes counted time from six o'clock in the morning, as did the Jews (R.C.H. Lenski, *Interpretation of St. John's Gospel,* p. 150).

> Most scholars think the other of the two disciples who met Jesus on this occasion was John the apostle and the author of this gospel. John never uses his own name in his gospel.

Jesus meets Philip and Nathanael (John 1:43-51):

On the day following His meeting with Andrew, with the "other" disciple (probably John), and with Peter, Jesus decided to return to Galilee. He found a man named Philip and said to him, "Follow me."

Philip was from Bethsaida, on the northeastern shore of the Sea of Galilee. Bethsaida was also the home of Peter and Andrew.

> NOTE:
>
> Philip was probably a disciple of John the Baptist, as were Andrew, John, and Peter. Jesus did not just walk up to Philip, a perfect stranger, and say, "Follow me." Obviously there was an earlier meeting between Jesus and Philip about which we are given no details. That meeting had been sufficient to convince Philip that Jesus was the Christ.

> Authorities used to think there were two Bethsaidas, one on the east and another

22

on the west side of the Sea of Galilee. Now most believe there was only one, the one on the northeastern shore of the Sea. (*Macmillan Bible Atlas*, maps 231, 232, 258; *Reader's Digest Bible Atlas,* pp. 177, 178, 180.)

Philip had an acquaintance named Nathanael. He found him and told him, "We have found the one Moses wrote about in the Law, and about whom the prophets wrote. He is Jesus of Nazareth, the son of Joseph."

Nathanael replied, "Nazareth! Can anything good come from there?"

"Come and see for yourself," Philip answered.

Nathanael went with his friend to find Jesus. When Jesus saw Nathanael coming to Him, He said, "Look, here is an Israelite in whom there is nothing false." What a comment on the character of Nathanael!

Nathanael was skeptical, though. He did not know Jesus, and he thought that Jesus had no way of knowing him. He said, "How do you know anything about me?"

Jesus answered, "I saw you while you were still under the fig tree before Philip called you."

Nathanael was very impressed. After his initial skepticism, he laid his heart at Jesus' feet. He declared, "Rabbi, you are the Son of God; you are the king of Israel." Note that this was one of the strongest confessions of faith one could make — and yet it was made after so short an acquaintance with Jesus.

Bemused, Jesus said, "You believe because I told you I saw you under the fig tree? You will see greater things than that. Really and truly, you will see the heavens opened, and angels of God ascending and descending on the Son of Man."

NOTE:
It is thought that this man Nathanael was the one called Bartholomew in the list of apostles (Matt. 10:1-4; Mark 3:13-19; Luke 6:12-16). There is no way to know for sure.

Jesus refers to Himself as the "Son of Man" in this passage. This term emphasizes His humanity. He was human as well as divine. Both sides of His nature were necessary for His mission to be accomplished. He was both the "Son of God" and the "Son of Man" —that is, God in human form.

First miracle in Cana of Galilee (John 2:1-11):

On the third day after His return to Galilee, Jesus went to a wedding in Cana. His mother was there helping with the festivities. Jesus and His disciples were among the invited guests. At this point, the association of Jesus and the disciples was informal. They were not yet spending all their time with Him.

While the feast was going on, an emergency arose. The wine gave out! It was not a major problem such as death, but it was a great embarrassment to the bridegroom because he was responsible for providing the supplies for the feast.

Mary came to Jesus and said, "They have no more wine."

"Woman, why do you involve me in this?" Jesus replied. "My time has not yet come."

NOTE:

Jesus' use of the term "Woman" in addressing His mother was very deliberate and needs to be noted. First of all, it was not at all comparable to the use of the word today. When a man addresses a woman today in such a fashion, he is being curt, very brusque, and bordering on the offensive. Such was not the case here. "Woman," used in this manner, was a polite form of address.

Second, Jesus did not say, "Mother," as we might expect Him to do. The point is that Jesus had to help her see that His powers were not given to Him to do the bidding even of His mother. In the use of these powers, He functioned, not as the son of Mary, but as the Son of God. Jesus had to be sure His mother understood this before He did anything.

There was nothing slow about Mary. She got the point and was not offended at all. She told the other helpers at the feast, "Whatever He tells you to do, do it."

There were six large jars sitting nearby, each holding twenty to thirty gallons. They were commonly used to hold the large quantities of water used for the Jews' ceremonial washings.

Jesus told the servants: "Fill these jars with water." The servants went to work and filled the jars to the brim.

Then Jesus said, "Now dip some out and take it to the master of the banquet."

The servants did so, and the master of the banquet tasted the water that had been turned to wine. He did not know where the wine had come from, but the servants knew. The master of the banquet called the bridegroom aside and said, "Usually everyone brings out the best wine first and saves the cheaper wine for later, after the guests have had enough to drink. But you have saved the best till now."

This was the first of Jesus' miraculous signs, done in Cana of Galilee. By it He began to manifest His glory, and His disciples put their faith in Him.

NOTE:

So far as the record goes, this was the first miraculous sign of any kind that Jesus performed. There is no indication at all that He performed miracles as He was growing up. Now, after His baptism, and after the Holy Spirit came upon Him at that time, He is ready to demonstrate His deity by the signs which He does.

Much has been said about this episode. Those who love alcholic beverages make use of this story to show that Jesus approved of the drinking of wine and strong drink. There are several facts that need to be considered, however, to understand Jesus' actions:

1. The strongest alcoholic content a wine of Palestine could have was about 5 or 6%. Such an alcoholic content is less than most alcoholic beverages today.
2. There is a much evidence to show that when wine was drunk in that day, it was cut or diluted with large quantities of water unless the point was to get drunk.
3. There is no evidence that the wine served at this feast was cut. The servants dipped into the new wine from water and took it to the master

of the banquet. This fact brings up a third point: the Greek word "oinos" refers to grape juice, ranging from fresh grape juice to a highly fermented substance.

4. Many people think that the "good" quality to which the master of the banquet referred was its fermented state. Though this is possible, it is more likely that it had the delicious taste of fresh grape juice. The people of the land could only enjoy fresh grape juice during harvest, so the privilege of fresh grape juice was a real treat.

5. Finally, if Jesus were demonstrating His powers in an indisputable miracle, what better way than to produce fresh grape juice at a time when such juice was absolutely unobtainable (it was not long before the Passover, in early spring)?

Jesus visits Capernaum for a few days (John 2:12):

Sometime after the wedding feast, Jesus, His mother, His brothers, and His disciples went to Capernaum for a few days. A little later in His work, Jesus made Capernaum His headquarters. This stay was temporary, "not many days."

Jesus attends the first passover in His ministry and cleanses the temple (John 2:13-22):

CHRONOLOGICAL NOTE:

The Passover was observed in the month Nisan. This was the first month of the religious year. Nisan corresponded to our March 15-April 15. No other feast has been mentioned since Jesus began His ministry. Also the events during this period are fairly well connected. It seems that the baptism of Jesus, His temptation, and the few events mentioned between His temptation and this feast occurred within the months immediately before this Passover. These few months are the time we add to Jesus' ministry above three years to get the usual estimate of three and one-half years for the length of His public work.

While Jesus was in Jerusalem for the Passover, He and His disciples went to the temple. As Jesus swept His eyes over the court of the Gentiles, He saw what resembled a market place. There were cattle, sheep, and doves for sale. In addition, there were money-changers sitting at their tables exchanging the various coins that were brought for the shekels that had to be used in the temple.

Without a word, Jesus picked up a few pieces of rope and twisted them into a whip. Then He drove all the sheep and cattle from the temple area. He turned over the tables of the money-changers and scattered their coins. He told the owners of the doves, "Get these out of here! How dare you turn my Father's house into a market place!"

His disciples were frightened at the action He had taken. They feared the consequences. They remembered the statement from Psalms 69:9: "Zeal for your house will consume me."

It is interesting that, because of the moral indignation Jesus showed, and because of the Jews' own guilt, nobody resisted Him at that moment. Everyone fled like naughty schoolboys. Nevertheless, the Jews were not long in coming to challenge Jesus for what seemed an outrageous action to them.

"What miraculous action can you show us to prove you have the authority to do all this?" they asked.

Jesus answered, "Destroy this temple, and I will raise it again in three days." Jesus, even this early in His ministry, was telling them of the greatest sign which He would give them — His resurrection. By this event, above all, His identity and His claims would be validated by God.

The Jews replied, "It has taken forty-six years to build this temple, and you are going to raise it in three days?" The Jews did not believe that Jesus could build or raise a physical structure such as the Herodian temple in three days. They proved to be even more unbelieving about His resurrection.

Even Jesus' disciples did not understand what He meant at this point. After His resurrection, however, they remembered His words and understood what He meant. Then they believed the scriptures and the words Jesus had spoken. In other words, it was after the resurrection of Jesus that everything came together for the disciples. Then they understood the various scriptures that foretold His resurrection, and they understood the various comments Jesus had made about it during His ministry.

> NOTE:
> According to Deuteronomy 14:22-26, the Jews were allowed to bring money with them when they came to the temple for special sacrifices or occasions and buy the necessary items for their worship. Jesus was not objecting to there being money-changers or animals available for sale. His objection was that they had picked the temple area to carry on their business: "How dare you turn my Father's house into a market!"
>
> Notice, also, that Jesus did not accuse these men of dishonesty. This cleansing took place early in Jesus' ministry, when He went to Jerusalem for the first Passover after His public work began. There was a later cleansing of the temple which occurred when He went to Jerusalem for the last Passover before His death (see Matt. 21:12-13; Mark 11:15-17; Luke 19:45-46). On that occasion, He accused the men of being thieves: "My house will be a house of prayer, but you have made it a den of robbers!"

Many believed on Jesus during the feast (John 2:23-25):

During the Passover, Jesus performed a number of miracles which are not described. Many believed in Him because of these signs. Jesus held Himself back, however, and did not place His affairs in the hands of the multitudes because He knew the hearts of men. He did not need anyone to tell Him about men, because He knew all about them.

Nicodemus visits Jesus (John 3:1-21):

One of the Pharisees named Nicodemus was a member of the Jewish Sanhedrin (ruling council). He came to Jesus one night to talk with Him.

NOTE:

The Bible does not say why he came at night. Some have said it was cowardice. It may be that he came then because the day's work was done, and he had time to do so. Or it may have been the best time for a private talk with Jesus. We should avoid attributing cheap or improper motives to people in the Bible unless there is clear proof.

Nicodemus was interested in Jesus, but he did not know how he should regard the Lord. So he began the conversation by saying, "Rabbi, we know that you are a teacher who has come from God, because no man could do the signs you have done unless God were with him."

Jesus did not respond directly to Nicodemus' statement. Instead, He went to the heart of what all men must do: "I tell you the truth, unless a man is born again he cannot see the kingdom of God."

No doubt Nicodemus stared at Jesus as he thought over this puzzling statement. He said, "But how can a man be born when he is old? Surely he cannot enter a second time into his mother's womb to be born!" Nicodemus knew that Jesus was not speaking of a literal, physical re-birth, but he had no idea what Jesus meant. How could a man be born again?

Jesus answered, "I tell you the truth, unless a man is born of water and the Spirit, he cannot enter into the kingdom of God. The flesh is born of flesh, but that which is born of the Spirit is spirit. Do not be amazed that I said you must be born again. The wind blows where it will. You hear its sound and know it is real, but you cannot tell where it comes from or where it is going. So it is with everyone who is born of the Spirit."

Nicodemus said, "How can this be?"

Gently chiding, Jesus asked:

You are a teacher in Israel, and you do not understand these things? Truly we speak of things we know and testify what we have seen, but still you do not receive it. I have spoken of things that take place on earth, and you do not believe. How will you believe if I speak of heavenly things? No one has ever gone into heaven but the One who came down from heaven — the Son of Man. Just as Moses lifted up the serpent in the wilderness, so the Son of Man will have to be lifted up so that everyone who believes in Him may have eternal life.

Indeed, this was the plan of God. He loved the world so much that He sent His only begotten Son into the world so that whoever believes in Him shall not perish but have eternal life. God did not send His Son into the world to condemn the world, but to save the world. All men are offered the chance to believe on Him and be saved. But all those who do not accept the testimony and believe on Him are condemned in God's plan. Each individual has the choice of believing or disbelieving. The verdict is that even though the Light has come into the world, many will not believe because their deeds are evil. They love darkness rather than the light because they do not want their deeds exposed. But whoever chooses to live by the truth will come into the light, so that it may be plainly seen that what he has done has been done through God.

NOTE:

It is not certain whether verses 16-21 are a continuation of Jesus' conversation with Nicodemus or the inspired comments of John, amplifying what Jesus said. All this passage is definitely based on the visit of Nicodemus, so we include all the verses under this heading.

Look back to Numbers 21:4-9 to find the story about Moses lifting up the serpent in the wilderness. What was the connection between the serpent being lifted up and Jesus' life? This was just one more reference Jesus was making to His death. At this point in His ministry, such statements sounded like riddles.

Jesus preaches in the countryside of Judea (John 3:22-24):

After the Passover, Jesus spent some time in Judea with His disciples, more or less sharing in the work of John the Baptist. He was teaching the people and baptizing, although Jesus Himself was not doing the actual baptizing (John 4:2). He was preaching and the disciples were baptizing people.

John was still preaching in the area, baptizing at Aenon near Salim because there was plenty of water there. Many people were still coming to him to be baptized. These events took place before John was put into prison.

John's testimony regarding Jesus (John 3:25-36):

About this time, an argument arose between some of John's disciples and the Jews over purifying. We are given no more information about this discussion.

John's disciples learned about the work Jesus and His disciples were doing. They were not sure how they should feel about it, so they went to John and said, "Rabbi, that man who was with you beyond the Jordan — the One about whom you testified — well, He is baptizing, and everyone is going to Him."

John replied, "A man must be satisfied with whatever lot he receives from heaven. You yourselves can testify that I said, 'I am not the Christ, but was sent to go before Him.' The one who has the bride is the bridegroom. The friend who assists the bridegroom gets his joy from helping the bridegroom. That is my joy and it is complete. He must become greater while I must become less important."

John continued with his testimony: "The One who comes from above is above all. The one who is from the earth belongs to the earth. The One who comes from heaven testifies to what He has seen and heard, but no one accepts His testimony. The man who has accepted it has certified that God is truthful. Because the One God has sent speaks the words of God. To Him God has given the Spirit without limit. The Father loves the Son and has put everything into His hands. Everyone who believes in the Son has eternal life, but whoever does not obey the Son will not have life. Instead, the wrath of God will abide upon him."

John rebukes Herod Antipas and is put in prison (Matt. 14:1-5; Luke 3:19-20):

NOTE:

Herod Antipas had two brothers named Philip. One was Philip the tetrarch of Ituraea and Trachonitis (Luke 3:1). The other, Herod Philip, was banished by his father Herod the Great. He was living in Rome with his wife Herodias and his daughter Salome when Herod Antipas visited his brother and managed to woo away

Herodias.

John the Baptist reproved Herod Antipas for taking Herodias, saying, "It is not lawful for you to have her."

Herod Antipas added to all his other sins by putting John in prison. Antipas would have slain John except that he feared the people because they considered John a prophet.

NOTE:
John was imprisoned at Machaerus, east of the Dead Sea. According to Josephus, the public reason given for John's imprisonment was that Herod Antipas was afraid John might decide to lead a revolution. Look for Machaerus on your map.

Jesus' reasons for leaving Judea (Matt. 4:12; Mark 1:14; Luke 4:14; John 4:1-4):

Two things happened that made Jesus decide to leave Judea. One was that the Pharisees learned that Jesus was making and baptizing more disciples than John. [We have already noted that the disciples were doing the actual baptizing.] John's imprisonment occurred about this same time. When Jesus heard of these things, He decided to go back to Galilee. He also decided to go straight north through Samaria.

NOTE:
Look on your map. Do you see that the most direct route from Judea to Galilee was straight through Samaria? Jesus chooses this direct route this time. The Jews hated the mixed race of the Samaritans and sought to avoid them. They often crossed the Jordan River at Jericho and traveled north on the east side of the river until they crossed back over a few miles south of the Sea of Galilee.

Look back to 2 Kings 17:24-41 to see who the Samaritans were and how they came to be living in the midst of the Jews. The hatred between the Jews and Samaritans only intensified after the people of Judah came back from captivity and tried to rebuild their city of Jerusalem. The Samaritans were among their worst enemies during that period (see the books of Ezra and Nehemiah).

On His way through Samaria, Jesus talks to a woman of Samaria and then to others of the city (John 4:4-42):

Sychar was a city of Samaria near the site of old Shechem. Jesus and His disciples came to this city about noon. Jacob's well was located near the city, and Jesus, being weary from His journey, sat down by the well. He sent His disciples into the city to buy food.

While Jesus sat there — hungry, thirsty, and tired — He looked up and saw a Samaritan woman coming to draw water. Under normal circumstances there would have been no communication at all between a Jewish man and a Samaritan woman. Each would have ignored the other. This is what the Samaritan woman intended to do. She was shocked, therefore, when Jesus said, "Will you give me a drink of water?"

She looked at Him and said, "You are a Jew and I am a Samaritan woman. Why do you ask me for a drink?"

Jesus answered her, "If you knew what the gift of God is and who it is that asks you for a drink, you would have asked Him and He would have given you living water."

The well was 105 feet deep. The woman swept her eyes over Jesus again and said, "Sir, you have nothing to draw with and the well is deep. Where do you get this living water?" The woman perceived that Jesus was referring to something other than ordinary water. She continued: "Are you greater than our father Jacob, who gave us this well and drank from it himself, as did also his sons and his flocks and herds?"

Jesus answered, "Everyone who drinks of this water will get thirsty again, but whoever drinks the water I give him will never get thirsty. In fact, the water I give him will become a spring of water welling up to eternal life."

Jesus had placed the invitation before the woman to ask Him and He would give her living water. He had piqued her interest so that she wanted the water. So she said, "Sir, give me this water so that I will not get thirsty and have to keep coming all the way out here to draw water."

He told her: "Go, call your husband and come back here."

Jesus had brought up something here that the woman was ashamed of. She said, "I have no husband." She thought this simple statement would hide what she did not want this man to know.

But Jesus said, "You are right when you say you have no husband because you have had five husbands, and the man you are living with now is not your husband. So what you have said is quite true."

The woman was startled by Jesus' knowledge of her affairs. "Sir," she said, "I can tell that you are a prophet. Our fathers worshiped on this mountain, but you Jews claim that Jerusalem is the place we ought to worship."

NOTE:

The mountain to which the Samaritan woman referred was Gerizim. It was opposite Mt. Ebal. The mountains were on either side of Sychar and old Shechem. Mt. Gerizim was where the blessings were read by Joshua and the Israelites when they entered Canaan (Deut. 27:11-13; Josh. 8:33-34). It was also the location of a temple which had was built by the Samaritans after the close of the Old Testament. That temple was destroyed by John Hyrcanus about 128 B.C., but the site continued to be holy to the Samaritans. The woman wanted to hear what this authentic prophet had to say on the subject.

Jesus said, "Woman, believe me; a time is coming when neither this mountain nor Jerusalem will be the exclusive place where men worship. You Samaritans worship what you do not know; we worship what we do know, because salvation is from the Jews. But a time is coming and has come when the true worshippers will worship the Father in spirit and truth for they are the kind of worshippers the Father seeks. God is spirit, and His worshippers must worship Him in spirit and in truth."

The woman said, "I know that Messiah is coming. When He comes, He will tell us about all things."

Jesus declared, "I who speak to you am He."

Just then the disciples of Jesus returned and were surprised to find Him talking with a woman. Not one of them would say anything about it, though. They just ignored the whole situation.

Then, leaving her water pot, the woman went back into the town and told the people, "Come! See this man I have met. He has told me everything I ever did! Could this be the Christ?"

Meanwhile the disciples offered Jesus food, saying, "Rabbi, eat something."

But He answered, "I have had food to eat that you know nothing about."

When the disciples had left Jesus at the well, He was hungry. That is why they had gone to buy food. Now He says He is not hungry. The disciples were mystified. They said among themselves, "Did someone else bring Him food to eat?"

Jesus then told them about His special "food." He said, "My food is to do the will of the One who sent me and to finish His work." He said, "Look around you. Do you think it is still four months until harvest? Let me tell you that the fields are already ripe for harvest."

Soon the Samaritans came out of the city. Having heard the woman's testimony, they urged Jesus to stay with them. He stayed two days. Though many had believed on Him because of the woman's word, many more believed because of His words which they heard. They told the woman, "We no longer believe just because of what you said; now we have heard for ourselves, and we know that this man really is the Savior of the world."

Jesus arrives in Galilee (Matt. 4:12-17; Mark 1:14-15; Luke 4:14-15; John 4:43-45):

After two days with the Samaritans, Jesus continued His journey to Galilee. This fact is stated in the verses given above, and then an overview is given of the great Galilean ministry. We are told the Galileans welcomed Him because they had been in Jerusalem during the Passover and had seen the miracles He had done there. News of His arrival soon spread throughout the region. He taught in their synagogues and everyone praised Him at this point. Matthew and Mark each summarize the lessons He was preaching by saying He was preaching the good news of God: "The time has come; the kingdom of God is near. Repent and believe the good news."

The Great Galilean Ministry
(Matt. 4:12-14:12; Mark 1:14-6:29; Luke 4:14-9:9; John 4:43-5:47)

Life of Christ

Preparation
Beginning Ministry

*Galilean Ministry

 *Capernaum
 *Apostles Called
 *Great Multitudes
 *Many Miracles
 *Sermon on the Mount
 *First Opposition
 *Many Parables
 *Limited Commission
 *John Beheaded

Retirement
Close of Ministry
Last Week
Resurrection
Exaltation

So far, we have studied the years of preparation and the beginning of Jesus' ministry. The years of preparation cover the time from the announcement of the birth of John to Zacharias until the baptism of Jesus. The beginning of His ministry deals with the time from the baptism of Jesus until His return to Galilee after the Passover. Look in your left column and review your broad outline again. Jesus has returned to Galilee from Judea and we are ready to begin telling the events of the great Galilean ministry.

The chronology of the first two periods is fairly easy to figure. From this point on, however, the exact chronology of the life of Christ is exceedingly difficult to determine. There are two difficult questions about the Great Galilean Ministry. How long did it last? And, what is the order of the events which occur during it? Neither of these questions can be fully answered. The evidence is largely circumstantial with some of the answers being purely a matter of judgment.

The question of the length of the ministry of Jesus hinges on what feast He visited in John 5:1 (see note given at that point). I believe that when all the evidence is considered, it is better to say it was a Passover. If it were, then the Galilean ministry lasted eighteen to twenty-one months, and the public ministry of Jesus lasted a few months over three years as we have already described.

There is no way to determine the exact order of the miracles and lessons during this period. More important, however, is the *progress* of the history as Jesus' activities are described. First, there is an increasingly intensive manifestation by Jesus of Himself as the Son of God. Second, the twelve apostles are gradually trained to carry on His teaching and work after His death. Third, there is a deepening and spreading hostility among the influential classes of the Jews and among the rulers of the people.

As a teacher takes a class into this period and the following periods of Jesus' life, it will be necessary to do some choosing of stories to tell, parables to teach, and miracles to describe. Just because they are all in this material does not mean you will have time to teach them all. Nor does it mean they would all be suitable for all ages. Some of the lessons of the parables, or some of the great sermons, for example, will be difficult to convey to small children. Keep a record of the episodes covered this time, and then the next time through, try to choose a different set of stories so that all can be taught at some time.

Your primary task as a teacher of the life of Christ, just as it was the primary task of the gospel writers, is to present Jesus to your students vividly enough to help them learn who He was and what He was like. That is the only way we can learn to love Him and to imitate Him. This is the section of His life where so many of His miracles, His sermons, and His parables are described. Make them come alive for your students.

Since Mark comes nearer following a chronology of events in Christ's life, we will use his account as our basic guide. We will then amplify and supplement by using Matthew, Luke, and John.

The healing of the Nobleman's son (John 4:46-54):

Jesus came again to Cana of Galilee where He had turned the water into wine. A certain nobleman came to Him from Capernaum. The nobleman's son was deathly ill, so when he heard that Jesus had returned from Judea he came to ask Him to come and heal his son.

Jesus had already seen the attitude of the Jews in Jerusalem concerning His miraculous signs. He said, "Unless you people see miraculous signs and wonders, you will not believe, will you?"

The nobleman said, "Please, Sir, come down before my child dies." It was obvious he was not demanding a sign for him to be able to believe. He had come believing. His supplication made that clear.

Jesus replied, "You may go. Your son will live." When the compassionate words were spoken, the man departed.

> NOTE:
> It was one o'clock in the afternoon when this happened. It was about a four hour walk from Cana to Capernaum, yet the man did not get back home until the next day. In faith, he had accepted Jesus' statement about his son and did not frantically rush home to check on him.

On his way home the next day, his servants met him with news that his son lived. He asked, "What time was it when he got better?"

The servants replied, "The fever left him yesterday at one o'clock."

The father realized that this was the exact time when Jesus had told him, "Your son will live." The nobleman and all his house believed in Jesus as the Christ because of this miracle.

> NOTE:
> This story is placed here because it is the second sign Jesus did in Galilee (v. 54). Remember the first sign He did in Galilee was the changing of water to wine at Cana. This is not the second sign He had done anywhere, however, because the book of John specifically states that "while He was in Jerusalem at the Passover Feast, many people saw the miraculous signs He was doing and believed in His name" (John 2:23). The Galileans welcomed Jesus into their midst because they had seen the things which He had done in Jerusalem (John 4:45).

The first rejection at Nazareth (Luke 4:16-36):

It is clear from many references that Jesus used Capernaum as His home base during this period. Matthew tells of His leaving Nazareth to go to Capernaum (Matt. 4:13), but Luke tells us why.

Jesus went to Nazareth where He had been reared. How often He had come and had worshiped at the synagogue at Nazareth! As His custom was, He went into the synagogue on the sabbath day and stood up to read. The scroll of the prophet Isaiah was handed to Him. He found the passage which says: "The Spirit of the Lord is upon me; because He has anointed me to preach good news to the poor, to proclaim freedom for the prisoners and sight for the blind, to release the oppressed, and to proclaim the year of the Lord's favor" (Isa. 61:1-2).

He rolled the scroll back up and handed it to the keeper of the scrolls. When He sat down, every eye was upon Him, waiting. He said, "Today this scripture is fulfilled in your hearing."

Everyone had something good to say at first, and all were amazed at the gracious words that came from His lips. "Isn't this Joseph's son?" they asked.

Jesus said to them, "You will surely quote the proverb to me: 'Physician, heal thyself! Do here in your home town what we have heard that you did in Capernaum.'

"I tell you the truth," He continued, "no prophet is accepted in his home town. I assure you, there were many widows in Israel in Elijah's time when there was drought and famine. Yet Elijah was not sent to any of them, but to a widow in Zarephath in the region of Sidon. There were many in Israel with leprosy in the time of Elisha the prophet, yet not one of them was cleansed except Naaman the Syrian."

When Jesus referred to the Gentiles who were objects of blessing in the days of Elijah and Elisha, the crowd became furious. They seized Jesus, drove Him out of town, and took Him to a cliff where they intended to throw Him down. But He walked right through the crowd and went on His way.

Jesus moves to Capernaum (Matt. 4:13-16):

During this period of Jesus' work, He uses Capernaum as His headquarters. He resides there part of the time and often returns there after a preaching tour in some other part of Galilee.

Capernaum was in the area where the tribes of Zebulun and Naphtali once had their territories. The beauty of this region is praised by ancient writers. Jesus' move there fulfilled the prophecy of Isaiah that said: "The land of Zebulun and Naphtali, the way to the sea, beyond the Jordan, Galilee of the Gentiles — the people living in darkness have seen a great light, and to those living in the land and shadow of death has the light begun to shine" (Matt. 4:15-16, quoting Isa. 9:1-2).

> NOTE:
>
> Here is one of those countless instances in the New Testament where a knowledge of the Old Testament is indispensable to understand the passage. Go back and read Isaiah 9:1-2: "But there shall be no gloom to her that was in anguish. In earlier times He made the land of Zebulun and the land of Naphtali contemptible..."
>
> What was it that brought such desolation, such darkness, upon the territories of these tribes? This was the first portion of the land on the west side of the Jordan to be devastated by the Assyrians. The Assyrian king Tiglath-pileser III invaded this area and took away captives not long before the fall of Israel (2 Kgs. 15:29).
>
> It was during this very time, when the land was invaded, that Isaiah prophesied

this message. It simply said that, though this area was a region of gloom, and darkness, and sorrow, the day would come when it would be a place of joy, and gladness, and light. It was there that the light of God would shine in the deeds and teaching of Jesus Christ.

Be sure to show your students where Capernaum was, and also show them where the old territories of Zebulun and Naphtali were.

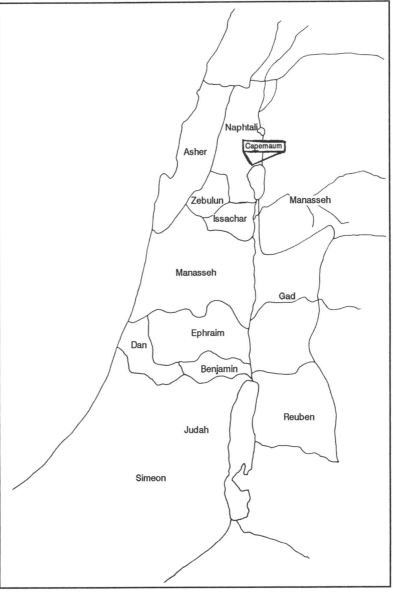

Jesus calls four disciples to follow Him (Mark 1:16-20; Matt. 4:18-22; Luke 5:1-11):

One day Jesus came walking by the Sea of Galilee. The multitude pressed upon Him so closely He hardly had room to stand to teach them. Nearby, the fishermen were washing and mending their nets, a job which had to be done after each fishing expedition. Jesus noticed two fishing boats at the water's edge. One of the boats belonged to Simon Peter and the other to Zebedee, the father of James and John.

Jesus got into Peter's boat and asked him to put out from shore just a little. From the boat, Jesus taught the multitude. When He had finished speaking, He turned to Peter and said, "Put out into deep water, and let down your nets for a catch."

Peter was tired. He said, "Master, we have worked very hard all night, and have caught nothing. But because you say so, I will let down the nets." It was obvious Peter did not have much hope of catching any fish.

The nets were gotten into the boat, and the fishermen put out into deep water. The nets were let down for a few moments, and then they began to haul them in. The nets have a certain weight as they are pulled in, even when they are empty. But — these nets were not empty! There were so many fish in the nets that the threads began to break as the men tried to pull them up. The other boat had to come out to help. There were so many fish that both boats were filled to the point they were sinking.

When Simon Peter saw this, his great and simple heart was so filled with faith and wonder, he fell to his knees and told Jesus, "Get away from me, for I am a sinful man, Lord." He was totally amazed at the immense catch of fish which they had taken. James and John, who were partners with Simon, were also amazed.

Jesus said to Peter, "Don't be afraid. From now on you will catch men." He also called Andrew, James, and John to come follow Him and to become fishers of men.

So these men turned their backs on what had been their lives and their livelihoods. As Peter would tell Jesus later, they forsook all to follow Him.

> NOTE:
> Remember that Jesus had already met these men when they were disciples of John. By now they had been with Him a good bit and knew Him well. The account in Luke is by far the fuller one, so we followed it in our story. Understand that the call of the men to follow Jesus came *after* the miraculous catch of fish and after the multitude had left.

Jesus teaches in the synagogue and heals a demoniac (Mark 1:21-28; Luke 4:31-37):

On the sabbath day, Jesus entered the synagogue at Capernaum to teach. The multitude was impressed with Jesus' teaching because He taught them as one who had authority, not as the teachers of the law among the Jews.

During the lesson, a man who was possessed by an unclean spirit cried out, "What do you want with us, Jesus of Nazareth? Have you come to destroy us? I know who you are — the Holy One of God!"

Jesus never wanted the demons' confessions. He said, "Hush!" Then He said, "Come out of him." The evil spirit shook the man violently and came out of him with a shriek.

Everyone was amazed and asked one another, "What is this? A new teaching! With authority He commands even the evil spirits and they obey Him." The news of this deed was circulated throughout all of Galilee.

> NOTE:
> This event and the healing of Peter's mother-in-law happened on the sabbath. Mark and Luke relate both of these events, while Matthew tells only of the healing of Peter's mother-in-law. Luke and Mark are almost exactly parallel at this point. Luke, however, tells of the call of the four disciples in the fifth chapter *after* these things. It seems more logical to follow Mark's order, so that the four have already been called and are accompanying Jesus regularly in the events recorded in Mark 1:21-39 and Luke 4:31-44.

Jesus heals Peter's mother-in-law (Mark 1:29-34; Matt. 8:14-17; Luke 4:38-41):

After leaving the synagogue, Jesus went to the house of Simon and Andrew. James and John were with them also. Peter's mother-in-law was suffering from a high fever. They told Jesus about her, and He took her by the hand and made the fever leave her. Immediately she was well and got up and waited on them.

That evening, when the sun was set, people brought all their sick, and those who were possessed by demons. Jesus healed every one of them, but He would not allow the evil spirits to speak because, though they knew He was the Christ, He would not have their confessions.

NOTE:

Notice that huge crowds are gathering to see and hear Jesus. The man possessed with the evil spirit was healed early in the day, and before night, others afflicted in the same way were brought to be healed. By now all those with sick relatives or friends were interested in bringing them to Jesus. Human nature has not changed. If Jesus came into our midst today, we would seek to bring our sick friends to Him.

In every crowd that gathered at this point in the Bible story, there were some who wanted to be healed themselves, plus friends who were very interested in the loved one being healed. In addition, there were many who gathered to see the marvel of the miracles, just as we might gather to see the marvels of some magician. Yet, all of Jesus' miracles were for the purpose of producing faith in the hearts of His listeners. When the crowds gathered, He taught as well as healed. Therefore, these that came, whether hoping to be healed or just curious, would soon become either believers or unbelievers. There would be no middle ground.

This early in His ministry, the unbelievers are still quiet. All of these miracles took place on the same day, and that day was a sabbath, because the story begins by telling that Jesus went into a synagogue on a sabbath to teach. Later His enemies will oppose His every action on a sabbath day. Now the strongest emotion among those who follow Him is amazement that He is capable of such teaching and such miracles.

Jesus tours Galilee, preaching and healing (Mark 1:35-39; Matt. 4:23-25; Luke 4:42-44):

Very early the next morning, while it was still dark, Jesus got up, left the house, and went to a solitary place to pray. Simon and the other disciples went to look for Him. When they found Him, they said, "Everyone is looking for you!"

Jesus replied, "Let us go somewhere else — to the nearby villages — so that I can preach there also. That is why I have come." So He traveled through Galilee, preaching in their synagogues and performing miracles.

NOTE:

This account, and other references such as Luke 8:1-3, indicate that Jesus made several preaching tours through the territory during the Galilean ministry. About some of these, such as this one in Mark 1:35-39, we are given no details. Just be sure you note that such tours were made. We are given only a sampling of the miracles and sermons from Jesus' life. "Jesus did many other signs *which are not written in this book*, but these are written that ye might believe that Jesus is the Christ, the Son of God; and that believing ye might have life through His name" (John 20:30-31).

Healing of a leper (Mark 1:40-45; Matt. 8:2-4; Luke 5:12-16):

While Jesus was going through one of the cities of Galilee, a man with a severe case of leprosy came to Him and knelt down. The man said, "If you are willing, you can heal me."

Jesus was moved with compassion at the terrible condition of the man. He said, "I am willing," and He touched him and said, "Be clean." Immediately the man was clean.

Jesus said, "See that you do not tell anyone about this. Be sure and go show yourself to the priest and offer the gift Moses commanded." (See Lev. 13:49; 14:2-32).

The man did not stay quiet as Jesus asked, however, but told everyone he saw what had happened to him. The word spread fast so that soon Jesus could not enter publicly into a city without being thronged by the crowds. Even in the countryside, multitudes sought Him to hear Him, and to be healed.

> NOTE:
>
> The word leprosy in the Bible referred to a variety of skin diseases. Some were contagious; some were not. The people had no means of determining whether any one case was contagious or not. The Law of Moses declared a leper unclean. Anything he touched was unclean. Even an object on which could be seen a patch of leprosy was to be either washed, burned, or destroyed (Lev. 13-14).
>
> This is the first time in the story when someone who was healed was told not to tell anyone what had happened. There will be more occasions. Why? Surely the one healed would be excited and would want to tell the news. Did not Jesus want to be known?
>
> Jesus gave this instruction on occasions when the crowds were thronging Him. He did His miracles in order to give testimony that He was indeed the Christ, but He did not want the people coming only for the purpose of seeing and experiencing miracles. He wanted time to teach them. The crowds were coming so constantly at this point, Jesus had very little time to rest or to teach the profound lessons He needed to preach. It is no wonder that Jesus often withdrew to lonely places and prayed, just as Mark described in Mark 1:35-37.

Jesus heals a paralytic in Capernaum (Mark 2:1-12; Matt. 9:2-8; Luke 5:17-26):

Soon after Jesus returned to Capernaum, the word was out that He was in the city, and a great crowd of people came together to hear Him teach. They were crowded into the house so much that there was no room for anyone else. Even the doorway was packed full.

Four men carrying a man who was spastic came to the house. They could not get in the door, so they went up on top of the house. They removed several tiles or flat stones from the roof. When the hole was big enough, they lowered the man into the house into the midst of the crowd.

Naturally Jesus' teaching had come to a halt as a hole appeared in the roof. Then, as the platform was lowered into the room, everyone's eyes were on the poor man with his shriveled, gnarled limbs. It was apparent that this man needed to be healed.

Jesus was impressed with the faith of the these men, but as He looked upon the palsied man, He saw something all men need even more than the healing of their bodies. Jesus said to the sick man, "My son, your sins are forgiven."

There were Pharisees and teachers of the law there, some from as far away as Judea and Jerusalem. They thought: "Who does this man think He is that He can forgive sins? Does He think He is God? He is blaspheming and dishonoring God because only God can forgive sins."

Jesus knew exactly what they were thinking. He asked them, "Why are you thinking these things in your hearts? After all, which is easier, to say, 'Your sins are forgiven,' or 'Get up! Take up your bed and walk'? But just so you will know that the Son of Man does have power on earth to forgive sins" — He turned to the spastic man — "Get up! Take up your bed and go to your house."

Immediately the man arose, having been fully healed right before their eyes, and took up his bed and went out through the crowd.

Everyone was amazed and glorified God saying, "We have never seen anything like this."

NOTE:

Jesus asked which of the two statements was easier to say. To say, "Your sins are forgiven," would be easy, because no one could tell by looking whether the sins were forgiven or not. But if Jesus said, "Get up. Take up your bed and walk," it would be immediately obvious to all whether He had power or not. So Jesus used power they could see in action to teach them He could do that which they could not see taking place. He could forgive sins!

Look at the reasoning that should have followed this miracle. God gives His power only to those whom He approves. This man can do miracles. Therefore God must approve of Him. Yet, this man says He can forgive sins. God would not approve of a liar or a blasphemer. Yet He approves of this man. Therefore this man must be telling the truth. But only Deity can forgive sins. Therefore, His claims to Deity must be true.

The people with honest and sincere hearts did reason this way. We will watch as the unbelievers begin to reason incorrectly. It was Jesus' use of this divine prerogative that began to arouse opposition.

The call of Matthew (Levi) and his feast in honor of Jesus (Mark 2:13-17; Matt. 9:9-13; Luke 5:27-32):

Again Jesus went out by the Sea of Galilee. A large crowd came to Him and He began to teach them. As He walked along, He passed by a place where Roman tribute was collected. The publican (or tax collector) in charge was a man named Matthew (Levi), the son of Alphaeus. Jesus said to him, "Follow me." Matthew left his business and followed Jesus.

NOTE:

No prior meeting of Jesus and Matthew is recorded, though there may have been one or more. Matthew was one of five apostles whose specific call is related. As a publican, he fit into a group which was hated by the Jews. Publicans were Jews who collected the tax for the Roman government. They were a constant reminder of the Roman domination and a profession which helped to exert Roman oppression. Publicans were counted as traitors to their people. They had a reputation for being dishonest, but some (such as Zachaeus) made an effort to be honest. There is no need to assume Matthew was a dishonest man. Nevertheless, it is remarkable that

Jesus could put together a group of men that included such diverse elements as a tax collector for the Romans and a Jewish zealot (Simon Zelotes). The zealots were the Jews most bitterly opposed to the Roman domination and could be compared to the terrorists of today.

Matthew made a great feast in his house, with Jesus as his invited guest. Many of the guests were publicans. The scribes and Pharisees who were now nearly always present in the crowds that gathered, observed Jesus and said to His disciples, "Why do you and your Master eat with publicans and sinners?"

When Jesus heard their question, He answered them saying, "A person who is well does not need a physician. It is the sick person who needs a doctor. I did not come to call righteous men but sinners. But you need to go and learn what this means: 'I desire mercy and not sacrifice'" (Hos. 6:6).

NOTE:
Jesus' point was that the Pharisees considered themselves perfect. They did not think they needed what He offered. Since they would not accept His help, He turned to those who would. When He did that, it was soon obvious that the Pharisees were so consumed by hatred for the publicans and others whom they deemed "sinners" that they did not want them saved. They needed to learn the lesson of Hosea 6:6 that God is more interested in men having the right attitudes than He is in ritualistic sacrifices men offer to hide their hatred and unkindness.

Jesus defends His disciples for their feasting instead of fasting (Mark 2:18-22; Matt. 9:14-17; Luke 5:33-39):

All three of the writers cited give this story next. Therefore, it apparently happened on the occasion of the feast at Matthew's house. The objection to Jesus and His disciples feasting instead of fasting came from a somewhat surprising source. It was the disciples of John who asked, "Why do we and the Pharisees fast often, but your disciples do not fast?"

Jesus answered, "Is it appropriate for the friends of the bridegroom to mourn while He is still with them? As long as they are together they rejoice. But when the bridegroom leaves them, then they will fast. No man patches a hole in an old garment with a new piece of cloth because the new piece will shrink when it is washed and tear out an even bigger hole. Neither do men put new wine into old wineskins because the new wine will expand and burst the old wineskins. The new wine has to be put into new wineskins."

NOTE:
All three of Jesus' illustrations make the same basic point. Some actions are not appropriate. It would not be appropriate for Jesus' disciples to fast, which was often a sign of grief, while their Lord was with them.
Fasting was an act of devotion which has never been emphasized in God's word as a thing of great importance. Only on the Day of Atonement which came once a year were the Jews commanded to "afflict their souls," (Lev. 16:29), which is taken to mean fasting.
When fasting was practiced as a product of genuine repentance and mourning for

sins, it was pleasing to God. But fasting easily became something that men could do to show how pious they were. It was considered to have merit of itself. Such a misconception was wrong. Jesus did not deal with the subject of fasting comprehensively. He dealt with it in the context of the question which had been asked.

Jesus attends a feast of the Jews and heals a lame man (John 5:1-47):

After these things, there was a feast of the Jews, and Jesus went up to Jerusalem.

> NOTE:
>
> There is no way of knowing exactly when this event occurred. The evidence is very scant. There is no place in the narratives of Matthew, Mark, or Luke which shows a definite break in the work in Galilee while Jesus goes to Jerusalem. This story deals with a conflict over the sabbath day. Therefore, we are grouping it with two other stories that involve a similar conflict.

At this time there was a pool called Bethesda located near the Sheep Gate in Jerusalem. This pool had five porches or porticoes surrounding it for shelter. Multitudes of sick people — some sick, blind, lame, or paralyzed — gathered in these porches. They were waiting for the water to be stirred, and then the first one into the water hoped to be healed. One of the crowd was a man who had been an invalid for thirty-eight years.

Jesus, observing the crowd of sick people, noticed this man and said, "Would you like to be made well?"

The sick man answered, "Sir, I have no one to help me into the pool when the water is stirred. While I am trying to get there, someone else gets in ahead of me."

Jesus said, "Get up! Take up your bed, and walk." At once the man was well. He picked up his mat and walked away.

> NOTE:
>
> This story has an interesting aspect. There were crowds of people here at the pool of Bethesda who wanted to be healed, but Jesus ignored them. He did not come into the world for the purpose of healing all physical maladies. Instead, His miracles were performed for specific reasons. On this occasion, Jesus deliberately selected someone to heal who would have a cot to pick up and carry so that He could have an opportunity to talk to the Jews about their misunderstandings concerning the sabbath law.

It was a sabbath day. When the Jews saw the man, they said, "It is the sabbath, and it is not lawful for you to carry your bed."

The man replied, "The man who healed me told me to take up my bed and walk."

The Jews did not ask, "Who healed you?" They blinded themselves to the display of genuine power which had been used to do this miracle. Instead they asked, "Who told you to take up your bed and walk?"

But the man had no idea who it was because Jesus had left quickly after the miracle was done. Later Jesus found the man in the temple and said, "See, you have been healed. Sin no more or something worse may happen to you."

The man promptly went and told the Jews that it was Jesus who had healed him. The Jews, therefore, persecuted Jesus because He had done this on the sabbath.

But Jesus took the opportunity to teach the Jews about the sabbath day. He reasoned with them saying, "My Father continues to work even until now, and I work." The divine activity continued even on the sabbath. No one thought of accusing God of breaking the sabbath. The Son was sharing in the work of God when He healed the man. He was no more breaking the sabbath than God was.

Nevertheless, the Jews tried harder to find a way they could kill Jesus. They were angry because they thought He had broken the sabbath. Now they were more upset because He called God His own Father, making Himself equal with God.

Jesus continued His speech:

The Son does nothing but what the Father shows Him and what the Father gives Him to do. You will be amazed when you see what greater things the Father is planning to give the Son. Just as God raises the dead and gives them life, even so the Son gives life to whom He will. Moreover, the Father judges no one, but has entrusted all judgment to the Son so that all may honor the Son as they have honored the Father. He who does not honor the Son does not honor the Father who sent Him.

Really and truly, I tell you that whoever hears my word and believes the One who sent me has eternal life and will not be condemned. He has passed from death to life. Truly, a time is coming and has come when the dead will hear the voice of the Son of God, and those who hear will live. Because just as God has life in Himself, so He has granted the Son to have life in Himself. He has also given Him authority to judge because the Son is a human being.

Do not be amazed at this. The time is coming when all who are in their graves will hear the Son's voice, and will come forth. Those who have done good will rise to live, but those who have done evil will rise to be condemned. By myself I do nothing; I judge only as I am instructed, and my judgment is just because I am not trying to please myself but Him that sent me.

If I testify of myself, my testimony is not valid. But there is another who testifies of me, and I know His testimony is valid.

You sent to John, and he told you the truth. But the witness which I am talking about is not from a human being, nevertheless I mention John's testimony that you may be saved. John was a lamp that burned and gave light, and you chose for a while to enjoy the light he gave.

I have greater testimony than John's. The very works which the Father has given me bear witness that the Father sent me. The Father who sent me has testified concerning me. You have never heard His voice nor seen His form, nor does His word abide in you, because you do not believe the One He has sent. You diligently study the scriptures because you think that by them you possess eternal life. These are the very scriptures that testify about me but you still refuse to come to me to have life.

I do not receive glory from men, but I know your problem: God's love is not in your hearts. I have come in the Father's name, and you do not accept me. If another comes in his own name, you will receive him. How can you believe if the only praise you care about is that which comes from men?

Do not think that I will accuse you before the Father. The one who will do that is Moses on whom you have set your hope. If you really believed Moses you would believe me because he wrote of me. But if you do not believe Moses' writings, how will you believe my words?

The disciples pluck grain on the sabbath (Mark 2:23-28; Matt. 12:1-8; Luke 6:1-5):

One time, Jesus and His disciples were going through the grain fields on a sabbath day. As the disciples went, they plucked grain, rubbed the kernels between their hands to remove the husk, and ate them.

The Pharisees objected, saying, "Look, your disciples are breaking the law of the sabbath."

> NOTE:
> The Pharisees were not objecting to the plucking of grain from someone else's field, because the law specifically commanded that such a practice be allowed (see Deut. 23:25). They objected because they considered the plucking to be reaping, the rubbing of the kernels to be threshing — primary works that could not be done according to the rabbinical interpretations of the law.

Jesus replied, "Have you not read what David did when he was hungry? He entered the house of God and ate the shewbread which was given him by the priest. He ate that which only the priests were allowed to eat. In addition, have you not read in the law how the priests desecrate the sabbath (by working, offering the commanded sacrifices) and are yet blameless? (see Num. 28:9-10). The fact is that there is One here who is greater than the temple. The sabbath was made for man, not man for the sabbath. But if you had known the meaning of this statement: 'I desire mercy, and not sacrifice,' you would not have condemned the guiltless. Because the Son of Man is Lord of the sabbath."

Jesus heals a man with a withered hand on the sabbath (Mark 3:1-6; Matt. 12:9-14; Luke 6:6-11):

On another sabbath, Jesus entered into a synagogue to teach. There was a man present who had a withered hand. The scribes and Pharisees watched to see if Jesus would heal the man on the sabbath day so that they might accuse Him.

Jesus knew exactly what was going on, but instead of seeking to evade the issue, He said to the man, "Get up and stand out here in front of everyone." The man got up and stood in the midst of the people.

Then Jesus said, "Is it lawful on the sabbath to do good or to do harm? To save a life, or to kill? Which one of you, if you had a sheep, and the sheep fell into a pit on the sabbath day, would not lift that sheep out? How much more valuable is a man than a sheep?"

No one would say anything. Jesus looked around at all of them, and His heart was stirred with anger at the hardening of their hearts. Then He said, "Therefore it is lawful to do good on the sabbath day."

He told the man, "Stretch out your hand." The man extended his hand, and bone and sinew were mended; flesh and skin filled out, and in an instant the man was healed.

But the Jews were very angry. They even met with their enemies, the Herodians, to plan how they could kill Jesus.

NOTE:

Did Jesus break the sabbath law? The three events we have just studied were all occasions when Jesus was accused of breaking the law. He denied that He did so. Let us be careful, as we study the passages, that we remember that Jesus did *NO* sin, neither was any guile found in His mouth (1 Pet. 2:22). Therefore, we must study the arguments Jesus made on these occasions to see what He was actually saying about His actions. Remember that these stories are in the Bible to create faith. As a teacher, *never* say, with doubt written all over your face, "Well, I don't know *why* Jesus did that!" Instead, study Jesus' arguments and learn the explanation.

As you tell these stories, stress that neither the disciples nor Jesus broke the law of Moses. With younger children, tell the story with little or no explanation. Then, among older students, explain the points to the degree they can understand.

In order that teachers may have badly needed information about the sabbath, we add the following notes:

The Jewish rabbis divided all work into thirty-nine general categories. Then they classified literally hundreds of activities under these thirty-nine headings and gave specific rules about each activity. We will look at a few examples.

In giving the rules regulating the sabbath, the law of Moses specified, "Ye shall kindle no fire throughout your habitations upon the sabbath day" (Exod. 35:1-3). The rabbis had taken that law and had forbidden anything that required concentration of the mind near a lighted lamp — lest one forget and incline the lamp to bring the wick nearer the oil and thus be guilty of "kindling." Under the same category, they had declared that it was permitted to tell a non-Jew to kindle a fire in a stove if the weather were cold, since the cold makes everyone suffer, but it is wrong to do so if it is not necessary. If the non-Jew happened to place cold food on the stove before he kindled the fire, it was all right if the food got warm. He could not, however, put the food on a stove where a fire was already burning. Neither could a Jew tell the non-Jew to put the food on the stove before he started the fire.

Another specific statement from the Old Testament about the sabbath law was "Take heed to yourselves, and bear no burden on the sabbath day, nor bring it in by the gates of Jerusalem" (Jer. 17:21-22). On the occasion when that passage was written, the prophet Jeremiah was rebuking the people of Judah for their total disregard for the sabbath day. They were going ahead with their normal work, as if there were no sabbath law. The rabbis had taken this restriction and had made the following rules.

If a house catches fire on the sabbath, one can carry out and save only such articles as will be used to keep the sabbath. One may, however, go into the house, put on as many clothes as he can wear, go outside, take them off, go back in and put on more clothes to carry out.

One was allowed to wear a bandage on a wound (if the bandage were made *before* the sabbath began), provided that the wound was bad enough to be in danger of bleeding. Otherwise, it was a burden.

The list of regulations the rabbis had made could go on and on. If one were wearing false teeth for appearance sake, it was all right. If he were wearing them for the purpose of chewing his food, then he was "grinding" and, therefore, doing wrong.

Jesus did *not break any law of God about the sabbath day.* Instead He broke the traditions and regulations that the rabbis had made up about the day. That is what made the Pharisees and others so angry, because they counted their traditions as binding as the law itself. (Rabbi Solomon Ganzfried, *Code of Jewish Law,* Vol. II, pp. 63ff.)

Now let us take a moment to look at the points Jesus made on these three occasions. In Jerusalem, He made the point that God continues to work on the sabbath day, and that Jesus was doing the exact work that He had been given to do by God Himself.

Then, in connection with the disciples plucking grain on the sabbath day, He referred to the time David ate shewbread. Even the Pharisees would have said that the action of the disciples would have been all right on any day except the sabbath. Yet, David's action would have gone against the law on any day of the week. The story referred to in David's life concerns the time when he fled from King Saul (1 Sam. 21). David went to Nob, a city of the priests. He asked Ahimelech for bread, and the only bread the priest had was the old shewbread which was replaced each sabbath day. The law specified that the old shewbread was to be eaten by only the priests (Lev. 24:5-9). Yet, David was in need, and Ahimelech gave the shewbread to David and to the men with him. Jesus did not express disapproval of what was done for David. The immediate point was that the Jews had never thought of criticizing David. The same God who commanded the priests to eat the shewbread also commanded the showing of mercy. When someone was sick, or starving, one should not refrain from helping them. No law of God was given to keep men from showing mercy. When Ahimelech gave David the shewbread, he was obeying a law of God, one which took precedence over the law of the shewbread on that one occasion.

Likewise, Jesus reminded the Pharisees that the priests work on the sabbath day. The law required that they prepare new shewbread on that day and that they offer specific sacrifices (Lev. 24:5-9; Num. 28:9-10). The same God who commanded a day of rest on the sabbath commanded the priests to perform these specific duties. Therefore, in the service of the temple, the priests labored on the sabbath and yet were not guilty of breaking the law. Jesus' disciples served One who was greater than the temple. Did the Pharisees believe that such a one would allow His disciples to break the very law He had given and which He came to fulfill?

The sabbath was given by God to be a blessing for the Israelites, to provide them a day of rest. The Jews had turned it into a day which bristled with minute regulations. God never intended that people go hungry on the sabbath, nor that they freeze to death. Such results violated the very purpose of the sabbath day.

The Jews needed to learn that God preferred righteousness, goodness, and mercy over ritual for ritual's sake. If the Jews had understood that principle, they would not have condemned the innocent. Jesus thus pronounced His disciples guiltless of breaking the sabbath law.

The Son of Man is Lord of the Sabbath. Jesus was not at all saying that since He was Lord of the Sabbath, He could break it if He pleased. It meant that He never forgot who He was. He was the Lord who had *given* the sabbath law in ages past. Of all men, He knew exactly what that law meant and how it should be kept. The Pharisees criticized Him because they did not believe He was the Son of God.

Note how the opposition from the unbelievers is growing. Jesus deliberately looked for a man to heal in Jerusalem in order to create the very discussion about the sabbath day which arose. Then by the time the man with the withered hand was healed in the synagogue, the teachers of the law were watching to see what Jesus would do so that they might trap Him. The Jews in Jerusalem were so angry about Jesus' statements, they wanted to kill him. In the third story, the teachers of the law were so angry they went out and began plotting to kill Him.

Notice the incorrect reasoning they were doing. They should have said: This man obviously has the approval of God because of the mighty miracles He can do. Yet He says our rules about the sabbath day are wrong. Therefore, we must be mistaken in our rules because He obviously knows God's will better than we do. Instead, they said: He breaks our traditions. Therefore, we do not like Him and we refuse to believe anything He does, even though He does do miracles we cannot deny.

Jesus teaches and heals great multitudes by the Sea of Galilee (Mark 3:7-12; Matt. 12:15-21):

The multitudes following Jesus were still very large and will continue to be large for some time yet, as we follow Him in His work. Jesus was aware of the plot the Pharisees were making to try to kill Him, so He withdrew to the Sea of Galilee with His disciples. A great multitude from Galilee, Judea, Jerusalem, Idumea, beyond Jordan, Tyre, and Sidon followed Him to observe the things which He did.

NOTE:
Find all these places on your map. Label them on your blank map. Particularly note the Sea of Galilee.

As He did more than once, He got into a boat and had His disciples put out from shore a little so that He could have room to teach. He also healed many people and cast out demons, forbidding them to tell who He was.

Jesus' method fulfilled the prophecy of Isaiah 42:1-4 that the Servant of Jehovah would not become known with fanfare and public outcry, but through the work He would do. He would nurture and minister to the bruised reeds and smoking flax among the people, till He would send forth judgment unto victory. And in His name the Gentiles would have hope also.

After a night of prayer, Jesus selects twelve apostles (Mark 3:13-19; Luke 6:12-16):

One of the most important things that Jesus did was to choose and train twelve men to carry on His work. It is no wonder that Jesus spent the night before He appointed the twelve praying. Until now, these men were followers, disciples. Now they would begin gradually to share in Jesus' work. The plan was for these men shortly to go out and preach. They would exercise power to cast out demons and to heal.

Matthew does not give the names of the apostles until they are ready to go out on the limited commission (Matt. 10:2-4). A fourth list is found in Acts 1:13, minus Judas Iscariot who, by that time, had committed suicide.

NOTE:

The word apostle means "one sent." The apostles were unique in the history of the church. They served as eye witnesses of the life of Christ, and were therefore uniquely qualified to tell the world the good news about Jesus. In addition, they were given the baptism of the Holy Spirit (on the day of Pentecost, Acts 2) to bring to their remembrance all things Jesus had said and done and to guide them into all truth. It was their task to lay the foundation of Jesus Christ upon which the church was built (Eph. 2:20; 1 Cor. 3:11).

```
Memorize the names of the
apostles:

Peter
Andrew
James
John
Philip
Bartholomew
Thomas
Matthew
James
Thaddaeus
Simon
Judas
```

As the apostles died, there was no effort at all to replace them. Paul was chosen as a very special apostle to work particularly with the Gentiles. The very way in which he is described as an "apostle out of due season" is evidence that God never intended to replace apostles. There is no evidence at all of apostolic succession.

Since the order of the apostles named differs slightly from one list to the other, let us all learn to name them from the same list to avoid confusion. The list in Matthew 10:2-4 is the one followed most often.

The sermon on the mount (Matt. 5-7; Luke 6:17-49):

NOTE:

The speech recorded in Luke is probably the same as the one recorded by Matthew. They begin in the same way; they follow the same order, and they end with the same warning. Sections of the sermon on the mount as recorded by Matthew are found elsewhere in Luke's account. It is, therefore, implied that Jesus taught many of these lessons in more than one setting.

Matthew describes the event as taking place on a mountain while Luke has it on a "level place" or plain. There is certainly no problem with having the sermon taught at a level place *on* a mountain. No one knows which mountain served as the site for the sermon, but tradition says it was the Horns of Hattin located a few miles west of the Sea of Galilee.

Weeks can be spent studying the sermon on the mount. For the purpose of this course, we need to study it lightly and summarize its teaching.

```
Memorize the Beatitudes:

Blessed are the poor in spirit:
for their's is the kingdom of heaven.

Blessed are they that mourn:
for they shall be comforted.

Blessed are the meek:
for they shall inherit the earth.

Blessed are they which do hunger and
thirst after righteousness:
for they shall be filled.

Blessed are the merciful:
for they shall obtain mercy.

Blessed are the pure in heart:
for they shall see God.

Blessed are the peacemakers:
for they shall be called the children
of God.

Blessed are they which are persecuted
for righteousness' sake:
for their's is the kingdom of heaven.

Blessed are ye, when men shall revile
you, and persecute you, and shall say
all manner of evil against you false-
ly, for my sake. Rejoice and be
exceeding glad:
for so persecuted they the prophets
which were before you.
```

A great multitude of Jesus' disciples were present for this lesson. Large crowds were following Him from Galilee, the Decapolis, Jerusalem, Judea, Syria, and from the region beyond the Jordan (Matt. 4:23-25). Jesus healed many, and then, finding a level spot upon the mountain, He sat down and His disciples came to Him. He began to teach them — directing His message specifically to His disciples with the larger multitude listening in the background.

Matthew 5; Luke 6:17-36:

Perhaps the most famous part of the sermon on the mount is the beatitudes. "Beatitude" is from a Latin word which means "happy" or "blessed." There are eight beatitudes with the eighth one repeated and amplified. The beatitudes show that blessedness (happiness) is not what the world thinks it is.

Also the beatitudes describe the character that each disciple of the Lord, each child of the kingdom, should have. But because true blessedness and godly character are so different from the world's concept of happiness, persecutions will come. Instead of being turned away from the service of God by such things, rejoice, realizing that the righteous people of long ago were persecuted also. As they were rewarded, so God's present children will be rewarded, and how great that reward will be!

Followers of God *must* be different from the world. Righteous people are the salt of the earth, the light of the world. Salt is *made* to be tasted; light is *made* to be seen. Do not suppress your impact and influence upon others, but let your light shine in such a way that men will see your good works and glorify God.

Jesus did not come to destroy the law, but to fulfill it. If Jesus had been talking about prophecy, then fulfill would have had a different significance here. Rather, He meant that He came to help men understand what obeying God's law was all about. This idea certainly fits far better with what follows than the idea of finishing the law so as to do away with it.

For example, anyone who wishes to obey the law, which teaches it is wrong to murder, will see that the teaching against murder also condemns hate and even scorn toward another.

Anyone who truly wants to avoid adultery will avoid lust. Sometimes one may say, "But I can't help it. When my eyes look upon a woman, they just lust in spite of everything." Jesus met this foolish excuse head on: "If your right eye causes you to sin, pluck it out and throw it away. It is better for you to lose one part of your body than for your whole body to be thrown into hell."

Jesus dealt with divorce, the swearing of oaths, the seeking of personal revenge, and the love of one's enemies in the same way.

Matthew 6:

Acts of worship should be offered to God, not done to be seen of men. Jesus said:

When you give to the needy, don't blow your horn so that everyone will be sure to notice how good you are. If that is what you're after, then that is all you will get.

Likewise, when you pray, don't be like the hypocrites who like to stand on the corner and pray so that everyone will see them. If that is what they want, then that is all they will get. When you pray, pray quietly, privately, and your Father will hear your prayer.

Also, when you fast, do not mark your face so that people will know you are fasting. I tell you the truth — that is all you will get from your fasting. If you fast, wash your face and anoint your head and let your fasting be between you and God.

Do not worry about accumulating money and material things which are often stolen or destroyed. Lay your treasures up in heaven.

You cannot have two masters. Either the world and its treasures, or God; that is the choice. Therefore, do not worry about your life, what you will eat or drink. Look at the birds. They do not sow or reap or gather into barns, yet your heavenly Father feeds them. Are you not much more valuable than they?

And why worry about clothes? Look at the lilies of the field, how they grow. They do not work or spin the thread for their garments. And yet, not even Solomon, in all his glory, was dressed as beautifully as these.

Therefore do not worry about tomorrow. It will take care of itself. Do what can be done today, and, above all, seek the kingdom of God and His righteousness first.

Matthew 7; Luke 6:37-49:

Finally Jesus warned against hypocritical judging. He said:

As you judge, you will be judged. If you are not merciful to others, do not expect mercy for yourself. Why do you look at the speck in your brother's eye and pay no attention to the plank in your own eye? First get the plank out of your eye and then you will be able to see clearly to get the speck out of your brother's eye.

He who really wants what God has for mankind can have it. If he asks, it will be given; if he seeks, he will find; if he knocks, the door will be opened. Your Father knows how to give you what you need. In everything you do, be sure to treat others as you would like to be treated because this rule sums up all that is involved in obeying the law and the prophets.

Be sure to enter the narrow gate. Wide is the gate and broad is the way which leads to destruction, and many will enter through it. But narrow is the gate and demanding is the way that leads to life and only a few will find it.

Look out for false prophets. They will pretend to be sheep, but inside they are ferocious wolves. You will be able to tell them by their fruits. A good tree does not bear bad fruit; nor does a bad tree bear good fruit.

Not everyone who says to me, "Lord, Lord" (that is, "Ruler, Ruler"), will enter into the kingdom of heaven. It is the one who does the will of my Father, that is, the one who accepts my rule, who will enter heaven.

Everyone who hears these words and puts them into practice will be like a wise man who built his house on the rock. The rain came down, the streams arose, and the wind blew and beat upon the house. Yet it did not fall because it was built upon a rock. But everyone who hears these words of mine and does not do them will be like a foolish man who built his house on the sand. The rain came down, the streams arose, and the winds blew and beat upon that house. It fell with a great crash because it was built on the sand.

Stories recorded in Matthew and Luke which fit into this period:

We come at this point to several stories related by Matthew and Luke which are not included in Mark. It seems best to include them here before the great day of parables found in Matthew, Mark, and Luke.

Jesus heals a centurion's servant at Capernaum (Matt. 8:5-13; Luke 7:1-10):

When Jesus finished His teaching, He entered into Capernaum. A centurion there had a servant who was deathly ill. The servant was greatly esteemed by the centurion. Having heard of Jesus, the centurion sent elders of the Jews to ask Jesus to heal his servant.

The Jews respected the centurion and told Jesus, "This man is worthy that you should do this for him because he loves our nation and has built our synagogue."

Jesus said, "I will go and heal him."

When they were almost to the centurion's house, the centurion sent friends to Jesus to give Him an important message: "Lord, I am not worthy to have you come into my house. You just say the word and my servant will be healed. I also am a man who exercises authority, having soldiers under me. I say to this one, 'Go,' and he goes. To that one I say, 'Come,' and he comes. I tell my servant to do a thing, and he does it."

Jesus was deeply impressed with the centurion. He told all the people around Him, "I tell you, truly, I have not met with such faith even in Israel. And I tell you that many will come and will sit down with Abraham, Isaac, and Jacob in the kingdom of heaven, while the sons of the kingdom will be cast out into the outer darkness."

Then Jesus told the friends of the centurion to tell him, "Let it be as you have believed." As soon as the friends of the centurion had returned, they found the servant completely well.

Jesus raises the widow's son at Nain (Luke 7:11-17):

Soon after (many ancient manuscripts read "the next day"), Jesus went to a city called Nain with His disciples. Nain was in the plain of Esdraelon about seven miles southeast of Nazareth. A great multitude accompanied Jesus and His disciples.

As Jesus approached the gate of the city, a procession of people came out bearing a dead man to his grave. The dead man was the only son his mother had, and she was a widow. When the Lord saw her He was filled with compassion for her. He told her, "Do not cry."

He walked up to the platform on which lay the body and touched it. The ones carrying it stood still. Then Jesus said, "Young man, I say to you, get up!"

Immediately the dead man sat up and began to speak. Then Jesus gave him to his mother.

Everyone was afraid and glorified God saying, "A great prophet is risen among us," and, "God has visited His people." News of this great event circulated in all the region round about and even in all of Judea.

Message from John the Baptist; Jesus praises John (Matt. 11:2-19; Luke 7:18-35):

NOTE:
It is Luke who tells the preceding story of raising the man of Nain. He connects that story and its far-reaching effects with the record of John's disciples telling him about these things. John was a prisoner at this time at Machaerus at the very southern end of Perea, east of the Dead Sea.

When John in prison heard about the works of Christ, he sent two of his disciples to ask Jesus, "Are you the one who comes, or should we look for another?"

When they came to Jesus they said, "John the Baptist has sent us to ask you, 'Are you the one who comes, or should we look for another?'"

Apparently Jesus did not answer them at first. He was very busy, as usual. While John's disciples were there, He cured many people of their diseases and of evil spirits.

Finally He turned to John's disciples and told them, "Go back and tell John what you have seen and heard: the blind have been given sight; the lame are made to walk; the lepers are cleansed; the deaf hear; the dead are raised; and the poor have the gospel preached to them. Blessed is that one, whoever he may be, who finds no cause to stumble over me and my work."

When the two men were gone, Jesus' thoughts were understandably about John. He decided to use the opportunity to make a point about John's work and also to teach a lesson about the blessedness of those in the kingdom. He said to the crowd:

When you went out to see John, what did you think you would find? A reed swayed by the wind? What did you go out to see? A man dressed in fine clothes? Those who wear expensive clothes and indulge in luxury live in palaces.

What did you go out to see? A prophet? Yes, John was a prophet. But he was more than just a prophet. He was the one of whom it is written: "Behold, I send my messenger before your face, who shall prepare your way before you" (Mal. 3:1).

I tell you, among those who are born of women, there has never been one greater than John. Yet he that is but little in the kingdom of heaven is greater than he. From the days of John until now the kingdom of heaven has been borne along with great force and energy, and men of energy and diligence enter into it.

All the prophets and the law prophesied until John. If you can grasp my meaning, this

John is Elijah, which was to come (Mal. 4:5). He who has ears, let him hear.

All the people, even the publicans, rejoiced and justified God, because they had been baptized of John. But the Pharisees and lawyers rejected the plan of God because they did not accept John's baptism. Therefore, Jesus said:

> To what can I compare the men of this age? They are like children sitting in the market place and calling out to one another: "We played the flute for you, and you did not dance; we wailed and you would not cry."
> John and I have not played your game to please you. John the Baptist came eating no bread, nor drinking wine, and you say, "He has a devil." The Son of Man has come both eating and drinking, and you say, "Look, He is a gluttonous man and a drunkard, a friend of publicans and sinners." So wisdom is justified by her children.

In other words, Jesus was saying that the plan not to try to please men was justified by the way things turned out.

Woes upon the cities of Galilee (Matt. 11:20-30):

> NOTE:
> Months have now been spent in Galilee. What is the result? We have been impressed with the multitudes that have followed Jesus. We have observed the teaching and the many miracles He has performed. How deeply has the work of Jesus reached into the heart of Israel?

Jesus began to reprove the cities where He had done His mightiest works, because they did not repent. He said:

> Woe to you, Chorazin! Woe to you, Bethsaida! For if the great miracles which have been done in you had been done in Tyre and Sidon, they would have repented long ago in sackcloth and ashes. It will be better for Tyre and Sidon in the day of judgment than for you.
> And you, Capernaum. Do you think you will be exalted as high as heaven? You will go down unto Hades! Because if the mighty works had been done in Sodom which have been done in you, it would still be here. So, I tell you, it will be more tolerable for the land of Sodom in the day of judgment than for you.

Even in the midst of the stubbornness and rejection Jesus found, He remembered those who had accepted Him and He gave an invitation to any who would come:

> I thank you, O Father, Lord of heaven and earth, that you have hidden these things from the wise and understanding and that you have revealed them to babes, because it was well-pleasing in your sight. All things have been delivered unto me from my Father, and no one knows the Son except the Father. Neither does anyone know the Father except the Son, and the one to whom the Son is willing to reveal Him.

Come unto me, all ye that labor and are heavy laden, and I will give you rest. Take my yoke upon you, and learn of me; for I am meek and lowly in heart: and ye shall find rest unto your souls. For my yoke is easy, and my burden is light.

Jesus attends a feast given by Simon the Pharisee; A sinful woman anoints His feet (Luke 7:36-50):

Jesus was invited by Simon, a Pharisee, to attend a meal at his house, so Jesus went to eat with him. A woman in the city, who was a sinner, heard that Jesus was eating there. She brought a little alabaster flask of ointment and entered into the house where the feast was going on.

The people eating were arranged around a central area, lying on their sides. They could reach the food while leaning on an elbow, and their feet were thrust away from the central area to the outside. Therefore the feet of Jesus were in easy reach of the woman.

The woman approached Jesus' feet. Ordinarily she could have gone right ahead and anointed His feet, because they would already have been washed by a servant as a common act of courtesy to a guest. Curiously, this courtesy had not been done on this occasion so His feet were still dusty.

Weeping, the woman caused her tears to fall upon Jesus' feet, and she wiped them with her hair. Tenderly she kissed His feet. Then she anointed them with her ointment.

The Pharisee, observing these things, thought: "If this man were a prophet, He would know what kind of a woman this is touching Him. She's nothing but a sinner."

Jesus, knowing Simon's thoughts, said, "Simon, I need to tell you something."

Simon replied, "Please do, Teacher."

"One time a certain man had two people who owed him money. One owed him five hundred pence (five hundred days' wages) and the other owed him fifty (fifty days' wages). When time came to pay, they did not have the money. Their creditor forgave them both of their debts. Which of them do you think would appreciate him the most?"

Simon answered, "I suppose it would be the one to whom he forgave the most."

Jesus said, "You have answered correctly." Then, turning to the woman, He said to Simon, "Do you see this woman? When I came into your house, you gave me no water to wash my feet, but she has wet my feet with her tears and wiped them with her hair. You gave me no kiss of greeting, but she, since she came in, has not ceased to kiss my feet. You did not anoint my head with oil, but she has rubbed my feet with ointment. Therefore, I tell you, her sins, though they are many, are forgiven, because she loved much. But to whom little is forgiven, that one loves little."

Jesus then spoke directly to the woman, saying, "Your sins are forgiven."

Jesus' statement caused questions to arise in the hearts of His companions at the meal: "Who is this who even forgives sins?"

But Jesus continued speaking to the woman: "Your faith has saved you; go in peace."

NOTE:

It is popularly thought that this woman was Mary Magdalene. This idea rests on very late tradition for which there is not the least historical evidence. The Bible does teach that Mary Magdalene was possessed with demons when Jesus found her, but it is nothing short of brutal and unfair character assassination to make her a prostitute.

Second tour of Galilee (Luke 8:1-3):

Luke says "soon afterward" Jesus went through the cities and villages preaching and carrying the good news of the kingdom of God. With Him were the twelve apostles and also certain women who had been healed of evil spirits and infirmities. Among these were Mary Magdalene, from whom seven demons had been expelled; Joanna the wife of Chuza who was Herod's steward; Susanna; and many others.

> NOTE:
>
> At least some of these women had money which they used to help support Jesus in His work. Some have thought that Chuza may have been the nobleman (literally, the king's officer) whose son Jesus healed at the beginning of His work in Galilee (John 4:46-54). This idea is attractive and reasonable, but without any definite proof.

Jesus' busy day

The next several stories all occurred on the same day. Most of the stories and parables are told in Matthew, Mark, and Luke. One or the other of the parallel accounts will make the point, "Now on the same day," or some such statement. It enhances all these activities to know that they did occur on the same day. There were undoubtedly many similar days which are not described, but the work of this day lets us know how busy Jesus was during His short public ministry.

Jesus is accused of casting out demons by Beelzebub (Mark 3:20-30; Matt. 12:22-37):

Jesus went into a house but the multitudes gathered again, so that there was no time even to eat a meal. Jesus' friends and relatives were worried about Him, thinking He was losing His mind because He allowed the crowds to come so constantly.

One was brought to Him who was possessed with a demon. The demon had caused the man to be blind and dumb. Jesus healed the man, and the multitude was very excited, saying, "Is this the Son of David?"

The Pharisees did not want the multitudes to be attracted to Jesus, so they moved to counter the budding belief. They said, "This man casts out demons by Beelzebub the prince of the demons!" The Pharisees were probably very grateful to the shrewd one of their number who came up with *some* way they could explain Jesus' miracles. It was not a very good argument, however, as Jesus soon showed.

> NOTE:
>
> Luke gives an account similar to this one which apparently happened later in Judea (Luke 11:14-32). Earlier, when Jesus cast out a demon, such an accusation was made by the Pharisees (Matt. 9:27-34). It is not surprising that the blasphemous charge was made more than once since some did not want to believe Jesus came from God. Neither is it surprising that Jesus would answer the charge in the same way each time.

Jesus responded:

Why is Satan casting out Satan? You have him casting out his own servants. If a kingdom is divided against itself, it will soon come to ruin. Every city or house which is divided cannot stand. If Satan is divided against himself, how will his kingdom stand? When I cast out demons, you say it is by Beelzebub. When your people cast them out, by whom do they do it?

But if I by the Spirit of God cast out demons, then the kingdom of God has come upon you. Otherwise how can one enter the house of a strong man and ransack his possessions unless he first ties up the strong man? Then he can spoil his house. Everyone is either for me or against me.

I tell you that every sin and blasphemy shall be forgiven of men, but the blasphemy against the Spirit will never be forgiven. Whoever speaks a word of criticism against the Son of Man, it can be forgiven, but whoever speaks a word against the Holy Spirit, it shall never be forgiven, neither in this world, nor in the world to come. He is guilty of an eternal sin.

You cannot have bad fruit and a good tree. The tree is known by its fruit. You offspring of vipers, you are so evil! How can you speak any good things, because men speak that with which their hearts overflow? I tell you that men will give account for every word they speak, even casual ones. By your words you will be justified, and by your words you will condemned.

Scribes and Pharisees ask for a sign (Matt. 12:38-45):

These strong words Jesus had spoken soon brought a challenge from the scribes and Pharisees: "Teacher, we need to see a sign from you."

Jesus replied, "It is an evil and adulterous generation that continually seeks a sign." Jesus had already given the Jews hundreds of signs. They ignored His miracles, and blasphemed the power by which He did them, and then they demanded a sign!

"There will be no sign given you," Jesus continued, "but the sign of Jonah the prophet. Because, as Jonah was in the belly of the whale three days and three nights, so shall the Son of Man be three days and three nights in the heart of the earth." (See Jonah 1:17.)

> NOTE:
>
> Back at the beginning of His public work, Jesus had been challenged to give a sign to show He had authority to cleanse the temple (John 2:13-22). At that time He said, "Destroy this temple, and in three days I will raise it up." He referred, of course, to His resurrection. In the present story, the crucifixion, burial, and resurrection are the sign to which Jesus refers. It would be the ultimate sign that He was God's Son. At this point, none of His listeners, even His closest disciples, understood what He meant.

Jesus reproved the Pharisees and scribes for turning down their opportunities to know the truth. He said:

The men of Nineveh will stand up in judgment against this generation and shall condemn it, because they repented when they heard the preaching of Jonah, and now a greater than

Jonah is here. The queen of Sheba came from the far corners of the earth to hear Solomon's wisdom, and yet a greater than Solomon is here.

The unclean spirit, when he is gone out of a man, passes through arid wastelands, seeking rest, and does not find it. So he says, "I will go back to my house from which I went out," and when he returns, he finds it empty, swept, and decorated. Then he goes and takes seven other spirits who are worse than he, and they all enter in and dwell there. The last state of the man becomes worse than it was at first. That is how it will be with this generation.

NOTE:

Jesus was telling the Jews that when men are confronted with the opportunity to be filled with good and they reject the opportunity, then evil will come in to fill the void. They will be much more evil than they were before. Such is the nature of evil.

Jesus' mother and brethren come to see Him (Mark 3:31-35; Matt. 12:46-50; Luke 8:19-21):

While Jesus was yet speaking to the crowd, His mother and brethren came seeking Him. The multitude was so great, however, they could not get to Him. Word was brought: "Your mother and your brothers are outside wanting to see you."

Jesus, like all of us, had precious memories of His family. His family was special to Him. He used this chance to make a point about who else was special to Him. He said to the crowd, "Who is my mother and my brothers?" He surveyed the people, and then stretched His hand out toward His disciples and said, "Look, these are my mother, and my brethren! Whoever does the will of God, he is my brother, my sister, and my mother."

Jesus teaches in parables:

An enormous crowd of people gathered by the Sea of Galilee to see Jesus. There were so many that He got into a boat and taught them while they stood on the beach. He taught them many things that day by way of parables.

NOTE:

A parable is nothing strange. We call a parable an illustration. The word translated parable means "something cast along beside." It is a story used to compare ("put along beside") and to illustrate. In addition to illustrating, Jesus used parables to conceal knowledge from those who did not want it.

Observe that very large crowds were still following Jesus, but by now, each individual was being called upon either to believe the message Jesus was preaching or to disbelieve. The opposition from the unbelievers was growing. Therefore, Jesus adopted the method of speaking in parables to confuse and confound those who did not want to accept His message. He was glad to explain the meaning of any of the parables to those who were humble enough to come inquiring.

Matt 13: parable
mark 4: chapter

Parable of the sower (Mark 4:3-25; Matt. 13:3-23; Luke 8:5-18):

Jesus told this story:

A farmer went out to plant his seed. As he sowed the seed, some of them fell on the path, and the birds came down and ate them. Other seed fell where the soil was thin over a rocky area. Since the soil was shallow, the seed sprang up quickly, but the roots could not go down very deep. When the sun came out, the little plants shriveled and died. Some seed fell in an area where thorns or brambles grew and they were choked out so that they bore no fruit. Still other seed fell on the good ground and produced a crop. Some areas brought forth thirty times as much as was planted; some sixty times, and some a hundred times as much. Let everyone who has ears listen to me.

The disciples were curious about Jesus' use of parables. When they were alone with Him later, they asked Him, "Why do you speak to them in parables?"

Jesus replied, "You disciples have been given the privilege of knowing the things about the kingdom of God which were hidden. Others do not have such a right because they do not want to hear the truth. Therefore I speak in parables so that they may hear what I am saying, but cannot know what it means. It is in reference to them that the words of Isaiah are fulfilled: 'This people's heart has become calloused, and their ears have gone deaf. Therefore they will hear, but they will not understand. They will see, but they will not understand. Otherwise they might really understand what is happening, and repent, and I would heal them'" (Isa. 6:9-10).

NOTE:
God never treated anyone this way until that one had repeatedly rejected His word. When, however, men refuse to listen to the truth, God will not only abandon them to their fate, He will allow strong delusions to be circulated so that those who do not want the truth may find a lie to believe. Thus they nail the lid of their coffins firmly shut. (See 2 Thess. 2:11-12.)

Jesus continued, "But your eyes are blessed because they see; and your ears are blessed, because they hear. Truly, I tell you that many prophets and righteous men have wanted to see and hear the things you see and hear, but they could not. Hear then the meaning of the parable of the farmer:

The farmer plants the word. The seed is the word of God. The seed that fell on the wayside are those who hear the word but do not understand it. Immediately the devil comes and snatches away the word.

The seed scattered upon rocky places are those who hear the word and receive it joyfully, but they have no depth. When tribulation or persecution arises, they falter right away.

Now the seed that was sown among the thorns is that one who hears the word, but the cares of the world and the deceptive nature of riches choke the word. He produces no fruit.

The seed sown upon good ground is that person who, having a good and honest heart, hears the word and clings firmly to it. He will bear fruit by perseverance.

Jesus continued, "Is a lamp brought to be set under the table, or under the bed? Is it not placed on a stand so that its light may be seen? Be careful, therefore, what you hear. Listen carefully. You dare not hide the truth from yourself or ignore it. If you do reject it, even the little knowledge you have will be taken away."

Parable of seed growing in the ground (Mark 4:26-29):

"The kingdom of God works like this. A man plants a seed in the earth. Then he goes on about his activities, sleeping at night, and rising in the day. The seed is growing under the soil, but the farmer does not see any evidence of activity until the seed puts forth. The little plant begins as a blade, then the ear forms on the stalk, and finally the ear of grain matures. Then the farmer takes his sickle and cuts the grain because it is time for harvest."

> NOTE:
>
> Remember that many of our young people are completely unfamiliar with the most simple facts of agriculture — especially the agriculture of Jesus' day. They will need a *brief* explanation of a sickle, etc. They will need to know that by the time a plant pushes up through the soil, a great deal of growth and development has taken place unseen. Jesus' point in this parable was that the influence of God's word will grow in heart of an individual without any noticeable sign until, one day, it pushes through into his outward activities and makes itself known.

Parable of the tares (Matt. 13:24-30, 36-43):

Jesus told them another parable saying:

The kingdom of heaven is like a man who planted wheat in his field. Then, while he slept, his enemy came to the field and sowed tares (weeds) among the wheat and then slipped away.

When the wheat grew up, there were the tares also. The servants of the farmer came to him and said, "Sir, didn't you sow good seed in your field? Where did these tares come from?"

He replied, "An enemy has done this!"

The servants asked, "Do you want us to go and take up the tares?"

But he said, "No, because if you pull up the tares, you will root up the wheat with them and we will have no harvest. Let them grow together until harvest. Then I will have the tares gathered first and tied into bundles to be burned. Then I will gather the wheat into my barn."

After Jesus left the multitude, His disciples said to Him, "Explain to us the illustration of the tares."

Promptly Jesus responded: "He who sows the good seed is the Son of Man, and the field is the world. The good seed are the sons of the kingdom. The tares are the sons of the evil one. The enemy who sowed them is the devil. The harvest is the end of the world, and the reapers are angels. As the tares are gathered up and burned with fire, so it will be at the end of the world. The Son of Man will send forth His angels, and they will gather out of His kingdom everything that offends, and those who commit iniquity, and will cast them into the furnace of fire. There will be the weeping and gnashing of teeth. Then the righteous will shine forth in the kingdom of their Father like the sun."

NOTE:

Notice that many of these parables are describing the kingdom of God, not the world in general. In the parable of the sower, some who accepted the word failed to produce fruit. In this story of the tares, both the wheat and the tares were in the same field — but only the wheat was harvested into the barn. In the story of the net of fishes, the net was the kingdom and the division was made between the good and bad within it.

It is a sobering thought to remember that just because we have been offered a chance to know the plan of God and to begin in our efforts to serve Him does not assure us a home in heaven. We must be sure we are producing fruit, that we are living as God would have us live as His children.

Parable of the mustard seed (Mark 4:30-32; Matt. 13:31-32):

Another illustration Jesus used was this: "The kingdom of God is like a grain of mustard seed which is the smallest of seed. Yet when it is planted, it grows into a large plant which puts out great branches, so that the birds can make their roost under its shade."

Jesus' point was that the kingdom of God would begin in a very small way and grow to be exceedingly great.

Parable of the leaven (Mark 4:33-34; Matt. 13:33-35):

Jesus spoke many parables to the people and then privately explained them to His disciples. His use of parables fulfilled the prophecy: "I will open my mouth in parables; I will tell things hidden from the foundation of the world" (Psa. 78:2).

Another of His parables was: "The kingdom of God is like leaven which a woman mixed in three quantities of dough till it was all leavened."

NOTE:

The leaven used by the ancients was basically the sourdough used by people today. The point of the parable is that the kingdom of God spreads by contact, by the spread of influence, not by the flashier methods that impress the multitudes.

Parable of the hidden treasure (Matt. 13:44):

Jesus continued: "The kingdom of heaven is like a treasure hidden in the field, which a man found and then put back. He was so thrilled over what he had seen, he went and sold everything he had so that he could buy the field in which the treasure was hidden."

Parable of the pearl of great price (Matt. 13:45-46):

"The kingdom of heaven is like a man who was a merchant dealing in pearls. He found the pearl of all pearls, a pearl worth a fortune. To get that pearl, he went and sold everything he had and bought it."

NOTE:
The point of both of these parables is that the kingdom of God is so valuable, it is worth everything we give to obtain it — no matter the cost.

Parable of the net (Matt. 13:47-50):

"Again, the kingdom of heaven is like a net which was cast into the sea and gathered in fish of every kind. When it was full, the fisherman drew it up onto the beach and gathered the good fish into vessels and threw the bad ones away. So it will be at the end of the world when the angels will go out and cut off the wicked from among the righteous and will cast them into the furnace of fire. There will be weeping and the grinding of teeth."

Parable of the householder (Matt. 13:51-53):

At the end of Jesus' teaching, He asked the disciples, "Have you understood all these things?" "Yes," they replied.

Jesus said, "Therefore every teacher of the law who becomes a disciple in the kingdom of heaven is like the master of a house. To supply the needs he faces, he brings forth out of his storeroom things old and new."

NOTE:
Jesus' point was that one who teaches in the kingdom of God will use things he knew before he became a disciple as well as new things he learned after becoming a disciple.

Jesus stills the storm at sea (Mark 4:35-41; Matt. 8:18,23-27; Luke 8:22-25):

On the same day that Jesus taught these great parables, He said to His disciples, "Let us go over to the other side of the Sea."

Leaving the multitude, they entered a boat and set out across the Sea of Galilee. Jesus, exhausted from His teaching, and from the earlier conflicts with the Pharisees, fell asleep in the stern. A fierce storm came down upon the sea and the waves crashed against the boat. So much water was being thrown into the ship it was rapidly filling. Finally, in desperation, the disciples went to Jesus and woke Him. They said, "Master, don't you care if we perish?"

Jesus got up and rebuked the wind, and said to the sea, "Quiet! Be still!" Immediately the wind died down, the waves stopped tossing, and the whole sea was completely calm.

Jesus asked His disciples, "Why are you so afraid? Have you still no faith?"

His disciples, however, were terrified. They said to one another, "Who is this? Even the wind and the sea obey Him!"

Jesus heals the Gerasene demoniac (Mark 5:1-20; Matt. 8:28-34; Luke 8:26-39):

When they reached the other side of the sea in the region of the Gerasenes, two demoniacs came out of the tombs to meet them. One of them talked to Jesus.

NOTE:

Mark says this story occurred in the country of the Gerasenes. Matthew says the country of the Gadarenes. Some of the manuscripts of Luke have Gergesenes, some Gadarenes, and some Gerasenes. Most authorities on manuscripts now believe that Gerasenes is the best reading in Luke's account. This term referred to a village called Gerasa. It was apparently in a district belonging to the city of Gadara. Thus the territory could quite properly be called the country of the Gerasenes or of the Gadarenes.

Also note that Matthew mentions two demoniacs. Mark and Luke mention only one. He was likely the more prominent one of the two, so Mark and Luke record only his conversation. We will follow the lead of Mark and Luke as they tell of that more prominent demoniac.

This man was possessed with demons and, for a long time, had lived in the hills among the tombs. He was very fierce and dangerous so that no one would go near. On occasion, he had been bound with chains and fetters, but he tore the chains apart and broke the fetters in pieces. No one had the strength to control him. Day and night among the tombs, and in the mountains, he would howl and cut himself with stones.

When he saw Jesus from afar, he ran to Him and worshiped Him. Crying out in a loud voice, he said, "What do you want with me, thou Son of God? Have you come to torment us before the time?"

This response of the demons was because Jesus was saying, "Come out of this man, you evil spirit."

Jesus asked, "What is your name?"

The demons replied, "My name is Legion, for we are many."

The demons begged Jesus not to send them to the abyss. A great herd of hogs was feeding nearby on the mountain side. The demons asked Jesus to let them enter the swine, and He gave them permission to do so. The demons came out of the man and entered the herd of swine. Immediately, the whole herd ran down the steep shore into the sea and were drowned. There were about 2,000 animals in the herd.

Those who kept the hogs ran into the city and told everything that had happened to the demoniacs and to the animals. So everyone in the city and in the surrounding country came out to see. When they arrived, they found the man who had had the demons sitting down, dressed, and in his right mind. The people were filled with fear and asked Jesus to leave.

Immediately, Jesus prepared to enter the boat. The demoniac came to Him and asked that he be allowed to go with Jesus. Instead Jesus told him, "No. Go to your house and to your friends and tell them what great things the Lord has done for you, and how He had mercy on you."

The man went forth and began to tell everyone in the Decapolis about the great thing Jesus had done for him. Everyone who heard was amazed.

NOTE:

What were these demons? Were they just the Jews' way of describing illnesses? Were they actual spirit beings? Do they still possess people today? What do we know about them besides the information given in the New Testament?

The period of the New Testament is the only period of Bible history when the demons are mentioned. Notice that sometimes the demons made people deaf and dumb, or subject to seizures similar to epilepsy, or insane, or afflicted in other ways. That means there was not just one manifestation (or symptom) of demon possession. Since they are not mentioned in the Old Testament, we have no information about them outside the New Testament. There is no specific explanation about them given in the scriptures, so our only way to understand them is to gather the little information we have and draw a few conclusions. Since very little information is given, let us be wary about speculating on the subject.

That the demons were spirit beings with intelligence and volition of their own is apparent from the following considerations:

1. Jesus talked to them as if they were demons, and not just sicknesses or infirmities of some kind. He Himself called them devils or unclean spirits. If they were not demons but mental psychoses of some kind, then Jesus was carrying on a charade and perpetuating a false concept.
2. No mental psychosis or aberration would have invariably caused the possessed person to know that Jesus was the Son of God. Without Jesus saying anything, those possessed with demons knew exactly who He was. (See James 2:19.)
3. The request given in the story above, where the demons begged Jesus not to send them into the abyss, cannot be explained by a mental aberration since the abyss is associated with the devil (Rev. 20:3).
4. Satan is called the prince of demons, the prince of the powers of the air. Satan will be cast into the abyss (Rev. 20:3). The demons over whom Satan is prince also view the abyss as their ultimate place. So, if the demons are viewed as mental illness, then their prince is a mental illness, and perhaps the abyss is nothing but a Tylenol or Advil! Such a conclusion would be contrary to all the plain teaching about the existence of Satan.
5. The demons gave the demoniac in the story above power beyond that of a normal human being, even a psychotic human being. He had broken chains and fetters of iron.

It seems that God allowed Satan the freedom of sending his demons into men during the era when God was demonstrating the greatest outpouring of His power in the history of mankind. During that era while Satan had that privilege, God's Son was always victorious over any demon, and the apostles after Jesus were also victorious by the help of the Holy Spirit. God's power is not being demonstrated miraculously today, and, therefore, Satan is not given the privilege of inflicting his demons upon men either. The danger from Satan today is through the temptation to sin which he puts before us regularly.

To avoid getting too deep in the subject, let us merely note that in every confrontation between Jesus and the demons, the power of Jesus was absolutely irresistible. By this means, He gave another great proof that He was the Son of God (see Matt. 12:28-29).

Healing of Jairus' daughter and the healing of the woman with an issue of blood (Mark 5:21-43; Matt. 9:18-26; Luke 8:40-56):

When Jesus had crossed back over the Sea of Galilee, He found a great multitude waiting for Him. Before anything else could take place, one of the rulers of the synagogue, Jairus, came to Jesus and fell at His feet. Jairus said, "My little daughter is at the point of death. I beg of you, please come and lay your hands on her so she may be made well and live." His daughter was about twelve years old. Jesus agreed to go.

As He was on His way to the house of Jairus, Jesus was thronged by a great crowd of people. The people surrounding Him jostled Him as they walked along.

A woman in the crowd began to work her way toward Jesus. She had suffered from a constant bleeding for twelve years and had spent all her money upon physicians. She had suffered many things at their hands, but had grown steadily worse instead of better. So when she heard of Jesus, she determined to get to Him. She believed that if she could just touch His clothes she would be healed. Finally she got close enough to reach out and touch His garments. Instantly the source of the bleeding was dried up and she felt her plague healed. Imagine her joy! Touching Jesus had worked!

But Jesus knew that power had gone forth from Him, so He stopped. Looking about Him over the crowd, He said, "Who touched my garments?"

No one knew what Jesus meant. Peter and the other disciples said, "Master, the multitudes press upon you and are constantly jostling you. And yet, you ask, 'Who touched me?'"

Jesus said, "I can tell that power has gone forth from me."

When the woman saw that she could not quietly slip away, she was afraid. Trembling, she came and fell down before Him and there, in the presence of everyone, told why she had touched Jesus and how she was healed immediately.

Jesus told her, "Daughter, your faith has made you well. Go in peace."

While Jesus was still speaking to the woman, messengers came from Jairus' house with bad news: "Your daughter is dead. There is no need to bother the Master any longer."

Jesus turned to Jairus and said, "Don't be afraid. Just keep believing and she will be made well."

When they reached the ruler's house, Jesus heard the tumult and wailing and crying of the mourners. The flute-players were playing. The mourning for the little girl's death was in full swing. Jesus said, "Clear the way. Why are you making all this noise and crying? The child is not dead, but sleeping."

The people laughed scornfully at Jesus because they knew she was dead. Jesus entered the house, taking only Peter, James, John, and the girl's parents inside with Him.

Going into the room where the little girl was, He took her by the hand and said, "Talitha cumi." (These were Aramaic words which mean, "Young lady, I say to you, get up!") Immediately the little girl got up and walked around. Jesus told them to give her something to eat.

The little girl's parents were amazed. Jesus told them to tell no one what had been done, but news of the event spread all through that region.

NOTE:

Why did Jesus compel the woman with the issue of blood to come forward and tell her story and then told Jairus' family not to tell what had happened to them?

Jesus' miracles were always done to promote faith in the hearts of the people. A miracle had been done secretly in the case of the woman with the issue of blood. Therefore, Jesus called her forward so that her story could help others believe that

He was the Son of God. Yet in the case of Jairus' daughter, there were many people around to know of the miracle. Many would have the opportunity to believe from their own observation of the miracle. Therefore, Jesus told the family not to spread the word lest the crowds throng him further.

Jesus heals two blind men and a mute demoniac (Matt. 9:27-34):

As Jesus went on His way, He passed by two blind men who followed Him, crying, "Have mercy on us, O Son of David."

Jesus did not respond at first, but went on into the house. The blind men did not give up. They followed Him into the house. When they came to Him, Jesus asked them, "Do you believe I am able to do this?"

They said, "Yes, Lord."

Touching their eyes, Jesus said, "According to your faith, let it be done unto you." Immediately, their eyes were opened.

Jesus told them, "See that no one knows of this." But they went out and spread His fame abroad in all that land.

As the men were going out, there was brought to Him a mute who was possessed with a demon. When the devil was cast out, the mute could speak. The multitudes were amazed and commented, "Nothing like this has ever been seen in Israel."

The Pharisees, however, repeated their charge: "By the prince of demons He casts out demons."

The last visit to Nazareth (Mark 6:1-6; Matt. 13:54-58):

Toward the end of His work in Galilee, Jesus went back to Nazareth. As He taught in the synagogue on the sabbath, those who heard Him said, "Where has this man gotten all these things He says, and this wisdom? And how does He do all these mighty works? Isn't this the carpenter, the son of Mary and the brother of James, Joses, Judas, and Simon? Aren't His sisters here with us?" They just could not believe that one from their own town, whom they had known all His life, could be the Christ.

Jesus said, "A prophet is not without honor, except in the country he comes from, and among his own kin, and in his own house."

Therefore Jesus did not do many miracles there except to heal a few sick people. He marveled at their unbelief.

Jesus' third tour of Galilee; The Twelve are sent on the limited commission (Mark 6:6-13; Matt. 9:35-11:1; Luke 9:1-6):

Jesus went about Galilee on a third general tour. Very few details are given about this tour, but when Jesus considered the multitudes, He was filled with compassion for them. They were like sheep that were scattered without a shepherd. He told His disciples: "The harvest is truly bountiful, but the workers are few. Pray, therefore, that the Lord of the harvest may send forth laborers to help."

It was then that Jesus called His disciples to Him for a mission. He gave them power to heal and to cast out demons. He told them:

Do not go to the Gentiles, nor to any city of the Samaritans. Go instead to the lost sheep of the house of Israel. As you go, preach that the kingdom of heaven is near. Heal the sick, raise the dead, cleanse the lepers, cast out demons. You have received freely; now go forth and give freely.

Do not take money with you. Do not carry a knapsack, nor extra coats, nor shoes except the sandals you have on, nor any staff but the one you already have. Take no bread with you either, because a worker is worthy of his food.

NOTE:

Mark's account distinctly says they could carry a staff and wear sandals, whereas the accounts of Matthew and Luke say no staff, and Matthew says no shoes. It is better to assume that Jesus meant that the apostles were not to go out and buy new shoes for the journey nor to get a new staff. Instead they were to use the ones they already owned, and not to take extra ones along.

Jesus continued: "When you go into a city, find in it someone who is worthy and stay with him until you leave to go to another city. When you enter a house, give a greeting of peace, and if the house is worthy, let your peace be upon it. If it is not, let your peace return unto you. If anyone will not welcome you or listen to your words, shake the dust off your feet when you leave that house or town. I tell you the truth, it will be better for Sodom and Gomorrah in the day of judgment than for that city."

NOTE:

The rest of the instructions Jesus gave are found in Matthew. These words go far beyond the scope of the limited commission. Some of the instructions, of course, do apply to the limited commission, but Jesus gave advice here which would be useful to the apostles, and in a general way to all His disciples, in those days when the gospel would go forth into all the world.

Jesus said:

I send you forth as sheep in the midst of wolves. Therefore be wise as serpents, but harmless as doves. Be careful in dealing with men because they will bring you before councils, and scourge you in their synagogues. You will be brought before governors and kings for a testimony to them and to the Gentiles.

When you find yourselves in such circumstances, do not worry about what you will say. At that time, it will be given you what to say. Because it will not be you who speaks, but the Spirit of your Father who speaks in you. You will be hated by everyone for my name's sake; you will cause strife wherever you go; families will be divided by your preaching. Do not let opposition silence you. What you hear in secret, shout from the housetops. Don't be afraid of those who can kill the body but are not able to kill the soul; be afraid of the One who is able to destroy both soul and body in hell. Everyone who confesses me before men, I will confess him before my Father in heaven.

Think not that I came to bring peace on the earth. I came not to bring peace but a sword. I came to set son against father and daughter against mother. My cause must come first. Whoever loves his father or his mother more than he loves me is not worthy of me.

Also, the one who does not accept the hardships the gospel brings to his life is not worthy of me. He who does everything to spare his life will lose it, but the one who loses his life for my sake shall find it.

He who receives you receives me, and he who receives me receives the One who sent me. One who receives a prophet will receive the reward of a prophet, and the one who receives a righteous man will receive a righteous man's reward. Even if someone simply gives a drink of cold water to one of my little ones because he is my disciple, that person will in no way lose his reward.

NOTE:

The main point Jesus made in Matthew 10:16-42 was a warning to His apostles that the preaching of His word would cause strife and persecution. They were not to let this deter them, but were to preach the gospel to all.

The apostles went forth preaching that men should repent. They went through all the cities and villages healing and casting out demons. Jesus also went through the cities preaching the message of repentance.

Herod Antipas hears of Jesus' work; The story of how Herod killed John (Mark 6:14-29; Matt. 14:1-12; Luke 9:7-9):

When Herod heard the things that Jesus did, he said, "John the Baptist is risen from the dead. That is why these powers work in this man."

Others said, "It is Elijah, or some such prophet."

Herod was sure it was John, though. "John, whom I beheaded, is risen from the dead!" Herod wanted to see Jesus.

In an earlier story, we learned that Herod Antipas took Herodias, the wife of his brother Philip, for his own wife. He was, therefore, living in adultery with her. John rebuked him for his action and John was imprisoned. [See page 29 of this material.]

Herodias hated John and wanted to kill him, but she could not because Herod feared him. He knew John was a righteous and holy man, and he knew the people believed John to be a prophet. So Herod kept John safe and heard him speak from time to time.

Finally the chance came that Herodias had been wanting. To celebrate his birthday, Herod gave a feast for his nobles and captains and for the chief men of Galilee. As part of the entertainment, the daughter of Herodias (history tells us her name was Salome), came in and danced before Herod and his guests. She pleased Herod so much that he said to her, "Ask anything of me that you wish and I will give it to you." He even swore with an oath saying: "Whatever you ask of me, I will give it to you, up to one-half of my kingdom."

Salome went to her mother and said, "What shall I ask?"

Herodias replied, "Ask for the head of John the Baptist!"

The girl rushed back to the king and said, "I want you to give me the head of John the Baptist on a platter!"

Herod was very upset at this request, but because he had sworn before all his guests, he felt he had to do as Salome asked. Herod commanded a soldier of his guards to go bring John's head. So the soldier went and beheaded John in prison and brought the head on a platter to Salome. She, in turn, took it to her mother.

When the disciples of John heard what had happened, they came and took the body away and buried it. Then they went and told Jesus.

Review your map

Take time to be sure you feel comfortable using your map. Notice that Jesus has been in or near Galilee for over a year by now. Some of the time He has been on the east side of the Sea of Galilee, but each time He soon returns to the cities on the west. The only recorded interruption in His stay in Galilee was His trip to Jerusalem for the feast that is recorded in John 5. There may have been other trips to feasts at their scheduled times, but the emphasis during this period of His work has been in Galilee.

But notice that people have come to hear Him from all over the land. Word of His work was wide-spread by this time.

The Period of Retirement
Matt. 8:19-22; 14:13-18:35; Mark 6:30-9:37; Luke 9:10-62; John 6:12-7:10

Life of Christ

Preparation
Beginning Ministry
Galilean Ministry

*Retirement

 *Feeding 5,000
 *Tyre and Sidon
 *Feeding 4,000
 *Bethsaida Julias

Close of Ministry
Last Week
Resurrection
Exaltation

We have come now to another main point in our broad outline of the life of Christ. Take time to look in your left column at that overall outline once more. Following the Great Galilean Ministry, Jesus sought to escape the multitudes by withdrawing into more remote areas in order to have time to teach His apostles special lessons that the crowds were not ready to hear. The multitudes have become used to coming to Him, however, so they seek Him out, even though their purpose for doing so was not always what Jesus wanted.

Though it has become customary to call this phase of Jesus' life the Period of Retirement, there were actually *four* separate times when He withdrew. The first of these involves the story of the feeding of the 5,000. The time is shortly before the Passover (John 6:4). If our chronology is correct, Jesus has one year left before His death, which will occur at the next Passover. He has been preaching for a little over two years. The Period of Retirement lasts for about six months — from just before the Passover Feast in the spring until the Feast of Tabernacles in the fall.

The First Retirement

The Twelve return from their mission; Jesus seeks rest across the Sea of Galilee; He feeds the 5,000 (Mark 6:30-44; Matt. 14:13-21; Luke 9:10-17; John 6:1-15):

The apostles returned from their preaching tour and gathered themselves to Jesus. They told Him all that they had done and what they had taught, but there were interruptions. So many people were coming and going around them that they could not even eat. Jesus told them, "All of you come into a quiet place and rest a while."

Jesus and His disciples got into a boat and went across the Sea of Galilee to a deserted place — that is, to a quiet place without multitudes. The place was Bethsaida on the eastern side of the Sea of Galilee. It belonged to the territory of Philip the Tetrarch and was often called Bethsaida Julias.

The multitudes saw Jesus leaving in the boat, and they ran on foot from all the cities and reached the other shore before Jesus and His disciples got there. So when Jesus arrived at Bethsaida, the multitudes were already waiting. Instead of being angry with the crowd, Jesus was filled with compassion. He healed their sick and taught them many things.

In the evening, the disciples came to Jesus and said, "This place is remote, and the day is almost over. Send the people away so they can go into the villages round about to buy food for themselves and find places to stay."

But Jesus asked Philip, "Where can we buy bread to feed them?"

Jesus already knew what He was going to do, but He wanted to see what Philip would say. In astonishment, Philip answered, "Two hundred days' wages would not buy enough for everyone to have even a bite!"

Andrew said, "There is a boy here who has five barley loaves and two fish, but what are these to be divided among so many?"

Jesus said, "Tell the people to sit down in groups of about fifty each." There was plenty of grass, so the people seated themselves as Jesus commanded. The grouping made it easy to count how many were there. The number was about 5,000 men plus women and children. The total number was probably 10,000 or more.

Jesus took the loaves and the fish and, looking up to heaven, He blessed them and broke them into pieces. He gave the portions to the apostles to distribute to the multitude. Jesus continued to do this until everyone was full. Then Jesus told the apostles to gather up the scraps. There were twelve baskets full. The portion left was far more than the original food supply! A notable miracle indeed!

Begin

Jesus withdraws to a mountain to escape being made king (Mark 6:45-46; Matt. 14:22-23; John 6:14-15):

This great miracle strongly moved the people. They said, "This truly is the prophet who is coming." Like a tidal wave, the popular support of Jesus reached its peak. The multitude intended to make Jesus king by force.

Knowing this, Jesus told His disciples to get into a boat and go on ahead of Him across the sea. Then He dismissed the crowd and withdrew into a mountain where He prayed alone.

NOTE:
    The crowds have been thronging Jesus for months. They have seen His miracles of healing many times. Now they see He can provide their physical needs miraculously. They want His blessings! What a person to have as ruler! They think they are complimenting Him when they intend to make Him their king. But He knows they do not understand His mission, nor do they know who He really is.

Jesus walks on the water (Mark 6:47-52; Matt. 14:24-33; John 6:16-21):

After the disciples set out in their boat, a sudden storm arose on the Sea of Galilee. They were in the middle of the sea and, because of contrary winds, could not make their crossing. They were greatly distressed. In the fourth watch of the night (about 3 to 6 a.m.), Jesus came to them walking on the water.

When the disciples saw Jesus, they were terrified! They cried out, "It is a ghost!"

But Jesus spoke and said, "Take courage; it is I; do not be afraid."

Peter answered Jesus saying, "Lord, if it is you, command me to come to you upon the water." Jesus said, "Come."

Peter stepped over the side of the boat and began to walk on the water. For a few steps he was all right. Then he looked at the wind as it tossed the waves and blew spray through the air, and he became afraid. As he began to sink, Peter cried out, "Lord, save me!"

Immediately Jesus stretched out His hand and took hold of Peter. He did not belittle Peter for trying. Instead He said, "O how little your faith is. Why did you doubt?"

> NOTE:
>
> Peter's faith had something to do with appropriating the miraculous power extended to him. In other words, Jesus did not perform the miracle and *make* Peter walk on the water. Instead, Peter had been given power to perform miracles along with all the other apostles when Jesus sent them out on the limited commission. Jesus is reminding Peter that he has the power to walk on the water if he so chooses. The faith in question was not that of a person upon whom a miracle was being done, but that of the person *doing* the miracle. On one other clear occasion, the lack of faith on the part of the apostles will explain their inability to do a miracle (Matt. 17:14-21).

As soon as Jesus and Peter got into the boat, the wind ceased. Also, immediately the boat was at the shore to which they were going. The apostles were amazed because they still did not grasp the implications of the miracle involving the five loaves. They could not yet understand the power that Jesus had continually at His disposal as the Son of God. They fell at His feet and worshiped Him saying, "Truly you are the Son of God."

The reception of Jesus at Gennesaret (Mark 6:53-56; Matt. 14:34-36):

When Jesus and His disciples got out of their boat, they found themselves at Gennesaret, a plain on the northwest shore of the Sea of Galilee. As soon as the people saw Jesus, they knew who He was and began to carry their sick to Him on beds. Wherever He went, into villages, or cities, or the countryside, the sick were brought and laid in the marketplaces. They begged Him to just let them touch the border of His garments, and as many as touched Him were made completely well.

The crowds begin to turn back (John 6:22-71):

The next day after Jesus crossed the sea by walking on the water, the multitudes found Him gone from Bethsaida. They knew that He did not go with His apostles when they left by boat; they knew of no other boat He had taken, but He was nevertheless gone.

The people got into boats which had arrived from Tiberias and made their way to Capernaum hunting for Jesus. When they found Him, they said, "Rabbi, when did you come here?"

Jesus did not answer the question asked, but dealt with the larger issue of why they had come looking for Him. "Really and truly, you hunt for me, not because you saw signs, but because you ate of the loaves and were filled. You should not be working so hard for food which is soon gone, but for the food which remains and gives eternal life, which the Son of Man will give you. And God has stamped the Son as being genuine."

NOTE:

Jesus' popularity was its very highest at the feeding of the 5,000, but He knew from the beginning of His work that one of the biggest problems He would face would be that most people would seek Him for healing and for other immediate benefits rather than for the truth He taught and for the redemption from sin which He offered. Jesus dealt with this problem at this time, and it cost Him a large part of His popular following.

The audience became antagonistic very quickly. They demonstrated the proof of Jesus' accusation. They said, "What must we do to work the works of God?" They wanted a list of actions they could perform and ignored their greatest failure — the failure to believe.

Jesus answered, "The work that God would have you do is to believe on the One whom He has sent."

The reply of the people was incredible. Remember that they had just observed a day of healing which was concluded by the miraculous feeding of a vast multitude. They said, "Well, what will you do for a sign which we can see and believe? Our fathers ate manna in the wilderness, as it is written, 'He gave them bread out of heaven to eat.'"

Jesus turned the discussion from the manna and from any kind of material bread to a spiritual bread. The eating of physical bread is necessary for physical life; the "eating" of spiritual bread is necessary for spiritual life. The spiritual bread, which is Christ, is "eaten" when men believe that He is the Son of God.

Jesus said, "Moses did not give you the bread out of heaven. It is my Father who gives you the real bread from heaven, because the bread of God is that which has come down out of heaven, and gives life to the world."

The people said, "Lord, give us this bread from now on."

Jesus answered, "I am the bread of life: he that comes to me will not get hungry, and the one who believes on me will never thirst, but you have seen me and still do not believe."

Then Jesus made a fervent plea for them to believe in Him, to accept Him as God's Son. "All those whom the Father has given me shall come unto me, and the one who comes, I will certainly not cast out. Because I have come down out of heaven, not to do my own will, but the will of the One who sent me. The will of my Father is that everyone who beholds the Son, and who believes on Him should have eternal life, and I will raise him up in the last day."

The Jews began to criticize Jesus because He said, "I am the bread which came down out of heaven." They said, "Isn't this Jesus, the son of Joseph, whose father and mother we know? What does He mean: 'I have come down out of heaven'?"

Jesus answered, "Do not murmur among yourselves. No man can come to me unless the Father who sent me draw him, and I will raise him up in the last day. It is written in the prophets, 'And they shall all be taught of God.' Everyone who has heard from the Father and has learned comes unto me. The one who believes is the one who has eternal life. I am the bread of life. Your fathers did eat the manna in the wilderness, and they died! There is the bread which came down out of heaven which a man may eat and not die. I am the living bread which came down out of heaven. If a man eat this bread, he will live for ever. The bread which I will give is my flesh, for the life of the world."

The Jews began to argue sharply among themselves: "How can this man give us His flesh to eat?"

Jesus told them: "The fact is: Unless you eat the flesh of the Son of Man and drink His blood, you have not life in yourselves. He who eats my flesh and drinks my blood has eternal life, and I will raise him up at the last day. The one who eats my flesh and drinks my blood remains in me and I in him. This is the bread which came down from heaven; not that which the fathers ate, and died; he who eats this bread will live forever."

These things were said in the synagogue in Capernaum.

At this point, many of Jesus' followers said, "This is a hard saying. Who can accept it?"

Jesus, knowing that His disciples murmured at this, said, "Does this cause you to stumble? What would you do if you beheld the Son going back to where He was before? It is the spirit that gives life; the flesh does not profit anything. The words that I have told you are spirit and are life, but there are some of you who do not believe."

Jesus knew from the beginning those who did not believe and who it was that would betray Him. He said, "For this reason, I said to you that no man can come to me unless it is given to him of the Father."

At this point, many of Jesus' followers stopped walking with Him. It must have saddened Jesus to see His followers walk away; yet He knew that when men follow Him for the wrong reason it is of no profit. It was a poignant moment when Jesus turned to the twelve and asked, "Would you also prefer to go away?"

It was Simon Peter who spoke simple words of profound faith: "Lord, to whom shall we go? You have the words of eternal life. And we have believed and know that you are the Holy One of God."

When Peter said, "We have believed," Jesus was moved to comment: "Did not I choose you twelve, yet one of you is a devil?" He spoke of Judas who would betray Him.

NOTE:

This event marked the collapse of Jesus' work in Galilee. In the next three retirements, we will see Jesus avoiding the territory of Herod Antipas and avoiding the crowds who had thronged Him. His visits in Galilee after this will be very brief and comparatively private. As we noted early in Jesus' public ministry, the crowds have consisted of some believers, some unbelievers, and some mere curiosity seekers. By now, the curiosity seekers must make their choice to believe or disbelieve. There is no middle ground. There will still be some big crowds for Jesus to speak to, but more often for the next few months, Jesus will be withdrawn somewhere with His intimate circle teaching them the things pertaining to the kingdom of heaven.

The Pharisees from Jerusalem criticize Jesus (Mark 7:1-23; Matt. 15:1-20; John 7:1):

After these things, there was much more opposition to Jesus than before. He had reached a distinct turning point. He avoided Judea because the Jews sought to kill Him (John 7:1), and we have seen that plots to kill Him have existed in Galilee as well (Matt. 12:14). In addition, Jesus was aware of Herod's attention. He sought to avoid confrontation with him by going into more remote areas, or areas that were not under Herod's rule.

A group of Pharisees and scribes came to Jesus with a criticism. They had observed that His disciples did not conduct the ritual washings of themselves that the Pharisees required. They had the tradition that when they had been in the marketplace, they could not eat until they had washed their hands and arms up to the elbows.

NOTE:

This was just one of many ritual washings the Pharisees practiced. Most of these washings probably originated from instructions in the law about washing after defilement (see Lev. 11:24-40). The primary motive for the washing of the hands here referred to was fear of defilement by Gentiles. The law and traditions of the rabbis were as minute, detailed, and far-fetched on this point as they were on other matters, such as the sabbath day. Jesus' disciples were not breaking the law of Moses. They were breaking the traditions of the Pharisees.

The Pharisees asked Jesus, "Why do your disciples not walk after the traditions of the elders? Why do they eat their bread with defiled hands?"

Jesus observed:

Well did Isaiah prophesy of you hypocrites when he wrote, "This people honors me with their lips, but their heart is far from me. But in vain do they worship me, teaching as their doctrines the precepts of men" (Isa. 29:13). You openly reject the commandment of God, so that you may keep your traditions.

For example, God said, "Honor your father and your mother," and, "He that speaks evil of father or mother, let him die the death." But you say that if a man says to his father or mother, "That which I would have used to help you is Corban" (which means "given to God"), then he cannot do anything for his father or mother. Thus you make the word of God meaningless by your traditions.

NOTE:

The statement Jesus quotes: "Corban, that by which thou mightest be profited by me," is an exact translation of the common formula of vowing, as given in the Mishnah and the Talmud. A person would use this vow to prohibit others from profiting from his possessions. Once the vow was made, even to parents, it had to be kept even if it involved breaking the commandment which told them to honor their parents, meeting whatever obligations that would entail. Some rabbis expressly taught that such a vow superseded the necessity of keeping the commandment to honor father and mother. Jesus' point was that these were not two commandments of God which came into conflict. The commandment to honor father and mother came from God, and the tradition surrounding the practice of Corban came from the rabbis. The Pharisees quite literally obeyed the traditions of the elders instead of the command of God.

Jesus came back to the question about whether His disciples were defiling themselves by not observing the ritual washings. He called the multitude closer and said, "Listen to me, everyone, and understand. Nothing which enters a man from without defiles him. It is the things that come forth from a man that defile him."

When Jesus went into the house, His disciples came and said, "Did you know that the Pharisees were offended by what you said?"

Jesus replied, "Every plant which my heavenly Father has not planted will be rooted up. Leave them alone. They are blind guides. If the blind lead the blind, both will fall into a hole."

Peter and the apostles said, "Explain your illustration to us."

Surprised, Jesus said, "Are you also still without understanding by this time? Do you not see that whatever goes into the mouth passes into the stomach and is then expelled from the body? But the things which proceed out of the mouth come from the heart, and they defile the man. Out of the heart come forth evil thoughts, murders, adulteries, fornications, thefts, false witness, and rantings. These are the things that defile a man, but to eat with unwashed hands does not defile anyone."

The Second Retirement

Jesus and His apostles go to the region of Tyre and Sidon (Mark 7:24-30; Matt. 15:21-28):

NOTE:

The first effort at retirement at Bethsaida Julias failed. The multitudes met Jesus and His disciples so that there was no time for rest nor for the teaching Jesus wanted to do with His disciples. He was more successful in the second retirement.

Look on your map and find Tyre, Sidon, Mt. Hermon, Decapolis, and Caesarea Philippi. Follow their route as the story proceeds.

Jesus and His apostles actually left the territory of Israel proper and went into the vicinity of Tyre and Sidon. There Jesus entered into a house and tried to keep anyone from knowing He was there.

A woman of that area, a Gentile, had a little daughter who had an unclean spirit. Having heard about Jesus, the woman came to Him and fell down at His feet begging Him to cast the devil out of her daughter. "Have mercy on me, O Lord, son of David."

But Jesus did not answer a word. His disciples came to Him and said, "Send her away because she keeps crying after us."

Jesus answered saying, "I was not sent to any but the lost sheep of the house of Israel."

The woman came worshiping Him, and said, "Lord, help me."

Jesus replied, "It is not fitting to take the children's food away and give it to the pet dogs."

The woman answered, "That is right, Lord, but the dogs do eat the scraps that fall from their master's table."

Jesus said to her, "O woman, your faith is great. Go on your way. Your wish is granted." The woman's daughter was healed from that hour.

NOTE:

Jesus was not pretending to be cruel to test the woman's faith. He had crossed over into Gentile territory. He had no intention of doing great works among the Gentiles which might appear to be the beginning of a campaign. So He said, "I was sent only to the Jews." He further stated His reservation by using an illustration. One does not take the food meant for the children and deliberately feed it to the pets. No insult was intended. Jesus' point was merely that His earthly mission was among the

Jews. The woman, by her reply, showed that she understood this and that this miracle would be regarded as an exception, not the beginning of a great work among the Gentiles.

The Third Withdrawal — Through Decapolis

Feeding the 4,000 (Mark 7:31-8:9; Matt. 15:29-38):

Jesus and His disciples went from the area of Tyre, up through Sidon, and around to the Sea of Galilee — possibly circling around by Mt. Hermon. Matthew mentions only the Sea of Galilee as their destination, while Mark also mentions the Decapolis. The borders of Decapolis reached a point about halfway up the east side of the Sea of Galilee. The events described therefore happened in the territory to the southeast of the Sea of Galilee in the borders of the Decapolis. Be sure you show your class a map of these areas.

The people brought a man to Jesus who was deaf and who also had a speech impediment. They asked Jesus to lay His hand upon him. Jesus took him apart from the crowd and put His fingers into his ears. Then He spat and touched the man's tongue. By these signs Jesus let the man know what He was doing.

Looking up to heaven, Jesus sighed and said, "Ephphatha," which means, "Be opened." The man's ears were opened, and his tongue was loosed so that he could speak plainly. Again Jesus sought to keep the news from spreading, but could not.

The people were astonished beyond measure and said, "He has done all things well. He even makes the deaf to hear and the mute to speak." Many others were also brought — lame, blind, mute, and injured. They were laid at His feet, and He healed them.

Jesus called His disciples to Him and said, "I feel sorry for this crowd because they have been here three days and have nothing to eat. I do not wish to send them away having had no food."

The disciples said, "Where are we going to get enough loaves here in this deserted area to feed such a great multitude?"

Jesus asked them, "How many loaves do you have?"

"Seven," they replied, "and a few small fish."

Having commanded the multitude to sit down on the ground, Jesus took the seven loaves and the few fish, gave thanks for them, and broke the food into pieces. He gave the pieces to His disciples and they distributed them to the multitude.

Everyone had plenty to eat. When they were finished, there were seven baskets of scraps. The number of people was about 4,000 men besides women and children. After this, Jesus sent the multitude away.

NOTE:

According to the Greek words used, the baskets in this story were large produce baskets, whereas the twelve baskets in the feeding of the 5,000 were smaller picnic-type baskets.

Remember to stress that though a miracle often showed the compassion of Jesus, or some other aspect of His character, *every* miracle provided evidence that He was the Son of God. Remember that "these are written, that ye might believe that Jesus is the Christ, the Son of God; and that believing ye might have life through his name" (John 20:30-31).

A brief visit to Dalmanutha (Magadan); Argument with the Pharisees and Sadducees (Mark 8:10-12; Matt. 15:39-16:4):

NOTE:
For the first time, the Sadducees join in the public opposition to Jesus. It is interesting to see how hatred of a common enemy can draw the bitterest of factions together. The cooperation of the Pharisees and Sadducees was only temporary.

After sending the multitudes away, Jesus entered a boat and crossed to the west side of the Sea of Galilee to a place called Dalmanutha (Matthew has Magadan of which nothing particular is known). When He arrived, the Pharisees and Sadducees sought Him out to try Him. They asked Him to show them a sign.

Jesus sighed deeply and said, "Why does this generation keep on seeking a sign? When it is evening you say, 'It will be fair weather, because the skies are red.' And in the morning, 'It will be bad weather today because the skies are red and overcast.' You know how to read the face of the skies, but you cannot read the signs of the times. It is an evil, adulterous age that keeps seeking for a sign. There is no sign that will be given to it but the sign of Jonah." Then Jesus left them and went away.

NOTE:
The signs of the weather mentioned by Jesus are those associated with Palestine. When the sky is fiery red in the evening, the wind has driven the clouds to the west out over the Mediterranean Sea. Therefore the day will be fair because the moisture-laden air is out to sea. On the other hand, when the fiery redness is seen in the morning when the sun rises above the eastern horizon, then foul weather can be expected because the air has come in from the Mediterranean.

The sign of Jonah is the one also referred to in Matthew 12:38-45. Again, Jesus was referring to His resurrection as the ultimate sign.

The Fourth Retirement — Back to Bethsaida Julias

Jesus rebukes the spiritual dullness of the disciples (Mark 8:13-21; Matt. 16:5-12):

Jesus and His disciples entered a boat to cross over to Bethsaida Julias on the northeast shore of the Sea of Galilee. The disciples forgot to take bread, and did not have more than one loaf with them. Naturally, this situation was upon their minds when Jesus said, "Watch out for the leaven of the Pharisees."

Jesus' thoughts were on His exchanges with the Pharisees. He meant beware of their influence and character. The disciples thought He was warning them not to get bread from the Pharisees. They explained His comment among themselves by saying, "It is because we took no bread."

Jesus heard them and could tell what they were thinking. They had missed His point. So He said, "O how little faith you have. Why are you reasoning among yourselves that you have no bread? Do you not yet understand? Do you not remember the five loaves I divided among the five thousand? How many baskets full of scraps did you pick up?"

"Twelve," they replied.

"And when I divided the seven loaves among the four thousand, how many basketfuls did you take up?"

"Seven," they answered.

"Why then did you not figure out that I was not talking to you about bread, but about the leaven of the Pharisees?"

Then they understood that He spoke to them regarding the teaching of the Pharisees.

Jesus heals a blind man at Bethsaida (Mark 8:22-26):

At Bethsaida, a blind man was brought to Jesus for Him to heal. He took the blind man by the hand and led him out of the village. Having spat upon his eyes and having laid His hands upon him, Jesus asked, "Do you see anything?"

The man said, "I see men, because I see them walking about as trees."

Then Jesus laid His hands upon his eyes, and the man gazed about and could see clearly. Jesus sent the man straight home. He said, "Do not even go into the village."

Peter's confession of Christ at Caesarea Philippi (Mark 8:27-30; Matt. 16:13-20; Luke 9:18-21):

Jesus and His disciples traveled on to the north from Bethsaida to Caesarea Philippi. This city was very close to Dan at the foot of Mt. Hermon, about twenty-three miles north of Bethsaida. Doubtless Jesus taught His disciples many things during this period, but we have only this one sublime conversation recorded.

As they traveled along through the villages and suburbs of Caesarea Philippi, He asked the disciples, "Who do men say that I am?"

The disciples answered, "Some say John the Baptist; others say Elijah; while some say that one of the Old Testament prophets has risen again."

Then Jesus asked them, "But who do you say that I am?"

Peter promptly answered, "You are the Christ, the Son of the living God."

Jesus answered Peter, "You are blessed, Simon son of Jonah, because flesh and blood has not revealed this truth to you, but my Father who is in heaven. And I also tell you that you are Peter (Greek for stone) and upon this rock (petra, a bedrock or ledge) I will build my church and the gates of Hades shall not prevail against it."

NOTE:

There is simply no way that Peter could be the rock upon which the church is built. Jesus is expressly said to be the foundation of the church; there can be no other (1 Cor. 3:11). In Greek, the word Peter means a stone such as one might pick up and hold in his hand, whereas petra, the rock upon which the church was to be built, was a great bedrock or ledge. The rock upon which the church would be built was the great truth which Peter confessed. The "gates of Hades" referred to the approaching death of Jesus. Not even His death would prevent the building of His church, because He would be raised from the dead.

Jesus continued speaking to Peter: "And I will give you the keys of the kingdom. Whatever you bind on earth shall already have been bound in heaven, and whatever you loose on earth shall already have been loosed in heaven." Then Jesus charged His disciples to tell no man He was the Christ.

NOTE:

Peter preached the first gospel sermon recorded. It was preached to Jews on the day of Pentecost (Acts 2). He also preached the first gospel sermon to Gentiles at the home of Cornelius (Acts 10; see also Acts 15:7). The "keys of the kingdom" was the preaching of the gospel. Peter would use these keys first. There is no Bible basis whatsoever for the popular idea that Peter guards the "pearly" gates of heaven.

Neither is it correct that Peter alone was given the right to bind and loose. In a later statement, Jesus makes the identical promise to all His apostles (Matt. 18:18).

We have shown the tense of the original language correctly. What the apostles would bind on earth would already have been bound in heaven. The idea that the apostles would speak on earth, and whatever they uttered would become law in heaven is exactly backward to the way it happened. The King James Version and the American Standard Version leave a false impression in their translation of this passage. Yet these same versions teach in an abundance of passages that the apostles bound and loosed the things they were given from heaven where those matters had already been made law (John 14:26; 15:26; 16:13; Matt. 10:19-20; Acts 10:28b; 11:17-18; Eph. 3:3-5).

Jesus Himself had told people He was the Christ. He demonstrated that His claim was correct by all kinds of proofs. He apparently did not think the apostles were ready to sustain the assertion that He was the Christ at this point. It would do more harm than good if they attempted to do so before they were ready. Therefore, He told them to tell no man that He was the Christ at this time. They would later risk their lives to tell people that very message.

Jesus foretells His death and resurrection (Mark 8:31-37; Matt. 16:21-26; Luke 9:22-25):

NOTE:

These periods of retirement covered approximately six months — from the Passover of John 6:4 till the Feast of Tabernacles in John 7. At this time it is less than a year till Jesus will die, so He begins to prepare His disciples for this ordeal.

Jesus began telling His disciples how He would be rejected, grossly mistreated by the elders, the chief priests, and the lawyers, and would be killed. He also said He would afterward be raised from the dead. He had hinted about these matters since the beginning of His public ministry, but now He speaks plainly about it to His apostles.

NOTE:
This news was like a bolt of lightning among the disciples. They knew He was the Messiah, the Son of God, but they still had no clear idea about what His ultimate mission was. They, like the multitudes around them, supposed the Messiah would be an earthly king. They were looking forward to an earthly kingdom with a king on a throne and themselves as officials in that kingdom.

The disciples were so shocked, the promise of the resurrection did not register. They heard only the fact that He would be mistreated and would die. Peter began to rebuke Jesus: "Don't talk that way! This will never happen to you."

Jesus turned to Peter and said, "Get behind me, Satan," or as we would say, "Get out of my sight, Satan; you are a stumbling block to me. You are not thinking of things from God's viewpoint, but only from men's."

Jesus called all of His disciples around Him. It must have been an emotionally charged moment for Jesus and His disciples. He told them, "If a man plans to follow me, he will have to put his wants second and accept whatever suffering he encounters because of the gospel. Whoever would save his life by avoiding responsibility will lose it, but whoever is willing to lose his life for my sake and for the gospel will save it. What will it profit after all, if a man gains the whole world and forfeits his life? What will a man give in exchange for his life?"

NOTE:
The principle of sacrifice is an alien concept to our generation. We need to have this lesson burned deeply into our hearts. So many of Jesus' questions were left hanging, as it were glowing in the darkness. Men must see these questions and answer them for themselves.

The coming of the Son of Man in His kingdom and in His glory within that generation (Mark 8:38-9:1; Matt. 16:27-28; Luke 9:26-27):

NOTE:
This speech of Jesus is given as a conclusion to the speech in which He warned of His death and resurrection. The humiliation of Jesus in death is contrasted vividly with the glory of His coming in His kingdom.

Jesus continued: "For whoever is ashamed of me and of my words in this adulterous and sinful generation, the Son of Man will be ashamed of him when He comes in the glory of His Father and with the holy angels. Then He will give judgment unto every man according to his deeds. Truly there are some standing here who will not die until they see the Son of Man coming in His kingdom with power."

NOTE:
Usually these passages are taken to prove that the kingdom of Christ came on

the day of Pentecost. The reasoning is that the kingdom would come with power; the power would come with the Holy Spirit; and the Holy Spirit came on Pentecost. It is definitely true that the church (or kingdom) was established on Pentecost, and it was established with and by the power of the Spirit. But it is doubtful that Jesus had the events of Pentecost in mind as He made this particular prediction.

Notice that Jesus is not speaking of a quiet, humble coming of the Son of Man. Rather He is predicting a time when He will be coming in judgment against an adulterous and sinful generation; a time when the Son of Man will show His feeling of shame for the fearful who have been ashamed to stand up for Him in that wicked generation.

Also consider the time frame mentioned. It was less than a year till the Pentecost when the church was to be established. Nearly everyone standing there hearing Jesus speak on this occasion would still be alive less than a year later. But Jesus says "some" standing here will not die until they see the Son of Man coming in power. It would have been an insipid statement to say some would still be alive a year from that time, but if He were speaking of an event that would happen about forty years later, then the statement is much stronger.

Look at the context and the statement itself. Jesus has just predicted that the rulers of the Jews will soon reject Him, will mistreat Him, and kill Him. Now He predicts that, though He will be humiliated by their treatment at this time, some of His disciples will live to see the wicked generation punished by the power of that same Son of Man. It was almost exactly forty years from the time of this prediction until Jerusalem was destroyed by the Romans, and the Jewish nation was no longer reckoned as God's chosen people. Indeed, the crucified-One returned as the punishing-One!

The transfiguration (Mark 9:2-8; Matt. 17:1-8; Luke 9:28-36):

NOTE:
The mount of transfiguration is not named. There is no mention or hint that Jesus had left Caesarea Philippi. The most likely candidate for the mountain in question would be Mount Hermon, but we really do not know.

Six days later Jesus took Peter, James, and John with Him onto a high mountain by themselves to pray. As He was praying, His appearance was changed before their eyes. His face shone as did the sun and His clothes became dazzling white.

Two men appeared to talk with Him: Moses the great lawgiver of the Old Testament and Elijah the great prophet of Israel. They also appeared in glorious form. They spoke of the death of Jesus which was to take place at Jerusalem.

Peter, James, and John were very sleepy and had probably gone to sleep while Jesus was praying. When they were fully awake, they saw the glory of Jesus and the two men who were with Him.

Peter said to Jesus, "Master, if you like, let us build three huts, one for you, one for Moses, and one for Elijah." But Peter did not really know what to say because he and his companions were very frightened.

While Peter was speaking, a cloud came and overshadowed them. Peter, James, and John were very afraid as they entered the cloud. Then they heard a voice say, "This is my beloved Son in whom I am well pleased. All of you, listen to Him."

When the disciples heard these words, they fell on their faces and were terrified. Jesus came and touched them and said, "Get up, and don't be afraid." When they lifted their heads and looked around, they were alone once again with Jesus. It can be said assuredly that no men ever got closer to heaven while on earth than these three men did.

NOTE:

Many years later, Peter recalled this experience and said, "We did not make up cunningly devised fables when we told you of the power and presence of our Lord Jesus Christ, but we were eyewitnesses of His majesty. For He received from God the Father honor and glory, when there was borne such a voice to Him by the Majestic Glory, 'This is my beloved Son, in whom I am well-pleased.' And this voice we ourselves heard out of heaven while we were with Him in the holy mount" (2 Pet. 1:16-18). What an exceedingly powerful impression this experience had on these three men!

The disciples question Jesus about Elijah as they come down from the mountain (Mark 9:9-13; Matt. 17:9-13; Luke 9:36):

As they were coming down the mountain, Jesus charged His disciples not to tell any one what they had seen until after He was risen from the dead. They wondered what He meant about rising from the dead, but they kept the matter to themselves as He had commanded them.

The disciples were puzzled about something. Here they had seen Elijah on the mountain, and Jesus had already been with them for over two years. Yet the scribes said that Elijah was supposed to come before the Christ. Therefore they asked, "Why do the scribes say that Elijah must come first, before the Christ?"

Jesus replied, "Elijah really does come first and will restore all things. But I tell you Elijah has already come, and they did not know him but did whatever they wanted to with him. In the same way, the Son of Man will suffer at their hands."

Then the disciples understood that He spoke to them of John the Baptist.

NOTE:

The Old Testament foretold that Elijah would come before the Christ (Mal. 4:5-6). The prophecy did not mean literal Elijah, but a forerunner who would come in the spirit and power of Elijah. When the Jews asked John if he were Elijah, he said, "No," because he knew they were asking if he were literal Elijah (John 1:21). But John the Baptist *was* the Elijah that Malachi foretold, as Jesus pointed out here.

Jesus heals a demoniac boy whom His disciples could not heal (Mark 9:14-29; Matt. 17:14-20; Luke 9:37-43):

The next day when Jesus, Peter, James, and John came down to join the rest of the disciples at the foot of the mountain, a great multitude had gathered. The scribes were questioning the disciples.

As soon as the multitude saw Jesus, they were astonished and ran to Him and greeted Him.

Jesus asked the people, "What were you asking them?" referring to His disciples.

One of the multitude came forward, kneeling to Jesus. The man said, "Master, I beg you to have mercy upon my son, for he is my only child. He has a spirit which throws him down, and he foams, and grinds his teeth, and then faints. He is bruised and sore all the time. I brought him to your disciples, but they could not cast the spirit out."

Jesus said, "O faithless generation, how long shall I be with you and bear with you? Bring your son to me."

They brought the son, and immediately the spirit threw him down violently. The boy fell to the ground and wallowed foaming.

Jesus asked, "How long has he been like this?"

The father replied, "From childhood. Often it has cast him into fire and water to destroy him. But if you can do anything, have compassion on us, and help us."

Jesus responded indignantly, "If you can! All things are possible to him who believes."

Immediately the father cried out: "I believe; help my unbelief."

When Jesus saw that the multitude was gathering around them, He said to the unclean spirit: "You deaf and dumb spirit, I command you, come out of him, and enter into him no more."

The spirit cried out, and, having convulsed the child, came out and left him as still as death. In fact, most of the people around said, "He is dead!" But Jesus took the boy by the hand, raised him up, and gave him back to his father. Everyone was astonished at the greatness of God.

When He had entered a house with His disciples, they asked Him privately, "Why could we not cast the demon out?"

Jesus said, "Because of your little faith. If you have faith as a grain of mustard seed, you will say to this mountain, 'Remove to that place over there' and it will move; nothing will be impossible for you. This kind of spirit does not come out by anything except prayer and fasting."

> NOTE:
> Jesus had given the apostles power to cast out devils (Matt. 10:1). This power was not temporary because if that had been why they could not cast out the demon, Jesus would have said that. The problem, Jesus said, was their own weakness in faith. They had succeeded in casting out demons on the preaching tour Jesus had sent them on (Mark 6:13). That proves they had strong enough faith to cast out some demons. Why not this one? Just as Peter, when frightened by the stormy waves, could not exercise the power available to him because of little faith, so the apostles were probably so frightened by the violent behavior of this demoniac that they could not exercise their power. Fear can drive out faith. The fasting and praying, therefore, have to do with the strengthening of faith and not with the working of miracles itself.

Jesus again foretells His death and resurrection (Mark 9:30-32; Matt. 17:22-23; Luke 9:43-45):

Jesus and His disciples left the area where He had been transfigured and went back into Galilee. On this trip, Jesus did not want anyone to know He was there. He continued to teach His disciples and to warn them of His coming death and resurrection. From the time He began telling them of His death, again and again He told them that He would be delivered into the hands of men who would kill Him, but that after three days He would rise again. But the message just did not sink in. It upset the disciples very much to hear this information, and they seemed to block it out of their minds. They did not understand what He meant, and they were afraid to question Him about it.

Jesus pays a half-shekel for the temple tax (Matt. 17:24-27):

NOTE:

There is some question about whether this episode took place before or after the discussion about who was to be the greatest in the kingdom. Matthew is the only one who tells this story about Peter. He places it *before* the discussion about greatness in the kingdom, but it seems the apostles had argued that subject on their way to Galilee (Mark 9:33). Jesus took time to deal with the subject soon after they arrived in Capernaum. This story happens about that same time, shortly after they arrived in Capernaum.

While they were in Capernaum, those in charge of collecting the tax for the temple came to Peter and said, "Doesn't your master pay the half-shekel?"

Peter promptly replied, "Yes."

As soon as Peter went into the house, Jesus said, "What is your thinking on this, Simon? The kings of the earth, from whom do they receive toll or tribute? From their sons, or from strangers?"

Peter answered, "From strangers." Peter knew that kings did not tax their own sons.

Jesus said, "Then are the sons free. But, lest we leave the wrong impression, go to the sea and cast a hook into the water. Take the first fish you catch and look in its mouth. There you will find a shekel. Take it and pay the tax for you and me."

NOTE:

The tax under consideration in this story was called the atonement money in the law. It was collected from every Jewish man above the age of twenty, and was used for the support of the temple service. (See Exod. 30:13-16.) In the Greek, the actual coin mentioned was a didrachmon, worth about forty cents, or over two days' wages for a common laborer.

Jesus was not present when the tax collectors came to Peter. Yet by anticipating the question that was on Peter's mind, Jesus showed that not only did He know what Peter was thinking, He knew what had happened to make him think about the tax. That in itself was amazing.

Let us look more closely at Jesus' answer. Peter had given an assured answer that "Yes, of course, Jesus paid the temple tax." But what kind of tax was it? It was a tax to keep up the service of the worship at the temple. In other words, a tax required by God's law to keep up worship to God. Jesus asks, "Are the king's sons required to pay the tax the king requires?" Peter had already affirmed that Jesus was the Son of God — so why should Jesus have to pay tax to His own Father? But, lest the Jews misunderstand, Jesus provided the money miraculously to pay the tax for Himself and Peter.

The Bible does not tell of Peter's going to the water, casting in his hook, and feeling the tug of the fish. Nor does it tell of his opening its mouth and finding the shekel Jesus had promised. Yet without doubt, he did so. Think of the powerful effect this interesting miracle would have had upon Peter.

The Twelve dispute over who would be the greatest in the kingdom of heaven (Mark 9:33-37; Matt. 18:1-14; Luke 9:46-48):

When Jesus and His disciples arrived in Capernaum, Jesus asked them, "What were you reasoning about on the road?"

They were quiet. They did not want to tell Jesus that they had been fussing about who would be the greatest in the kingdom of heaven.

Jesus sat down and said, "If any man wants to be first in rank, he will have to be servant to everyone." He called a little child to Him, took him into His arms, and said, "Unless you change and become as little children, there is no way you can enter the kingdom of heaven. Whoever will receive one such little child in my name, receives me as well. And whoever receives me, receives the One that sent me."

John said, "Master, we saw someone casting out demons in your name, and we told him he could not do that because he was not one of us."

Jesus answered:

Don't forbid him. There is no man who can do mighty works in my name who will quickly speak evil of me. He who is not against us is for us. Anyone who gives you a cup of water to drink because you belong to Christ, truly I tell you, he will certainly have his reward.

On the other hand, whoever causes one of these little ones to stumble, it would be better for him if someone had tied a great millstone around his neck and had cast him into the sea.

Woe to the world because of occasions of stumbling. Such occasions will come, but woe to the one who causes the occasions!

If your hand or your foot causes you to stumble, cut it off and throw it away. It is better to enter into life maimed than to have two hands or two feet to be cast into the unquenchable fire.

If your eye causes you to stumble, pluck it out and throw it away. It is better for you to enter into life with only one eye than to have two eyes and be cast into the hell of fire.

See that you do not look down on these little ones because I tell you that in heaven their angels always look upon the face of my Father.

How do you figure it? If a man has a hundred sheep, and one of them wanders away, does he not leave the ninety-nine and go into the mountains to hunt for the one which is lost? And if he finds it, there is more rejoicing over that one than over the ninety-nine which did not wander away. Just so, it is not the will of your Father that one of these little ones perish.

NOTE:

The "little ones" Jesus refers to are His followers. They are all to be as little children — which brings Him back to His original illustration.

How to deal with a brother who has sinned against another brother; Duty of forgiving the penitent (Matt. 18:15-35):

NOTE:

This discussion immediately follows Jesus' discussion of avoiding occasions of offense. The sin of one brother against another, and the failure to deal with such sins properly, has probably caused more trouble among the saints than any other single problem.

Jesus said, "If your brother sins against you, go to him and show him what he has done. Let there be just the two of you there alone. If he will listen to you, you have gained your brother. If he will not listen, then take one or two more with you so that there will be witnesses to uphold every word said. If he will not listen to them, tell the matter to the church. If he will not hear the church, then consider him as if he were a Gentile and a publican.

"Truly I tell you, whatever you bind on earth will have been bound in heaven, and whatever you loose on earth will have been loosed in heaven. I also tell you that if two of you agree on earth regarding anything you may ask, it will be done for you by my Father in heaven. Because where two or three are gathered together in my name, there I am in the midst of you."

This discussion about forgiveness moved Peter to ask, "Lord, how many times should I forgive my brother, up to seven times?" Peter probably felt that seven was a generous number. Jesus replied:

Not seven times, but seventy times seven! In this respect, the kingdom of heaven is like a certain king who decided to check the accounts of his various servants. When he began, one servant was brought in who owed ten thousand talents (several million dollars). Since the servant was not able to pay his debt, the king ordered him to be sold along with his wife, his children, and his possessions, to raise the money to pay it. The servant fell down and begged, "Lord, be patient with me, and I will pay you everything." The king was moved with compassion and canceled the man's debt.

But the servant went out and found one of his fellow servants who owed him about seventeen dollars. He seized the man, taking him by the throat, and said, "Pay me what you owe." His fellow servant fell down and begged, saying, "Be patient with me and I will pay you." But the man would not listen. He cast his fellow servant into prison till he should pay his debt.

When the other servants saw what was done, they were very sorry. They went to their master and told him what had happened. His lord called the servant back before him and said, "You wicked servant! I forgave you all your debt because you asked me to do so. Should you not have had mercy on your fellow servant, as I had mercy on you?" The lord was very angry and delivered the servant to the tormentors, till he should pay all that was due.

This is what my heavenly Father will do to you if each of you does not sincerely forgive his brother.

Christ's followers must give up everything to follow Him (Matt. 8:19-22; Luke 9:57-62):

As Jesus and His disciples were on the road, a scribe came up to Him and said, "I want to follow you wherever you go."

Jesus said, "The foxes have dens, and the birds have nests, but the Son of Man does not have a place of His own to lay His head."

To another, Jesus said, "Follow me."

The man replied, "Lord, give me time to go and bury my father."

Jesus answered, "Let the dead bury the dead; but you go and tell everyone about the kingdom of God."

Another said, "Lord, first let me say goodby to those of my family."

But Jesus said, "No man, having put his hand to the plough, and looking back, is fit for the kingdom of God."

NOTE:

All of these stories make the point that one's service in the kingdom of God is so important it must come before all earthly concerns. It must not be thought, however, that Jesus was making a law that one could not bury his dead or say goodby to a loved one. Jesus was not harsh or cruel. In the work He was doing, He had to go on. If these men wanted to go with Him, they could not stay to do things that were not really essential.

Jesus' brothers tell Him to show Himself to the world (John 7:2-9):

The Feast of Tabernacles took place in October. The time drew near and Jesus' brothers said, "Leave here and go to Judea so that your disciples can watch you do these works you are doing. No man does things secretly if He wants to be known openly. If you are going to do these things, show yourself to the world." Even His brethren did not believe on Him at this point.

Jesus answered, "My time is not ready. The time does not matter to you. The world cannot hate you, but it hates me because I testify that its works are evil. You go on up to the feast. I am not going yet because my time is not yet fulfilled." So Jesus remained in Galilee a little longer.

NOTE:

Later, in the book of Acts, one of the leaders in the church at Jerusalem was a man named James (Acts 15). James, the brother of John, was already dead by chapter 15. The James mentioned might possibly be James the son of Alphaeus who was another apostle. However, the book of Galatians tells us it was James, the brother of Jesus, and that he was counted as a "pillar" in the church at Jerusalem (see Gal. 1:19; 2:2:9). It is also thought that it was this same James, the brother of Jesus, who wrote the book of James. Jude identifies himself in the book he wrote as "the brother of James." Therefore, it is thought that Jude was a brother to the prominent James in the book of Acts — and was, therefore, another brother of Jesus.

Jesus goes privately to Jerusalem through Samaria (Luke 9:51-56; John 7:10):

When Jesus' brothers had gone on to the feast, He left Galilee and sent messengers before Him. They went into a village of the Samaritans to make ready for Him, but the Samaritans would not let Him stay because He was headed for Jerusalem.

Angrily, James and John said, "Lord, do you want us to call for fire to come down from heaven and burn them up?"

But Jesus turned and rebuked them, "You do not know what manner of spirit you are of. The Son of Man did not come to destroy men's lives, but to save them." They just went on to another village to stay.

Take time to review:

Take time to review what has happened so far during Jesus' life on earth. Think of the announcements before His birth; think of the miraculous birth and of those who came to worship the child; think of the years of growing up in Nazareth. Think of the beginning of His work as He was baptized and publicly proclaimed as God's beloved Son; think of those disciples who first met Him and recognized this was the One the prophets had foretold. Think of His first miracle in Cana and then the ones that soon followed in Jerusalem. Then think of His months in Galilee when crowds thronged Him to see or to experience His miracles. Remember the awe in the hearts of those first multitudes as they heard His sermons and knew they had never heard anyone speak like this man. Then remember how the first opposition arose: at Nazareth, then in the hearts of those who heard Him say He could forgive sins, and then as they saw Him disobeying their traditions about the sabbath day. Remember how they could not deny that miracles were occurring, but they accused Him of performing the miracles by the power of Beelzebub. Twelve of His early disciples have been chosen as His special servants, His apostles, and now He has taken some time during the last six months to take those twelve men aside to teach them lessons they will need to carry out the work before them. There are still crowds seeking Him out, but He has begun to scold them for their motives in seeking Him. By now the curiosity seekers must choose whether to believe He is the Messiah, or to turn back from following Him. The majority of His work in Galilee is behind Him. Most of the remaining time before His death, He will spend in other parts of the land. He will say many of the same things He has already said in Galilee to the new multitudes that will gather. Try to have a full, rich overview of His life so far in your mind.

The Close of Jesus' Ministry
Matt. 19:1-20:34; Mark 10:1-32; Luke 10:1-19:28; John 7:1-11:54)

Life of Christ

Preparation
Beginning Ministry
Galilean Ministry
Retirement

*Closing Ministry

 *Multitude Divided
 *Opposition Strong

 *Feast of Tabernacles
 *Feast of Dedication

 *In Jerusalem
 *In Judea
 *In Perea

Last Week
Resurrection
Exaltation

By now we have studied the first four parts of the outline of Jesus' life on earth. The Galilean ministry ended about six months ago and now we have come to the close of the period of retirement when He withdrew from the crowds in order to have time to teach His disciples. It is almost time for the Feast of Tabernacles in Jerusalem. It is fall — about our October. Jesus will die in the spring, during the feast of the Passover. It is, therefore, about six months before His death at this time.

Notice that in this period, the Close of Jesus' Ministry, there are many more direct conflicts between Jesus and the Jewish officials. There had been conflicts earlier, and the Pharisees in Galilee had plotted to kill Him on one occasion (Matt. 12:14). The Jews of Jerusalem had tried to kill Him during one of the earlier feasts (John 5:18). By now, however, the opposition is much more organized and determined. Jesus meets the opposition head-on and carries on many discussions with the Jews. Some of His strongest assertions about His deity were made in the temple area to the Jewish officials themselves. They saw the evidence He presented that should have produced faith, and they heard His mighty lessons — but they refused to believe and continued on their plan to destroy Him.

In Jerusalem

Feast of Tabernacles; Great excitement about the Messiah (John 7:1-8:1):

The Feast of Tabernacles was the last feast in the yearly cycle of feasts commanded in the law of Moses. It was celebrated in the seventh month in connection with the Day of Atonement. The entire seventh month was a special month to the Jews. They had two calendars that they used regularly: their religious year started in the spring in the month

Nisan when they celebrated the Feast of Passover; their civil year started in the fall in the month Tishri when they celebrated the Feast of Tabernacles.

It was also the time to celebrate the end of the harvest for the year, to remember their sins, to offer their special atonement sacrifices on the Day of Atonement. The seven days immediately following the Day of Atonement were designated as the Feast of Tabernacles to remember the years when they lived in booths or tabernacles while they wandered in the wilderness. (See Lev. 23:23-43).

As time for the feast approached, Jesus deliberately waited late to go to Judea because the Jewish officials were plotting to take His life. They were sure He would be at the feast. That is why Jesus did not go when His brethren first taunted Him about going to show Himself to the crowds. Instead of going publicly with the multitudes, as He had traveled so often in the preceding months in Galilee, He waited and traveled quietly through Samaria. He arrived in Jerusalem secretly.

Meanwhile, the Jews were watching anxiously for Him and were asking, "Where is that man?" The crowds were also wondering about Him. Some were saying, "He is a good man." Others said, "No. He leads the multitudes into error." Though there were questions about Him on every side, no one dared speak openly about Him because of their fear of the Jewish officials.

NOTE:
All Israelites were called Jews by now. That means that all the people gathered for this feast were Jews. Yet the word "Jews" is used in a special sense throughout the story of Christ. When the Bible speaks of the multitudes' "fear of the Jews" or the fact that the "Jews were waiting to take His life," it is using the word "Jew" to refer to the Jewish officials. The common people heard Jesus gladly on most occasions. It was their leaders who hated Him and sought to destroy Him.

It was not until the midst of the eight-day feast that Jesus went to the temple courts and began to teach. It is ironic that the Jews had been seeking for Him, yet when He began teaching in full view of all, they were amazed at His teaching. They said, "How did this man get such learning without having studied?" (They meant, How did this man get such learning without formal rabbinical training?)

Jesus told them how: "My teaching is not mine, but His that sent me. If a man determines to do God's will, he will come to know whether my teaching is from God or whether I have made it up. The one who speaks what he thinks seeks his own glory, but He who seeks the glory of the One who sent Him, that one is true and there is no unrighteousness in Him. Did not Moses give you the law, and yet none of you follows the law? Why do you seek to kill me?"

The multitude replied, "You have a demon! Who is trying to kill you?" The multitude generally did not know of the plans of the Jewish leaders to kill Jesus.

Jesus did not respond to their question. He knew that even though the multitude did not know of their leaders' plans to kill Him, when the time came, their spirit would move them to join their leaders in rejecting Him.

Jesus said, "I did one work and all of you are amazed. Nevertheless, because Moses gave you circumcision — although it is not of Moses originally, but of the fathers — you will circumcise a child on the sabbath. If a child can be circumcised on the sabbath so that the law of Moses will not be broken, why are you enraged at me because I made a man completely well on the sabbath? Do not decide by mere appearance; make correct judgment."

NOTE:

Obviously there had been some miracle performed in Jerusalem on a sabbath. There is the account of a man healed in John 5. That was on a sabbath and it had enraged the Jews, but that was at an earlier feast. There were other miracles performed on sabbath days. Possibly, the one Jesus is referring to on this occasion is one of the many signs that we are not told about specifically. That should not hinder our understanding of the passage.

Some in Jerusalem knew that their leaders were seeking to kill Jesus. They said, "Isn't this the one they want to kill? Look, He speaks openly, and they say nothing to Him. Can it be that the rulers know that He really is the Christ? The only problem is, we know where this man comes from, but when the Christ comes, no one will know where He comes from."

Therefore Jesus, still teaching in the temple, cried out: "Yes, all of you know me and you know where I came from. I am not here on my own, but He that sent me is true. You do not know Him, but I know Him because I am from Him and He sent me." At this statement, there were those who tried to seize Him, but they did not lay a hand on Him because His hour to be delivered over to them had not yet come.

Many of the multitude did believe on Him. They argued, "When the Christ does come, will He do more signs than the ones this man has done?" When the Pharisees heard the people saying these things, they sent officers of the temple to take Jesus into custody.

Jesus calmly continued His teaching. "Just a little while longer I will be with you, then I will go to the One who sent me. You will hunt for me and will not find me, and where I am, you will not be able to come."

So the Jews discussed among themselves what He meant: "Where will He go that we will not be able to find Him? Will He go out among our people scattered among the Greeks [the dispersion], and teach the Greeks? What does He mean by saying, 'You will hunt for me and will not find me,' and 'Where I am, you cannot come'?"

On the last day of the feast, when the whole crowd gathered for a public assembly, Jesus stood forth and proclaimed, "If any man thirst, let him come to me and drink. He who believes on me, as the scripture has said, 'From within him shall flow rivers of living water.'" By this figure, Jesus meant the Holy Spirit which those who believed on Him were to receive. As yet the Spirit had not been given because Jesus had not yet been glorified.

NOTE:

The ability to do miracles had been given to the apostles (Matt. 10:1) and would be given to the seventy whom He sent out just after this (Luke 10:1, 17-20). This possession of the Spirit was temporary and is referred to as authority over unclean spirits, to cast them out, and authority to heal (cf. Mark 3:15; Luke 9:1; 10:19).

In several passages, the glorifying of Jesus is shown to be His resurrection and ascension to heaven (John 12:16,23; 13:31-32). At that time, the Holy Spirit would be given by the Father in Jesus' name (John 14:26). Jesus said that then *He* would send the Spirit to them from the Father (John 15:26) and that the Spirit would glorify Him (Christ) because He would take of Christ's and would declare it to the apostles (John 16:13-14). In his sermon on Pentecost, Peter said that since Jesus was by the right hand of God exalted and since He had received of the Father the promise of the Holy Spirit, that He had poured forth the Holy Spirit upon them (Acts 2:33).

Thus one of the prerogatives of the Christ, upon His ascension and glorification, was the right to send the Holy Spirit upon whomsoever He wished. It is to this right that John 7:39 refers.

When the crowd heard these words of Jesus, some said, "Without a doubt, this is the prophet" (see Deut. 18:15). Others said, "This is the Christ." Some disputed with them. They said, "What? Does the Christ come out of Galilee? Don't the scriptures say that the Christ comes of the seed of David and from Bethlehem, the village which was David's home?"

So there was a division in the multitude concerning Him. Some wanted to seize Jesus, but no one did.

NOTE:
It is plain that the multitude knew Jesus was from Nazareth in Galilee, but they did not know the story of His birth in Bethlehem.

Even the temple officers who had been sent to take Jesus did not take Him into custody. When they returned without Him, they were asked, "Why did you not bring Him?"

The officers replied, "No man ever spoke like He does."

The Pharisees were angry and said, "Are you also led astray? Have any of the rulers believed on Him, or the Pharisees? No! But this multitude that knows nothing of the law — there is a curse on them."

One of the rulers who was a Pharisee protested. It was Nicodemus, who had visited Jesus early in His ministry. He asked, "Does our law judge a man before it first hears from the man himself and determines what he is doing?"

The other Pharisees answered with sarcasm: "Are you also from Galilee? Look it up and see that no prophet arises from Galilee."

After this, everyone returned to his own home, but Jesus went out to the Mount of Olives.

NOTE:
The Pharisees were mistaken in their own argument. Tradition says that "Capernaum" means "tomb of Nahum." In addition the scriptures clearly teach that Jonah was from Gath-hepher (2 Kings 14:25) which was a city of Zebulun, definitely in the region of Galilee (Josh. 19:10,13). Also, of the Messiah Himself, Isaiah foretold that He would prophesy in Galilee (Isa. 9:1-2).

An adulteress is brought to Jesus for judgment (John 8:2-11):

Early the next morning, Jesus came into the temple area and people gathered to hear Him. He sat down and taught them. The scribes and Pharisees interrupted the teaching of Jesus by pretending that they wanted to consult Him on a point of law.

They had with them a woman who obviously was there against her will. To her shame, she was set in the midst of everyone, and the Pharisees said, "Teacher, this woman has been taken in adultery, in the very act. Now, in the law, Moses commanded us to stone such a one. What do you say about her?" They said this to try to find some grounds on which they could accuse Jesus.

Jesus surprised them. He made no comment, but stooped down and began to write on the ground with His finger, acting as if He had not even heard them.

NOTE:

It is important to see the issues involved here. The woman had committed adultery. The Pharisees came pretending to be interested in the law when all they were really seeking to do was to find some grounds on which they could accuse Jesus. They were not interested in the law, nor in the sin of the woman. Jesus knew all of this and acted accordingly. The very fact that the partner of the woman was not brought indicated the Pharisees were not truly concerned about obeying the law. Only the woman was there. There is some question about whether the Romans would have allowed the Jews to stone the woman if they had wanted to do so. Most authorities say they could not have. If that be the case, then they were counting on Jesus' objecting to the idea; then they could accuse Him of breaking the law without their having had the least intention of stoning the woman themselves.

Therefore, Jesus was faced with the sin which the woman had committed, with the demands of the law that she be stoned (Lev. 20:10; Deut. 22:22-24), with the hypocrisy of the Pharisees, and with His own compassion and mercy toward the woman. How could all these conflicting problems be solved?

When the Jews continued to press Him for an answer, Jesus stood up and said, "Let him that is without sin among you cast the first stone." The law required that the witnesses should be the first to stone the wrong-doer (Deut. 17:7). Thus, Jesus was telling them to go ahead and fulfill the law by stoning her, but to be sure that the first stone came from one who had brought her because of a genuine concern that justice be done for the adultery committed.

Jesus again stooped down and began writing on the ground. This gave the Pharisees no target against which to vent their anger. Jesus had called their bluff and had convicted them of sin. Thus He dealt with the first problem — the Jews' hypocrisy.

Beginning from the oldest to the youngest, the Pharisees began to depart. Without a word, all the men gradually left. The woman stood as if rooted to the spot, watching as all her accusers left.

Finally Jesus stood and asked her, "Woman, does no one condemn you?"

"No one, Lord," she replied. No one had stepped forward to say, "I am a witness of her sin. I will cast the first stone." Since the law required the witness to be the first to stone her, and there was no witness to do so, the woman could not be stoned. Thus the law was obeyed.

Jesus said to the woman, "Neither do I condemn you. Go your way. From now on, sin no more." In this statement Jesus solved the last two problems. He dealt with the woman's sin by forgiving her. He showed His compassion and mercy by forgiving instead of condemning.

NOTE:

This story about Jesus has been used to cancel passages in the New Testament which teach that the church is to discipline unruly members (Rom. 16:17; 1 Cor. 5; 2 Thess. 3:6,14). Jesus does not contradict Himself. This story was not about justice and chastisement of sin. Rather it was a story of hypocrisy of the Pharisees and of the mercy of Jesus.

Jesus' statement concerning the one without sin is taken by some to mean that if the members of a church have *ever* committed sin, then they cannot withdraw from a sinful brother. While the scriptures do require that acts of discipline be done sincerely and for the right reasons, they do not require sinless perfection on the part of those who carry out such actions. If, however, those who are reproving a sinner are currently guilty of flagrant sins themselves, then they need to straighten out their own lives before they try to straighten out the faults of others (Matt. 7:1-5). The Pharisees were *not* without sin in this matter. They were trying to lay a plot for Jesus and were using the sin of the woman as merely a tool. That is why Jesus made His statement.

Jesus claims to be the light of the world (John 8:12-20):

Jesus taught, saying, "I am the light of the world. The one who follows me will not walk in darkness but will have the light of life."

The Pharisees said, "You appear as your own witness. Your testimony is not valid."

Jesus answered, "Even if I do appear as my own witness, my testimony is true because I know where I came from and where I am going. You do not know where I came from nor where I go. You judge as men think; I judge no one. But if I do judge, my judgment is true because I am not alone. I have the Father on my side. In your law it is written that the witness of two men is true (Deut. 19:15). I bear witness of myself and the Father who sent me bears witness of me also."

The Jews asked, "Where is your Father?"

Jesus replied, "You do not know me or my Father. If you knew me, you would know my Father also."

This exchange took place in the treasury as He taught in the temple. No man seized Him, because it was not yet time.

NOTE:

It is interesting to read the comments of various authorities about the ceremonies conducted during the evenings of the Feast of Tabernacles. According to the Midrash of the Jews, the court of the women was brilliantly lighted as a symbol that God would "kindle for them the Great Light" in the days of the Messiah. The Rabbis also spoke of the "original light" in which God had wrapped Himself as a garment. According to them, it was from this light that the sun, moon, and stars had been kindled. They said that this light was then reserved under the throne of God for the Messiah, in whose day it would shine forth once more. In such a context, the statement of Jesus that He was the light of the world would have special significance to the Jews.

Sometimes the teachings of Jesus appear to us to have come out of thin air. We wonder why He said that particular statement at that particular moment. If we had all the facts, we would surely see that His teaching was usually based on some circumstance present at the time.

Jesus compares His Father and the Jews' father (John 8:21-59):

Once again Jesus told the Jews, "I am going away. You will hunt me, and you will die in your sins. Where I am going, you cannot come."

The Jews wondered, "Will He kill Himself? Is that what He means by saying, 'Where I go you cannot come'?"

Jesus replied, "You are of this world; I am not of this world. That is why I said that unless you believe that I am the Christ, you will die in your sins."

They pressed Him: "Who are you?"

"The same one I have said I am all along. I have many things to say and to judge concerning you. I do exactly what my Father wants me to do." As Jesus spoke, many believed on Him; but from their subsequent response, it is evident that they did not believe very deeply.

To those Jews who believed in Him, He said, "If you remain in my word, then you will really be my disciples. You will realize the truth, and the truth will make you free."

The implication that they were in bondage sparked a bitter retort: "We are Abraham's seed and have never been in bondage to any man." (They conveniently forgot Egypt, Assyria, Babylon, Rome, and a dozen or so other masters!)

Jesus told them exactly what bondage He had in mind: "Anyone who keeps on sinning is the slave of sin. You say you are Abraham's seed, but you are making efforts to kill me because you do not freely and fully accept my words. I tell you the things I have heard from my Father, and you do the things which you have heard from your father."

The Jews said, "Our father is Abraham."

Jesus replied, "If you were really Abraham's children, you would do the deeds of Abraham. Instead you want to kill me, a man that has told you the truth which I heard from God. Abraham did not act like this. You are acting like your father."

"We were not born of fornication. We have one Father — God," they said.

"If God were your Father, you would love me because I have come from God. Why can you not understand the things I say to you? It is because you cannot perceive my message. You are acting like your father, the devil, and are trying to imitate his lusts. He was a murderer from the beginning and did not stand in truth because he has nothing to do with truth. Because I tell you the truth, you do not believe me. Which one of you convicts me of sin? If I tell you the truth, why don't you believe me? He who is of God hears my words. You do not hear them because you are not of God."

The Jews said, "Didn't we say it well? You are a Samaritan and have a demon!"

Jesus answered, "I do not have a demon. But whereas I honor my Father, you dishonor me. Really and truly, I tell you, if a man keeps my word, he will never see death."

"Now we know you have a demon," answered the Jews. "Abraham is dead, as are the prophets, and you say, 'If a man keep my word, he shall never taste of death.' Are you greater than our father Abraham, who is dead? And the prophets, who are also dead? Whom do you make yourself?"

Jesus answered, "If I glorify myself, it amounts to nothing. But it is my Father who glorifies me, the same One whom you claim as your God, but you have not known Him. I know Him. If I were to say I do not know Him, I would be what you are, a liar, but I know Him and keep His word. Your father Abraham rejoiced to see my day coming. He saw it and was glad."

Scornfully, the Jews said, "You are not fifty years old. Do you mean to say you have seen Abraham?"

In measured tones Jesus replied, "The fact is, before Abraham was born, I am." Jesus' words provoked an immediate and violent response. The Jews picked up stones to stone Him on the spot, but Jesus hid Himself and left the temple area.

NOTE:

The reason for the Jews' anger was that again Jesus had claimed to be divine. Not only did He claim to exist before Abraham was born, but He appropriated for Himself a designation which clearly said He was to be identified with the covenant

God of the Jews — Jehovah — for when God spoke to Moses from the burning bush and told him the name by which to identify Himself to His people, He said, "Tell them I Am hath sent you" (Exod. 3:14).

Notice that the Jews *want* to kill Jesus at this point. They have already tried to take Him into custody; they have tried to stone Him; they have laid traps for Him. But they cannot take Him. It was not yet time in God's scheme for Him to be taken — therefore they were unable to do so. The time will come when Jesus delivers Himself into their hands — but it will be because Jesus was *ready* to die, not because He could not avoid them longer.

Jesus heals a man born blind (John 9:1-41):

Some time later, Jesus chanced to see a man who was born blind. The disciples asked the Lord about the man: "Lord, who sinned, this man or his parents, that he should be born blind?"

Jesus replied: "Neither this man, nor his parents sinned. His blindness merely furnishes an opportunity to display the works of God. We must work the works of Him that sent me, while it is day. The night is coming when no man can work. When I am in the world, I am the light of the world."

Having said this, Jesus went over to the man and spat on the ground. He made clay of the spittle and anointed the man's eyes. He told the man, "Go, wash in the Pool of Siloam" (Siloam means "Sent").

The blind man made his way to the Pool of Siloam and washed his eyes. Immediately, he could see. His acquaintances and all who knew him as a beggar said, "Isn't this the one who sat and begged?" Some said, "Yes, it is!" But others were incredulous: "No, it just looks like him."

The man settled the dispute: "I am the man."

All of his acquaintances said, "How did you get your sight?"

He replied, "The man named Jesus made clay and rubbed it on my eyes and told me to wash in Siloam. So I went away and washed, and I received my sight."

"Where is this Jesus?" they asked.

He said, "I do not know."

The people brought the man to the Pharisees. Jesus had healed the man on the sabbath day so the Pharisees were not pleased. They asked the man to tell his story again of how he was healed.

This time the man told his story very concisely: "He put clay on my eyes, and I washed, and I see!"

Some of the Pharisees, overlooking the miracle staring them in the face, said, "This man Jesus cannot be from God, because He does not keep the sabbath."

Others said, "How can a man who is a sinner do such signs?" So they disagreed.

They turned again to the blind man. "What do you have to say about the one who healed you?"

He replied simply, "He is a prophet."

The Jews were stalemated. If the man had really been healed, his answer was the only logical explanation. *If* he had really been healed.... They decided that he had not really been blind, so no miracle had really been performed. So they called in the man's parents. The Pharisees asked them, "Is this your son who you say was born blind? If so, how does he now see?"

His parents were afraid. They said, "This is our son, and he was blind, but how he has come to see, we do not know. He is a grown man, ask him." They did not want to take a strong stand because they were afraid of the Jews. The word had already gone out that if anyone confessed Jesus to be the Christ, he would be expelled from the synagogue.

So they called the man before them a second time. "Why don't you give the glory for your healing to God? We know that this man you are talking about is a sinner."

The man said, "Whether He is a sinner, I do not know. But one thing I do know — I was blind and now I see!"

In desperation, the Jews decided to comb the case over to see if they could spot anything that would enable them to condemn Jesus. "What did He do to you? How did He open your eyes?"

He answered, "I have already told you, and you would not listen. Why do you want to hear it again? Do you intend to become His disciples?"

The Jews were very angry and began to revile the man. "You are His disciple, but we are disciples of Moses. We know God spoke unto Moses, but as for this fellow, we do not know where He comes from."

The man replied: "This is an amazing thing, that you do not know where He is from, and yet He opened my eyes. We know that God will not do the bidding of sinners, but if any man is a worshiper of God and does His will, God hears him. Since the world began, nobody ever heard of anyone opening the eyes of the blind. If this man were not from God, He could do nothing!"

Unable to answer such clear reasoning, the Jews said, "You are altogether born in sin. Is someone like you going to teach us?" Then they promptly cast the man out of the synagogue.

Having heard that he had been cast out, Jesus found the man and said, "Do you believe on the Son of God?"

The man said, "Who is He, Lord, that I may believe on Him?"

Jesus answered, "You have already seen Him, and He is speaking with you now." (When Jesus said, "You have already seen Him," He meant that by his faith and understanding the man had perceived Him.)

The man said, "Lord, I believe," and he worshiped Jesus.

Jesus then said, "For judgment I came into the world so that those who do not see may see, and those who see may become blind."

Pharisees who were nearby asked, "Are we blind?"

Jesus replied, "If you really were blind, you would have no sin, but now you claim, 'We see,' so your sin remains."

Jesus is the good shepherd (John 10:1-21):

NOTE:
  We are given no details about when or where the following speech was made.
  Probably it was in Jerusalem shortly after the other speeches recorded.

Jesus said, "Really and truly, I tell you that one who does not enter by the door of the sheep pen, but climbs up another way is a thief and a robber. But the one who enters by the door is the shepherd of the sheep. The guard at the door opens to him, and when he calls his own sheep by name, they come to him and he leads them out. When he has brought all his sheep out, then he goes before them and they follow him because they recognize his voice. They will not follow a stranger;

instead, they will flee from him because they do not recognize the stranger's voice." The Jews did not understand what Jesus was talking about.

Jesus continued His lesson:

Really, I say to you that I am the door of the sheep. All those who came before me were thieves and robbers, but the sheep did not hear them. I am the door. If any man enters by me, he will be saved. Then he will go in and out and find pasture. The thief comes only to steal, to kill, and to destroy. I came so that the sheep may have life and may have it richly.

I am the good shepherd. The good shepherd will die for his sheep. The hired hand is not the shepherd who owns the sheep. He sees the wolf coming, and he abandons the sheep and runs away. Then the wolf attacks the flock and scatters it. The man runs away because he is a hired hand and cares nothing for the sheep.

I am the good shepherd. I know my sheep and my sheep know me, just as the Father knows me and I know the Father. I lay down my life for the sheep.

I have other sheep that are not of this sheep pen. I must bring them also. They too will listen to my voice, and there will be one flock and one shepherd.

This is why my Father loves me: because I lay down my life so that I may take it up again. No one can take my life from me. I lay it down of my own free will. I have the authority to lay it down and I have the power to take it to me again. This authority I received from my Father.

Jesus' teaching continued to generate a tempest. The Jews were divided over Him. Many said, "He has a devil and is crazy. Why do you even listen to Him?" But others said, "These are not the statements of a man possessed by a devil. Can a devil open the eyes of the blind?"

NOTE:
Take time to notice again that Jesus is saying He will *lay down His life*. He will die because He *chooses* to do so. He did not lose His life as a helpless victim of the mob, but rather as a willing sacrifice to fulfill the scheme of redemption.

CHRONOLOGICAL NOTE:
One of the difficulties in the study of a chronology of the gospel accounts is to decide how the information in Luke 9:51-18:30 fits with the other accounts. Luke 9:51 says: "...when the time was come that He should be received up, He steadfastly set His face to go to Jerusalem." Therefore, some say these things all happened on Jesus' final journey to Jerusalem. (See Farrar, *The Life of Christ,* pp. 425-426.) This idea is contradicted by Luke 10:38-42, which indicates Jesus was just outside Jerusalem; by Luke 13:22, which refers to His journeying to Jerusalem; and by Luke 17:11, which refers to another journey to Jerusalem. Also, it is in Luke 18:31-34 that Jesus tells His disciples, "We go up to Jerusalem, and all the things that are written through the prophets shall be accomplished unto the Son of Man."

These factors, along with others, lead us to believe that the stories in Luke 9:51-18:30 occurred during the last six months of Jesus' life — but not during the very last few weeks and not during just one journey to Jerusalem. This period of time was after He left Galilee to go to the Feast of Tabernacles and before His death the following spring. There were at least three trips to Jerusalem during these months: the trip to the Feast of Tabernacles in the fall (John 7:2); the trip to the Feast of Dedication in the winter (John 10:22); and His final trip to the Passover in the spring.

It is impossible to decide which passages go with which journey to Jerusalem. Neither do we know exactly where Jesus was in each story during this period of time. The next story in Luke's account is the mission of the seventy (Luke 10:1-24). This account simply does not fit in the journey toward Jerusalem for the Feast of Tabernacles because of the secrecy of Jesus' journey, and because of the limited time. The seventy may have been sent out from Galilee because there is a repetition of the woes against Chorazin, Bethsaida, and Capernaum. It would seem logical for these statements to be made in a Galilean setting. Thus it may be that Jesus returned to Galilee for a short time after the Feast of Tabernacles and sent His disciples out into the cities and villages to prepare for His coming. Or, it may be that they were sent out into cities and villages of Judea to teach where Jesus had not yet spent much time. Perhaps the woes were expressed again as a warning to the Judean villages not to follow the example of their non-believing brethren in Galilee. The location of the work is simply not given in the story.

Stories in Luke — Location Uncertain

Mission of the seventy (Luke 10:1-24):

Jesus selected seventy of His disciples and sent them out two by two into the various cities and villages where He Himself planned to come. He impressed upon them the urgency of their work: "There is an abundant harvest, but the workers are few. Pray therefore to the Lord of the harvest that He will send forth laborers to help in His harvest."

The instructions Jesus gave this time were the same as the ones He gave His apostles on the limited commission (Matt. 10; Mark 6:6-13; Luke 9:1-6):

Go out to your work. I am sending you out like lambs among wolves. Take no knapsack or extra sandals with you. And hurry! Do not stop to talk with people on the road.

When you enter a house, say, "May there be peace upon this house." If a man of peace is there, let your peace rest upon him. If not, let it return to you. Stay at that house, eating and drinking whatever they give you, because the worker deserves the wages he gets. Do not move about from house to house for your living quarters.

When you enter a town and are welcomed, eat what is given you. Heal the sick and tell the people, "The kingdom of God is near." But if you are not welcomed in a town, go into its streets and say, "Even the dust of your town that sticks to our feet we wipe off against you. Be sure of this: the kingdom of God is near." I tell you it will be more tolerable on the day of judgment for Sodom than for that town.

Woe to you, Chorazin! Woe to you, Bethsaida! Because if the miracles which were performed in you had been done in Tyre and Sidon, they would have repented long ago in sackcloth and ashes. It will be more tolerable for Tyre and Sidon at the judgment than for you. And you, Capernaum, will you be lifted up to heaven? You will be brought down to Hades!

The one who listens to you listens to me; he who rejects you rejects me; but he who rejects me rejects the One who sent me."

The seventy went forth and then returned with joy. They were elated and said, "Lord, even the demons submit to us in your name."

NOTE:

It is obvious that this mission accomplished many things. Not only was much preaching done, but the confidence of the disciples was much increased. They were not just practicing; they were actually doing the work which foreshadowed the great work they would do after the ascension of Christ.

Christ was also elated at their progress and at the success of their work. He said, "I saw Satan fall like lightning from heaven. I have given you authority to tread on snakes and scorpions, and to overcome all the power of the enemy. Nothing will harm you. However, do not rejoice that the spirits submit to you, but rejoice that your names are recorded in heaven."

At that time, Jesus, full of joy through the Holy Spirit, said, "I praise you, Father, Lord of heaven and earth, because you have hidden these things from the wise and learned, and have revealed them to little children. Yes, Father, because this is what you wanted to do.

"Everything has been given to me by my Father. No one knows who the Son is except the Father; and no one knows who the Father is but the Son and those to whom the Son wills to reveal Him."

Then Jesus turned to His disciples and said to them, "Blessed are the eyes that have seen what you have seen. Many prophets and kings wanted to see what you see but did not see it, and to hear what you hear but did not hear it."

Parable of the good Samaritan (Luke 10:25-37):

On one occasion a lawyer stood up to test Jesus. "Teacher," he asked, "What must I do to inherit eternal life?"

Jesus replied, "What is written in the Law? How do you read it?"

The man answered, "Love the Lord your God with all your heart and soul and strength and with all your mind, and your neighbor as yourself."

Jesus said, "You have answered correctly. Do this and you will live."

The lawyer realized he was not doing too well in testing Jesus so he made one more effort to justify himself for having raised the question. He said, "But Lord, who is my neighbor?"

Jesus answered with a story:

A certain man was traveling from Jerusalem down to Jericho when he was attacked by thieves. They stripped him of his clothes, beat him, and fled, leaving him half dead.

By chance a priest was going that way. When he saw the man, he passed by him on the other side. Later a Levite came. When he got to the place and saw him, he also passed by on the other side.

Then a Samaritan, traveling along, came to the man. When he saw him, he took pity on him. He went to him and bandaged his wounds after pouring wine and oil on them. Then he put the man on his own donkey, took him to an inn, and took care of him. The next day the

Samaritan took out two silver coins and gave them to the innkeeper. "Take care of him," he said, "and when I come back, I will repay you for any extra expense you may have."

Then Jesus asked the lawyer, "Which of these three do you think acted as a neighbor to the man who fell into the hands of the robbers?"
The lawyer replied, "The one who showed him mercy."
Jesus told him, "You go and do likewise."

NOTE:
In asking his question, the lawyer wanted to see what commandments Jesus would say would *have* to be obeyed in order to go to heaven. When Jesus chose to ask the lawyer what the scriptures said, the man answered exactly as Jesus taught. The lawyer sought to limit the application of the great principles he had cited by asking, "But who is my neighbor?" He wanted a restricted list of some kind. Jesus' lesson was, "Anyone you have the opportunity to help should be considered your neighbor."

Jesus visits Mary and Martha (Luke 10:38-42):
As Jesus and His disciples traveled, they came to the home of a woman named Martha who opened her house to Him. She had a sister named Mary who sat at Jesus' feet listening to what He had to say. Martha was distracted by all the preparations that had to be made. Finally she went to Jesus and said, "Lord, don't you care that my sister has left the work for me to do by myself? Tell her to help me."
The Lord answered, "Martha, Martha. You are worried and bothered about many things, but one thing is really necessary. Mary has chosen the better thing, and it will not be denied her."

NOTE:
From John 11:1 we know that Mary and Martha lived in Bethany which was just over the Mount of Olives from Jerusalem. So Jesus may have arrived near Jerusalem for the Feast of Dedication, or this may just have been one of many Judean villages that He was visiting during this period. Luke does not tell us what the occasion was.

Jesus encourages His disciples to pray (Luke 11:1-13):
The examples of Jesus' many prayers had a powerful impact on His disciples. Once when He had finished praying, they said to Him, "Lord, teach us how to pray, as John taught his disciples."

NOTE:
It is interesting to consider this request. Did the disciples not know how to pray? Had they not heard prayers in the synagogues, etc.? Yes, but they did not know how to pray personally to God, as Jesus prayed. That is what they wanted to learn. How do *you* pray to the Father?

Jesus said, "When you pray, say: 'Father, may your name be held in reverence; let your kingdom come. Give us our food one day at a time. Forgive us our sins as we also forgive everyone who sins against us. And lead us not into temptation.'" Jesus continued the lesson on prayer by saying:

Suppose one of you had a friend, and you went to him at midnight and said, "Friend, lend me three loaves, because a friend of mine has come in from a journey and I have nothing to set before him."

Would your friend say, "Don't bother me now; my door is shut, and my children are all in bed. I cannot get up and give you anything"? The fact is, even if the friendship were not strong enough for the neighbor to do it out of pure friendship, he would go ahead and get up and give as many loaves as needed to keep you from disturbing more in the middle of the night.

So I say to you: Ask and it will be given to you; seek and you will find; knock and the door will be opened to you. Because everyone who asks receives; he who seeks will find; and to the one who knocks, the door will be opened.

Which one of you fathers, if your son asks for a fish will give him a snake instead? Or if he asks for an egg, will give him a scorpion? If you, being evil, know how to give proper gifts to your children, how much more will your Father in heaven give the Holy Spirit to those who ask Him.

NOTE:

Jesus gives a model prayer here, similar to the one found in Matthew 6. Jesus was not giving a "formula" to be repeated word for word as the ideal prayer for all circumstances. Too often we miss the point of Jesus' lessons on prayer.

Jesus' illustration of the neighbors does not at all mean that God answers our prayers to get rid of us. The illustration is a contrast: how much more readily God answers our prayers. The whole point is that God is ready and willing to bless us in answer to our prayers. He will bless us with good gifts, the chief of which is the Holy Spirit which is given to every believer through the Spirit's revelation.

Blasphemous accusations against Jesus (Luke 11:14-36):

NOTE:

This event is very similar to the one recorded in Matthew 12. The accusation that Jesus cast out demons by Beelzebub was made several times (Matt. 9:34; 12:22-37). This situation is simply another time the Jews sought to discredit Jesus in like manner. It is not surprising that Jesus would use the same arguments to deal with their blasphemous accusations that He had used before.

Jesus cast out a demon that had made a man mute. When the demon was cast out, the man could speak, and the multitude was amazed.

Some of the people, however, said, "It is by Beelzebub the prince of demons that He casts out demons." Others, testing Him, pressed Him for a sign from heaven.

Jesus answered them:

Every kingdom which is divided will come to destruction, and a house divided against itself falls. So, if Satan is now divided against himself, how will his kingdom stand? Besides, if I cast out demons by Beelzebub, by whom do your sons cast them out? We will let them be your judges. On the other hand, if I by the finger of God cast out devils, then that means the kingdom of God has come upon you.

When a strong man fully armed guards his own place, everything is undisturbed. But when a stronger one comes along and overcomes him, the stronger one takes away the armor the man was counting on for his defense and takes away the man's possessions also. Everyone is either for me or against me.

When an unclean spirit goes out of a man, he roams the waterless places seeking rest. Finding none, he says, "I will go back to my house which I just left." When he gets back, he finds it cleaned and decorated. Then he goes and takes seven more spirits, each more evil than he, and they all go and dwell in the place. The last state of the man is worse than the first.

NOTE:

    Jesus used the parallel of a demon's being cast out of a man to make the point that when a man or a generation has the opportunity to be freed from the yoke of sin, and does not take it, the yoke will be far heavier than it was before.

As He said these things, a woman in the multitude cried out, praising Him: "Blessed is the womb from which you were born, and the breasts which you sucked."
Jesus replied, "Much more importantly, blessed are those who hear God's word and keep it."

NOTE:

    Here and in other places, the scriptures show that Mary was never the focus of emphasis. Jesus consistently directed attention away from His mother to things that were more important.

The multitude gathered around and Jesus said:

This generation is an evil generation. It demands a sign, but the only sign that will be given is the sign of Jonah. The Son of Man will become a sign to this generation as Jonah did to the Ninevites. The queen of the south will rise up to judge the men of this age and will condemn them because she came from the ends of the earth to hear the wisdom of Solomon, and a greater than Solomon is here. The men of Nineveh will also stand up in the judgment to condemn this generation because they repented at the preaching of Jonah and now a greater than Jonah is here.

No man lights a lamp and then puts it in a cellar, or under a basket, but on a stand so that those who come in may see the light. The lamp of the body is the eye. When the eye sees as it is supposed to see, your whole body is illuminated. But when one's eye is bad, then his body is full of darkness. Be careful, therefore, to make sure that the light which is in you is not darkness. That way, if your body be full of light with no part of darkness, it will be completely filled with light.

NOTE:

    The point Jesus made about the eye being the lamp of the body is that we must be careful about the things we see and the way we perceive the things we see. If our attitude is a critical, cynical, unbelieving, or blindly stubborn outlook, then every fact we encounter will be shaded by our bad attitude. The people were all hearing Jesus and seeing His miracles. Some were believing in Him; others were not. The difference was not because they saw different evidence; it was rather how they treated that evidence because of their own pre-existing attitudes.

While eating with a Pharisee, Jesus condemns the Pharisees and arouses their wrath (Luke 11:37-54):

A Pharisee asked Jesus to eat breakfast with him (the word "eat" or "dine" that is used in this passage means to eat breakfast in the Greek) and Jesus agreed to go. When it was time to eat, the Pharisee was amazed that Jesus did not wash before eating. The point was not sanitation, but the traditions of the elders (see also Matt. 15:1-20; Mark 7:1-23).

Jesus, knowing the thoughts of the Pharisee, said:

> You Pharisees wash the outside of the cup and of the plate, but you leave the inside full of cheating and wickedness. You foolish ones, didn't the same one make the inside and the outside? If, however, you honestly give to the poor such things as you have, then all things will be clean to you.
>
> But woe unto you Pharisees, because you tithe mint and rue and every herb, and skip such things as justice and the love of God. You ought to do these things also and not leave the others undone.
>
> Woe to you Pharisees, because you love most of all the chief seats in the synagogues and the greetings in the marketplaces.
>
> Woe to you because you are like unmarked graves which men walk over without knowing.

A lawyer spoke to Him, saying, "Teacher, what you are saying rebukes us, also." To which Jesus replied:

> Woe unto you lawyers also. You load men down with burdens too difficult to carry, yet you yourselves will not touch the burdens with one of your fingers.
>
> Woe to you! Because you build the tombs of the prophets, and yet it was your fathers who killed them. So you are witnesses and consent to what your fathers did. You are all in cooperation: they killed the prophets, and you build their tombs. This is why God in His wisdom said, "I will send unto them prophets and apostles, and some of them they will kill and persecute so that the blood of all the prophets may be required of this generation, from the blood of Abel unto the blood of Zachariah who died between the altar and the temple" (Gen. 4:8; 2 Chron. 24:20-21). Yes, I tell you, it will be required of this generation.
>
> Woe unto you lawyers! Because you took away the key of knowledge. You did not enter in yourselves and those who would have entered, you stood in their way.

Jesus' words were very upsetting to the scribes and Pharisees. They began to attack Him fiercely, trying to provoke Him to make a mistake.

NOTE:

The comment regarding Abel and Zachariah is puzzling because people wonder why Jesus did not refer to the prophets who died after Zachariah. The explanation is not chronology, but the arrangement of the Hebrew Old Testament. In the original, it began with Genesis which tells of Abel's death at the hands of Cain, and it ends with 2 Chronicles which tells of the death of Zachariah, the son of Jehoiada, at the command of Joash king of Judah. In other words, the Hebrew Old Testament does not end with Malachi, but with 2 Chronicles. Jesus, therefore, included every instance from cover to cover in which prophets were persecuted and killed.

Jesus preaches to great multitudes:
Warnings and encouragements (Luke 12:1-12):

NOTE:

Some of the things found here in Jesus' speeches are found in the Sermon on the Mount. It is not at all surprising that Jesus would teach the same lessons at different times. Here we find Him speaking to His disciples, telling a parable in answer to a question from the multitude, responding specifically to a question of Peter, and then addressing the multitude.

Thousands of people gathered together so closely they hardly had room to stand. Jesus taught His disciples in the midst of the multitude:

Look out for the yeast of the Pharisees, which is hypocrisy. There is nothing covered up that shall not be uncovered. Whatever you have said in the dark will be heard in the daylight; and what you have whispered in the ear in the inner rooms will be proclaimed from the housetops.

I tell you, my friends, do not be afraid of those who kill the body, and after that can do no more. But I will warn you whom you should fear: Fear Him who, after killing the body, has the power to cast into hell. Yes, I tell you, fear Him. Are not five sparrows sold for two pennies. (A penny was 1/16 of a denarius, which was a common man's wages for a day.) Yet not one of them is forgotten by God. Indeed, the very hairs of your head are all numbered. Do not be afraid. You are worth more than many sparrows.

I tell you, everyone who will confess me before men, the Son of Man will also confess him before the angels of God. But he that denies me before men will be denied in the presence of the angels of God.

Everyone who speaks a word against the Son of Man will be forgiven. But to one who blasphemes against the Holy Spirit, it will not be forgiven.

And when you are brought before synagogues, and rulers, and authorities, do not worry about what to say, or how to answer, because the Holy Spirit will teach you in that very hour what you should say.

Parable of the rich fool (Luke 12:13-21):

Just then, someone cried out from the multitude: "Teacher, make my brother divide the inheritance with me."

NOTE:

What was it that Jesus said that provoked such a response? We could pick out several possibilities. It could have been the idea of taking a dispute which was private and settling it publicly, shouting it from the housetop, as it were. Or the man may have felt that Jesus was a righteous man of authority who could settle the issue between him and his brother. Really, only Jesus and the man knew why the request was made.

Jesus answered, "Man, who appointed me a judge or an arbiter between you?"
Then Jesus told the crowd, "Watch out! Be on guard against all kinds of greed. A man's life does not consist in the abundance of his possessions." To illustrate, Jesus told this parable:

The fields of a certain rich man brought a great harvest. He thought to himself: "What shall I do since I have no place to store my crops?"

Then he said, "I know. I will tear down my barns and build bigger ones, and there I will store all my grain and my possessions. And I'll say to myself, 'You have many possessions put away for many years to come. You do not have a thing to worry about. Take it easy. Eat, drink, and have fun.'"

But God said to him, "You fool! This very night your life will be required. Then, to whom will all these things you have stored up belong?"

So will it be with everyone who stores up treasure for himself and is not rich in the things of God.

Lessons on attitudes toward material things (Luke 12:22-34):

Continuing His theme, Jesus said to His disciples:

Therefore I tell you, do not worry about your life, what you will eat, or about your body, what you will wear. Life is more fundamental than food, and the body more than clothes. Think about the ravens: they do not sow or reap; they have no storeroom or barn; yet God feeds them. And how much more valuable are you than birds! And which one of you by worrying can add a single hour to his life, or a cubit to his height? If you cannot do even such a small thing as that, then why worry about the rest?

Think about the lilies, how they grow. They do not work or spin thread to make their clothes, yet I tell you that not even Solomon in all his glory wore such beautiful clothes as they. But if God so beautifully dresses the grass in the field, which today is standing, and tomorrow is thrown into the oven, how much more will He dress you, O you of little faith? Do not spend your time wondering what you will eat, and what you will drink. Do not have any doubts about it. These are the things the people of the world run after, but your Father knows you need these things. Rather, you seek His kingdom, and these things will be given to you as well.

Do not be afraid, little flock, because your Father has made up His mind to give you His kingdom. Sell what you have and give to the poor. Make yourselves wallets that will not wear out, a treasure in heaven which will not run out, where thieves cannot rob you and the moth cannot destroy. Because where your treasure is, that is where your heart will be also.

In the next portion of His teaching, Jesus impressed His disciples with the need to be prepared for the return of the Son of Man. He said:

Stay dressed for work and keep your lamps burning. Behave like men who look for their master to return from a wedding feast, so that when he comes and knocks, they may open the door for him promptly. It will be good for those servants whose Lord finds them watching for him. I tell you the truth, he will dress himself to serve and will seat them at his table to eat and will come and serve them. If they are ready in the second watch, and in the third, they will be well off indeed. But be aware of this, that if a house owner had known what time the thief was coming, he would have watched and would not have abandoned his house to be broken into. You be ready also, because in a hour when you think He won't, the Son of Man will come.

Parables about the waiting servants and the wise steward (Luke 12:35-48):

Peter said, "Lord, are you telling this illustration particularly to us or to everyone?" Jesus answered,

Who then is the trustworthy and wise manager whom his master sets over his household, to give to everyone his portion of food at the proper times? Blessed is that servant whom his Lord will find doing what he has been appointed to do. Truly, his Lord will set him over everything he has.

But if that servant says to himself, "My master is staying away a long time," and begins to beat the menservants and the maidservants, and to eat and drink and get drunk, his master will come back on a day the servant is not expecting him and at a time unknown. Then the master will cut the servant to pieces and assign him a place with the unfaithful ones. And that servant who knew his Lord's will, and did not get ready, and did not do what his Lord wanted him to do, will be beaten with many stripes. The one who did not know, and did things worthy of punishment, will be beaten with few stripes. Of the one to whom much is given, much will be required.

Jesus said He came to bring division, not peace; The signs of the times (Luke 12:49-59):

Then Jesus briefly considered the consequences of His work, both upon the world and upon Himself. He said,

I came to throw fire upon the earth, and how I wish it were already kindled! But I have a baptism to be baptized with, and how distressed I am until it be accomplished! Do you think that I came to bring peace in the earth? I tell you: no! I came to bring division.

Because there will be found five in one house divided, three against two, and two against three. Family members will be divided and set one against another.

When you see a cloud rising in the west, right away you say, "There is going to be a shower," and so it happens. A south wind starts blowing and you say, "There is going to be scorching heat," and so there is. You hypocrites. You know how to interpret the sky and the earth, but how is it you cannot interpret the times?

And why don't you judge for yourselves what is right? As you are going with your adversary to the magistrate, try hard to be reconciled to him on the way, or he may drag you off to the judge, and he will turn you over to the officer, and the officer will throw you into prison. I tell you, you will not get out until you have paid the last penny.

The necessity of repentance for all; Parable of the fig tree (Luke 13:1-9):

Some people who were with Jesus told Him about some Galileans, whose blood Pilate had mixed with their sacrifices.

> NOTE:
>
> We do not know the circumstances of these deaths. It was probably the result of a clash between the Jews and the Romans. Since the blood of these men was mingled with their sacrifices, this implies that the killing was done at the temple where sacrifices were offered.

Jesus' answer indicates that He was told this information to prove some special wrongdoing on the part of the Galileans. He said:

> Do you think these men were sinners more than all other Galileans because they suffered this way? I tell you, no, but unless you repent, all of you will likewise perish. What of those eighteen who were killed when the tower of Siloam fell upon them? Do you think they were sinners more than all the other people living in Jerusalem? I tell you, No! In fact, unless you repent, you will all likewise perish.

> One time a man had a fig tree planted in his vineyard. He came to get the tree's fruit, and there was none. He told the vinedresser, "For three years now I have come seeking fruit from this tree and have found none. Cut it down; why should it take up space in my vineyard?" The vinedresser said, "Lord, let it alone this year too. Let me loosen the soil around it and fertilize it. Then if it bears fruit, fine. If not, cut it down."

> NOTE:
>
> Why did Jesus use the figure of *three* years? The vineyard owner was not waiting for the tree to grow up. He had been expecting fruit for three years. I believe Jesus used this figure because for three years now He had been trying to gather fruit from the fig tree of Israel. If it did not bear fruit soon, it would be cut down. This parable takes its place alongside Matthew 3:11-12, the judgment parables in Matthew 25, and other passages, as a warning of judgment about to come upon Israel because they will not repent.

Jesus heals a crippled woman on the sabbath; Repetition of the parables of the mustard seed and of the leaven (Luke 13:10-21):

Jesus was teaching in one of the synagogues on the sabbath day, and a woman was present who had been crippled eighteen years. She was bowed over and could not straighten up. When Jesus saw her, He said, "Woman, you are released from your infirmity." He laid His hands on her, and immediately she was made straight and she glorified God.

The ruler of the synagogue, being very upset because Jesus had healed on the sabbath day, said to the crowd, "There are six days when men should work. Come to be healed on one of them and not on the sabbath."

Jesus responded forcefully: "You hypocrites! Doesn't each one of you loosen his ox or his donkey from the stall on the sabbath and lead him away to get water? And should not this woman, a daughter of Abraham, whom Satan has bound for eighteen long years, be loosed from her bonds on the sabbath?"

All Jesus' enemies were put to shame and silenced by His words. The multitude rejoiced because of all the wonderful things He did.

He said therefore, "Unto what is the kingdom of God like? To what shall I compare it? It is like a grain of mustard seed which a man planted in his garden. It grew, became a tree, and the birds perched in its branches."

He spoke again, saying, "To what shall I compare the kingdom of God? It is like yeast which a woman took and mixed into a bushel of flour until it worked all through the dough."

Jesus teaches as He journeys toward Jerusalem; He is warned about Herod Antipas (Luke 13:22-35):

As Jesus went along through the villages and cities on His way to Jerusalem, someone asked Him, "Lord, are there going to be few who are saved?"

Jesus answered, "Try hard to enter in by the narrow door, because many will try to get in and will not be able to do so. Once the master of the house has closed the door, and you come to the door and knock saying, 'Lord, open the door,' then he will say to you, 'I do not know where you are from.' And you will begin to say, 'We ate and drank with you, and you taught in our neighborhood.' He will say, 'I tell you, I do not know you. Get away from here, you workers of iniquity.' There will be crying and the grinding of teeth when you see Abraham, Isaac, Jacob, and all the prophets, in the kingdom of God, and yourselves thrown out of it. People will come from the east and west, from the north and south, and will sit down in the kingdom of God. Think about this: there are those who are last which will be first and there are some who are first which will be last."

At that same time, certain Pharisees came to Him and said, "Leave here; go away, because Herod would very much like to kill you."

Jesus replied, "Go tell that fox, 'Behold, I am casting out demons and performing cures today and tomorrow, then on the third day I am to be completed.' Nevertheless, I must go on my way today and tomorrow and the next day because it just would not do for a prophet to die out of Jerusalem.

"O Jerusalem, Jerusalem, which kills the prophets, and stones those who are sent unto you! How often I would I have gathered you unto myself as a hen gathers her brood under her wings, and you would not! Look, your house is left desolate. I tell you, you will not see me until you say, 'Blessed is He who comes in the name of the Lord.'"

NOTE:

Notice Jesus' attitude. Even though the Jewish officials of Jerusalem were rejecting Him, and, though His death was approaching when He would suffer such agonies at the hands of these officials, yet His feeling for the city is deep grief rather than anger. Oh, that we could learn to be more like Him!

Feast of Dedication (John 10:22-39):

NOTE:

We do not know at what point among the stories of Luke the Feast of Dedication comes, but certainly before the end of the section of Luke 9:51-18:30. This is as good a place as any for us to include it. In the reference above, Jesus was moving through towns and villages on His way to Jerusalem. Luke does not tell why He was going to Jerusalem at that moment, but we know from the book of John that at some point He went there to attend the feast. So this may be that time. At the end of this story, Jesus goes into Perea. Some of Luke's stories fit into that period.

The Feast of Dedication is not mentioned in the Law of Moses or in any other part of the Old Testament. It was of later date, celebrating the rededication of the temple and the relighting of the sacred lamps by Judas Maccabeus in 164 B.C. after he re-took the city of Jerusalem from the Syrians. It was an eight-day festival in December. Obviously Jesus approved of the feast as part of Jewish history or He would not have been there. This is the feast called Hanukkah today.

It was time for the Feast of Dedication. This feast was in late December, so it was winter. Jesus was walking in the temple grounds in Solomon's porch when the Jews came to Him and said, "How long are you going to hold us in suspense? If you are the Christ, tell us plainly."

Jesus answered, "I told you and you would not believe. The works that I do in my Father's name, these bear witness for me. You do not believe me because you are not of my sheep. My sheep hear my voice, and I know them, and they follow me, and I give them eternal life. They will never perish nor will anyone be able to snatch them out of my hand. My Father who has given them to me is greater than all, and no one is able to snatch them out of the Father's hand. I and the Father are one."

The Jews promptly began picking up stones to kill Him. Jesus said, "I have shown you many good works from the Father. For which one of these are you going to stone me?"

The Jews replied, "We are not stoning you for a good work but for blasphemy, because you, a mere man, are making yourself God."

Jesus said, "Is it not written in your law, 'I said ye are gods' (Psa. 82:6). If He called the magistrates and judges of the law gods (and the scripture is undeniable), then how can you say of Him whom the Father specially chose and sent into the world, 'You blaspheme,' because I said I am the Son of God? If I do not do the works of my Father, do not believe me. But if I do them, even though you will not believe my words, believe the works I do so that you can know and understand that the Father is in me, and I am in the Father."

Once again they tried to take Him, but He escaped.

NOTE:

The Jews had known to look for a Messiah (Christ), but they had not realized that the Christ would be divine, the Son of God. They wanted the Christ to come, but they thought he would be an ordinary man with the ability to lead them to military victory over their enemies. That is why it was so hard for them to accept Jesus as the Christ. He did not meet any of their pre-conceived ideas of what the Christ would be like. The humble people were willing to see the evidence Jesus presented and realize they had been mistaken in their ideas. They could see that this man was all He claimed to be — the Christ, the divine Son of God. The leaders saw the same evidence, but they refused to change their original ideas, and were therefore lost.

In Perea

Jesus withdraws to Perea (John 10:40-42):

After the Feast of Dedication, Jesus crossed over the Jordan to the region of Perea where John baptized in the early days. Many people came to hear Him, and He carried on the same type activities He had in other places — preaching and healing.

The people said, "John indeed did no miracles, but everything John said of this man is true." Many believed on Jesus.

NOTE:

At the end of the Feast of Dedication, there were three months left until Jesus' death. It is logical to assume that many of the episodes recorded by Luke occur in this period of time, even though we are not sure where to divide this section of Luke into the period between the Feast of Tabernacles and the Feast of Dedication (October through December), and between the Feast of Dedication and the Passover (January through March).

Look back at your map to see that Perea was on the east side of the Jordan River, extending from just south of the city of Pella in the Decapolis all the way down to include the fortress of Machaerus where John was beheaded. Perea's southern border came out at the Arnon River. It, along with Galilee, was ruled by Herod Antipas.

Jesus eats with a ruler of the Pharisees and heals a man on the sabbath; He defends Himself and tells three parables (Luke 14:1-24):

Jesus went into the house of a ruler of the Pharisees on a sabbath to eat. His enemies were there watching when a man was brought in who had dropsy. Jesus, knowing their thoughts, said, "Is it lawful to heal on the sabbath or not?" But they would not answer Him. So Jesus took the man, healed him, and sent him on his way.

Then He spoke to the Jews again, saying, "If any of you had a donkey or a cow to fall into a pit, would you not go and get him out — even on a sabbath day?" No one answered Him a word.

Later Jesus observed that the guests were all trying to pick places of honor at the table. He said,

"When you are invited to a marriage feast, do not sit in the chief seat because a more honorable man than you may be invited. Then your host may come to you and say, 'Give this man your place.' You will be humiliated as you make your way to the lowest place. Instead, when you are invited, go sit in the lowest place. Then when your host sees you, he will say, 'Friend, go up to a better seat.' Then you will have glory before all the guests. Because every one who exalts himself will be humbled, and the one who humbles himself will be lifted up."

Jesus turned to His host and said, "When you prepare a feast, do not call your friends, nor your brothers, nor your relatives, nor your wealthy neighbors. They would invite you in return and you would be paid back. Instead, when you make a feast, invite the poor, the crippled, the lame, and the blind. Then you will be blessed because they will not be able to pay you back. Instead you will be recompensed in the resurrection of the just."

When one of Jesus' fellow guests heard Jesus teaching these things, he said, "Blessed is he that will eat bread in the kingdom of God." Jesus replied:

One time a man prepared a supper and invited many guests. When it was time to eat, he sent his slave to tell the invited guests, "It is time to eat; everything is ready." But every one, without exception, began to make excuses. One said, "I have bought a field and I really have to go and look it over. Please accept my apologies." Another said, "I have bought ten oxen and I am on my way to check them out. Please excuse me." Another said, "I have married a wife, so I cannot come."

The servant came back and told his master what the people had said. The master of the house was very angry. He told his servant, "Go out quickly into the streets and lanes of the city. Bring in the poor, the blind, and the crippled." Later the servant said, "Lord, what you have ordered has been done, and there is still room." The master said, "Go out into the highways and the hedges in the countryside and have them come in so that my house will be filled. Because I tell you that none of the men who were invited will taste my supper."

Jesus warns the multitudes about the cost of discipleship (Luke 14:25-35):

Great multitudes continued with Jesus. He taught them, saying:

If anyone comes to me, and does not hate his own father, and mother, and wife, and children, and brothers, and sisters — yes, even his own life — he cannot be my follower. And anyone who will not carry his cross and follow me cannot be my disciple.

For which one of you would start out to build a tower without first sitting down to estimate the cost to see whether you had enough to complete it? Otherwise, when you have laid the foundation and are unable to finish it, everyone will begin to make fun of you, saying, "This man started building and was unable to finish!"

Or suppose a king is planning to meet another king in war. Will he not first sit down and meet with his advisers to see whether he will be able to take an army of ten thousand to meet the man who has twenty thousand? If he is not able, he will send a delegation while the other is still a long way off and ask for terms of peace.

In the same way, any of you who does not give up everything he has cannot be my disciple. Salt, therefore, is good; but if it loses its salty quality, how can you make it salty again? It is not fit either for the field or the compost heap; it is thrown out as worthless. Anyone who has ears to hear, let him hear.

Three great parables: the lost sheep, the lost coin, and the lost son (Luke 15:1-32):

NOTE:

The point Jesus was making in telling these stories was to reprove the Pharisees about their attitude toward sinners who repent. There are three parables, two of which have been the subject of poems and songs. Particularly the stories of the lost sheep and of the prodigal son have reached deeply into the hearts of men. They call to those who are lost and alone to come to One who loves them and who will save them to the uttermost.

The tax collectors and sinners were coming to Jesus to hear Him. The Pharisees and scribes murmured, saying, "This man receives sinners and eats with them." Jesus responded with these stories:

Which man of you, if you have a hundred sheep, and one of them is lost, will not leave the ninety and nine in the wilderness, and go after that which is lost, until he finds it? And when he finds it, he joyfully puts it on his shoulders and goes home. Then he calls his friends and neighbors together and says, "Rejoice with me; I have found my lost sheep." I tell you that in the same way there is more rejoicing in heaven over one sinner who repents than over ninety-nine righteous persons who do not need to repent.

Or, suppose a woman has ten silver coins and loses one of them. Won't she light a lamp and sweep the house and search diligently until she finds it? Then when she has found it, she calls her friends and neighbors and says, "Rejoice with me, because I have found the coin which I lost." Even so, I tell you, there is joy among the angels of God over one sinner who repents.

A certain man had two sons. The younger son came to his father and said, "Father, give me the part of your estate which is coming to me." The father gave the young man his portion, and, not many days later, the younger son gathered his things together and traveled to a far-away country. There he wasted his money, living wickedly. When his money was gone, a terrible famine arose and he fell into great need, so he went and hired himself to work for a citizen of that country. That citizen sent him to the field to feed his hogs. The young man was so hungry, he wanted to eat the pods that the hogs were eating, but no one would give him any.

One day, the boy came to his senses and said to himself, "How many hired servants of my father have food to spare, and here I am starving to death! I am going to go back to my father's house and I am going to say: Father, I have sinned against heaven, and in your sight also. I am no longer worthy to be called your son. Just make me one of your hired servants."

NOTE:

This alternative was nowhere near as good as being a faithful son beloved of his father, but he knew he had forfeited that right. Nevertheless, being a hired servant of his father was so much better than his present condition, he immediately set out to return to his father. It was a far-away country to which he had gone, so it was a long way back, especially since he had no provisions to help along the way.

Meanwhile, back at home, there was a father who had spent months wondering about his son whom he loved with all his heart. What had happened to him? How many times had he looked out down the road, wishing that his son would return?

One day the father looked up and saw a bedraggled figure. He bore little resemblance to the well-fed, well-fixed young man who had left some time before, but that father knew it was his son come home.

Jesus continued:

While the son was still far off, the father was moved with compassion toward him. He ran to meet him and hugged him and kissed him.

The son said, "Father, I have sinned against heaven and in your sight as well. I am no longer worthy to be called your son..."

But the son got no farther. The father called to his servants, "Hurry, and bring the best robe and put it on him. And put a ring on his hand and shoes on his feet. Prepare the fatted calf for a feast. Let us eat and celebrate because this son of mine was dead and is alive again. He was lost and has been found." Soon the celebration was underway.

The elder brother was in the field when the younger son returned. As he was coming back toward the house, he heard music and dancing. Calling a servant to him, he asked what was going on. The servant said, "Your brother has come! Your father has killed the fatted calf because he has his son back, safe and sound."

The elder brother became angry and would not go in. His father came out to reason with him. But the son answered, "All these years I have served you, and I never disobeyed your orders. Yet you never gave me even a kid of the goats that I might have a party with my friends. But when this son of yours came, the one who took the money you gave him and used it on harlots, you kill the fatted calf for him!"

His father replied, "Son, you are always with me. Everything I have is yours. But it is only right that we should celebrate and be glad now. Your brother was dead, and is alive again; he was lost and has been found."

NOTE:

These parables address a too-common problem. Many times those who do live good lives may look with scorn upon a sinner who repents. They may be jealous of the attention he receives. On the other hand, when someone "comes forward" to make his monthly "confession," while continuing in his ungodly practices, there is an equally scriptural point that applies: "Bring forth therefore fruit worthy of repentance" (Matt. 3:8).

In this parable of the prodigal son, the younger brother *did* repent. He pulled his wickedness out by the roots and cast it behind him. He came back making no claims to the status he once had, but begged his father to let him be just a hired servant.

Those who are faithful have the blessings of God. No one can take those blessings away from them. They should desire that those blessings be shared with others. It never robs us of God's blessings for them to be extended to others.

The first of three parables on stewardship: Parable of the unjust steward (Luke 16:1-18):

The first of these parables was told to the disciples of Jesus:

There was a rich man who had a manager working for him. Someone accused the manager of wasting his master's money. So, the rich man called the manager in and said, "What about these charges I have heard concerning you? You get an account together of all your transactions, because you cannot work for me any more."

To himself, the manager said: "What am I going to do since I have been given notice that I am to be fired? I do not have the strength to dig ditches, and I am ashamed to beg. I know what I will do, so that when I am fired, others will let me stay in their houses."

He called in each one of the debtors of his master. To the first one he said: "How much do you owe my master?"

"Eight hundred gallons of olive oil," the man replied.

The manager told him, "Take your note and change it to four hundred."

Then to the second, "And how much do you owe?"

"A thousand bushels of wheat," he replied.

The manager told him, "Take your note and make it eight hundred bushels."

When the master found out what his dishonest manager had done, he commended him for acting shrewdly.

"You see," Jesus said, "the people of this world are more shrewd in dealing with their kind than are the children of the light. Use your worldly possessions to gain friends for yourselves so that when the possessions run out, they may receive you into eternal dwellings.

"Anyone who is conscientious in little things, will certainly be conscientious in the big things. In the same way, if someone is dishonest with little things, he will also be dishonest in the big things. If, therefore, you have not been conscientious in handling worldly wealth, who will trust you with the true riches? And if you have not been trustworthy with someone else's property, who will give you property of your own?

"No slave can serve two masters. Either he will hate one and love the other, or he will be devoted to one and despise the other. You cannot serve God and mammon (possessions)."

When the Pharisees, who were lovers of money, heard this, they scoffed at Jesus. He told them, "You are the ones who justify yourselves before the eyes of men, but God knows your hearts. What men prize highly is an abomination to God. The law and the prophets were proclaimed until John; from his time the good news of the kingdom of God is preached and everyone enters into it with great energy. But it is easier for heaven and earth to pass away than for the least stroke of a pen to drop out of the law. Everyone who divorces his wife and married another commits adultery; likewise he who marries one who has been put away from a husband commits adultery."

NOTE:

This parable, and Jesus' comments, have caused a great deal of puzzlement. We need to make sure we understand the points He made. There are different explanations given, but we will give what appears to be the most sensible one.

1. Remember that "disciples" does not mean just the apostles. The disciples, or

followers, in this context included the *tax collectors* and *sinners* mentioned in 15:1. Note that the Pharisees were present also, but not, of course, as His disciples.

2. The *sole* point of the story of the dishonest manager is how shrewdly he used his resources to prepare for the future.

3. The tax collectors were usually men of wealth. Not much else mattered to them. They were both shrewd and single-minded in pursuing their goals. Jesus said that the men of this world tend to be more shrewd and dedicated to achieving their goals than the children of light.

4. The mammon of unrighteousness: "Mammon" is not a god in contrast to Jehovah. It is a word derived from the Syriac and Rabbinic word "mamon." It just means possessions. The possessions of the children of the world are often used unrighteously. This was true of those who were now followers of Jesus. He was, therefore, encouraging them to use the same diligence in following spiritual goals that they had used in dealing with their possessions of unrighteousness.

5. When He said "make friends by the mammon of unrighteousness," He called upon them henceforth to use their possessions, which had been possessions used in unrighteous pursuits, to make friends who would welcome them into eternal dwellings when their possessions failed.

6. In the parable and in His comments, Jesus made two points to His followers:
   (1) Use the shrewdness and diligence you have used in your worldly interests to seek your spiritual goals.
   (2) Those possessions which were formerly used in an unrighteous manner must now be used to help others.

7. In His comments to the Pharisees, Jesus made these points:
   (1) The Pharisees justified themselves, but the things that they so highly prized were an abomination to God.
   (2) They considered themselves to be the custodians of the law, but the law and the prophets reached unto John who began to preach the good news of the kingdom. Since that time everyone had to enter it by personal resolution and energy.
   (3) And, while it is true that the law could not fail in one tittle, yet, in their lives, the Pharisees commonly broke the law — for example, in divorcing their wives.

Second of the stewardship parables: The rich man and Lazarus (Luke 16:19-31):
Jesus told another story:

There was a rich man who dressed only in the very finest clothes and lived in mirth and splendor every day. But there was a beggar named Lazarus who was laid at the rich man's gate. The beggar was sick and covered with sores, and so hungry that he longed to be given scraps from the rich man's table. The dogs would come and lick the beggar's sores.

After a time, Lazarus died and angels carried him away into the arms of Father Abraham. The rich man also died, and was buried.

In Hades where he was in torment, the rich man looked up and saw Abraham far away with his arm around Lazarus. So he called to Abraham, "Father Abraham, have mercy on me and send Lazarus to dip the tip of his finger in water and cool my tongue, because I am in agony in this fire."

But Abraham replied, "Son, remember that in your lifetime you received your good things, while Lazarus received bad things. But now he is comforted here and you are in agony. And besides all this, there is a great canyon between us so that no one can cross over."

The rich man said, "Then I beg you, Father, send Lazarus to my father's house, because I have five brothers. Have him warn them, so that they will not also come to this place of torment."

Abraham replied, "They have Moses and the prophets. Let them hear them."

"No, Father Abraham, but if someone from the dead goes to them, they will repent."

Abraham answered, "If they do not listen to Moses and the prophets, they will not be convinced even if someone rises from the dead."

NOTE:

This story is not actually called a parable, but the same can be said about many other stories of Jesus. Also, this is the only parable in which a character is actually called by a personal name. Some have thought, therefore, that this story was not a parable but a factual story. Frankly, the main reason why this position has arisen is because some religious people dismiss the information on Hades because, as they say, this is just a parable. To counteract this point, others say, this story is not a parable but a true event. That Lazarus is called by name is very scant evidence on which to argue that this was a true story. The fact is there is no need to argue that Lazarus was a real character in order to answer the false doctrine mentioned. Jesus never told any parable that was not based squarely on reality. Jesus would never have spun a fanciful yarn involving Hades, Abraham, Lazarus in Paradise, and the Rich Man in torment, merely to illustrate that one should be unselfish with one's possessions.

One other point: Very often one encounters the name Dives applied to the rich man in this story. Dives is found in Latin Bibles in this parable as the name of the rich man because "dives" in Latin means "wealthy."

The third parable on stewardship: The unprofitable servant (Luke 17:1-10):

Jesus said to His disciples: "It is unavoidable that occasions will arise where one causes another to sin, but woe to that person who does so. It would be better for him to be thrown into the sea with a millstone tied around his neck than for him to cause a person of the least significance to sin. So watch yourselves.

"If your brother sins, rebuke him; and if he repents, forgive him. If he sins against you seven times in a day, and seven times comes back and says, 'I repent,' forgive him."

The apostles, perhaps feeling the difficulty of this command, said to the Lord, "Increase our faith."

Jesus replied, "If you have faith as small as a mustard seed, you can say to this mulberry tree, 'Be uprooted and planted in the sea,' and it will obey you.

"Suppose one of you had a servant who was plowing or looking after the sheep. When the servant comes in from the field, would you say, 'Come over here and sit down to eat'? Would you not say instead, 'Get my supper ready, then you get ready and wait on me while I eat and drink. After that you may eat and drink'? Would you thank the servant because he did what he was told to do? So you also, when you have done everything you were told to do, say, 'We are unprofitable servants; we have done only our duty.'"

> CHRONOLOGICAL NOTE:
>
> In Luke 17:11, Jesus begins His last journey toward Jerusalem. He will travel through Perea and will approach Jerusalem from Jericho (Matt. 19:1-2; Mark 10:1; Matt. 20:29; Mark 10:46; Luke 18:35). When He arrives at Bethany outside of Jerusalem, He will remain there for two days before entering Jerusalem in the triumphal entry.
>
> But at this point in our history, we have not yet had the story of the death and resurrection of Lazarus which is told about in John 11. The story of Lazarus has to take place before Luke 17:11, for there is no time for it afterward. Also, after Jesus raised Lazarus from the dead, He went to a village called Ephraim for a short time (John 11:54).
>
> Jesus was in Perea when He was informed of Lazarus' illness. He came to Bethany where Lazarus was buried, raised him from the dead, and departed to Ephraim. From Ephraim, it seems He went to Galilee and traveled with the multitudes on their way to Jerusalem for the Passover. They traveled down through Perea, crossed the Jordan at Jericho and came finally to Jerusalem for the triumphal entry. Look back at your map again and trace their journey.

Jesus raises Lazarus from the dead (John 11:1-44):

Lazarus, the brother of Mary and Martha, became sick. He and his sisters lived in Bethany, just outside of Jerusalem. The sisters sent word to Jesus, saying, "Lord, the one you love is sick."

When Jesus heard the news, He said, "The point of this sickness is not death, but the glory of God. God's Son will be glorified through it." Jesus loved Mary, Martha, and Lazarus, but He did not hasten to their side when He learned of the sickness. He stayed where He was for two more days. Then He said to His disciples, "Let us go back to Judea."

The disciples said, "Rabbi, the Jews tried to stone you to death just a short time ago, and yet you are going back there?"

Jesus answered, "Are there not twelve hours of daylight? If a man walks in the day, he will not stumble because he sees this world's light. But if a man walks at night he stumbles because he has no light."

Then Jesus said, "Our friend Lazarus has fallen asleep, and I am going to wake him up."

The disciples replied, "Lord, if he has fallen asleep, he will be all right." Jesus had spoken of the death of Lazarus, but they thought He was speaking of normal sleep.

Therefore, Jesus said, "Lazarus is dead. And I am glad for your sake that I was not there, so that you will have an opportunity to believe. Now let us go to him."

It was Thomas who said to his fellow disciples, "If He is going back, let us go with Him so that we may die with Him."

When Jesus and His disciples reached Bethany, Lazarus had been in the tomb four days. Bethany was less than two miles from Jerusalem, and many of the Jews had come to Mary and Martha to comfort them in the loss of their brother. When Martha heard that Jesus was coming, she went out to meet Him, but Mary remained at the house.

Martha said to Jesus, "Lord, if you had been here, my brother would not have died. And even now, I know that whatever you ask of God, He will give you."

Jesus said, "Your brother will rise again, Martha."

"I know he will rise again in the resurrection at the last day," Martha replied.

Jesus told her, "I am the resurrection and the life. He who believes in me will live, even though he dies; and whoever lives and believes in me will never die. Do you believe this?"

"Yes, Lord," she told Him. "I believe that you are the Christ, the Son of God, who was to come into the world."

Having said this, Martha went and called her sister Mary aside and told her, "The Teacher is here and is asking for you."

Mary quickly got up and went to meet Jesus. Jesus had not yet entered the village, but was still at the place where Martha had met Him. When the Jews who had been comforting Mary in the house noticed how quickly she got up and went out, they followed her. They supposed she was going to the tomb to mourn.

When Mary came to the Lord, she fell at His feet and said, "Lord, if you had been here, my brother would not have died."

When Jesus saw her weeping, and the Jews who had come with her weeping, He was deeply moved and troubled. "Where have you laid him?" He asked.

"Come and see, Lord," they replied.

Jesus wept also. The Jews said, "Look how much He loved him." Some of them, however, said, "Could not this man, who opened the eyes of the blind man, have prevented this man's death?"

Jesus, deeply moved again, came to the tomb. It was a cave with a stone over the opening.

> NOTE:
> Many of the tombs of that day were made from natural caves. Places to lay the bodies were chiseled out of the sides. A track of sorts was hewn out for a large, round rock to roll up and down in front of the opening to the cave. The stone usually rolled slightly downhill to rest in front of the opening. A small depression was hewn out in front of the door. The stone would drop into this small depression, and would then require several people to roll it back should entrance to the tomb be desired.

Jesus said, "Take away the stone."

Martha objected: "Lord, by this time his body will smell bad because he has been dead four days." One can imagine the pain it gave Martha to realize this and to say it.

Then Jesus said, "Did I not tell you that if you believed, you would see the glory of God?"

So they took away the stone. Jesus looked up and said, "Father, I thank you that you have heard me. And I know that you always hear me, but because of all those standing around, I have said this that they may know that you did send me."

When He had said this, Jesus called out in a loud voice, "Lazarus, come forth!" Imagine the suspense as everyone watched the dark opening. Then Lazarus came out! His hands and feet were wrapped with strips of linen and a cloth was around his face — as he had been prepared for his burial.

Jesus ordered, "Take off the grave cloths and let him go."

> NOTE:
> Think of the very powerful effect this miracle would have had. When the stone was rolled back, the smell of decay would have made its way out of the tomb and among the people present. While the odor of death is still in their nostrils, they hear Jesus command the dead man to come forth. The dead awakens and comes out, healthy and alive, with the smell of his previously dead body still in evidence. What a mighty lesson: there is always hope with God!

The effect of the raising of Lazarus (John 11:45-54):

Many of the Jews which had come to comfort Mary and Martha believed on Jesus when they saw the miracle. But some went away and told the Jewish officials what Jesus had done.

The chief priests and Pharisees called a meeting of the Sanhedrin and raised the question, "What are we going to do, because this man does many signs? If we let Him alone, everyone will believe on Him, and the Romans will come and will take away both our place and our nation."

> NOTE:
> Supposedly, the fear of the Jews was because they thought Jesus would become the leader of a national Messianic revolution which would result in the destruction of Jerusalem, the temple, and of the nation. Yet Jesus had refused to be made a political king (John 6:15). Ironically, their rejection of Jesus brought about the very thing they feared.

One of the council, Caiaphas, who was high priest that year, said, "You know nothing at all! Nor do you realize that it is much more convenient that one man die for the people, and spare the nation from destruction."

Caiaphas did not say this just of himself, but in his office as high priest, he prophesied that Jesus would die for the nation and not for the nation alone, but that He might gather together the children of God that were scattered over the earth.

So, from that day on, the Jewish officials made definite plans to kill Jesus.

> NOTE:
> Caiaphas was not aware that he had made this "prophecy." He meant that it was better that Jesus die than that Jerusalem and the temple be destroyed and the Jewish nation perish. His words were, however, true in a greater sense than he realized. Jesus would, indeed, die for the people as a sacrifice for their sins. This application of Caiaphas' words never entered his mind.

Jesus knew of the plot against Him, so He no longer circulated freely among the Jews around Jerusalem. He withdrew to a city called Ephraim near the wilderness where He waited with His disciples.

> NOTE:
> For a time the location of the village of Ephraim was unknown. Eusebius, the earliest of the church historians, reported that it was eight miles from Jerusalem. Its site has now been identified about four or five miles northeast of Bethel, about where Eusebius indicated.
>
> As we noted earlier, Jesus apparently traveled from that village to the borders of Galilee to make His way down to Jerusalem with the throngs of pilgrims on their way to the Passover. We observe Him speaking to the crowds and performing miracles as He makes this last journey.

Journey to Jerusalem

Ten lepers are healed (Luke 17:11-19):

As Jesus and His companions were on their way to Jerusalem, they passed along the border of Samaria and Galilee. As He entered a village, ten lepers met Him. They stood at a distance and shouted, "Jesus, Master, have mercy on us."

When He saw them, He said, "Go show yourselves to the priests." At first they were not well, but as they went toward Jerusalem to show themselves to the priests, as the Law commanded (Lev. 13:49; 14:1-3), they were cleansed.

One of them, when he saw he was healed, turned back. He went along glorifying God in a loud voice. He made his way back to Jesus and fell at His feet, giving thanks. This man was a Samaritan.

Jesus responded, "Were not ten cleansed? Where are the nine? Did no one else return to glorify God except this stranger?" (The word stranger literally meant alien, because this man was a Samaritan.) Then Jesus said to the man, "Get up and go on your way. Your faith has made you completely well."

> NOTE:
> Jesus Himself had told the ten to go show themselves to the priests. The reason the Samaritan returned to Jesus was that his heart was bursting with gratitude to God. The other nine could have returned also, if they had been grateful enough, and then could have completed their journey to the temple. The bottom line is that the nine were not properly grateful for the truly great blessing they had received.

Jesus explains the nature of the kingdom and predicts judgment (Luke 17:20-37):

Some Pharisees asked Jesus when the kingdom of God was coming. He said, "The kingdom of God is not coming in a visible way. Nor will people say, 'Look, here it is,' or 'There it is!' because the kingdom is within you."

NOTE:

The principle here is fundamental and powerful. It was not that there would be no outward indication of the coming of the kingdom of God. But Jesus' point was that, in contrast to the kingdoms of men, which are almost altogether external in domain and in function, the kingdom of God is almost altogether internal. Its primary domain is in the hearts of men. In other words, there is no political boundary for the kingdom of God, no physical army to fight to conquer or defend territory. Rather, as individuals all over the world give their allegiance to God and to Christ, they become subjects of God's kingdom.

Then Jesus told His disciples:

The time is coming when you will long to see one of the days of the Son of Man, but you will not see it. People will tell you, "Look, it is there!" or "Look, here it is!" Do not be carried away by such things or follow after such people. As the flash of the lightning reaches from one horizon to the opposite one, so will the Son of Man be in His day. But first He has to suffer many things and be rejected by this generation.

As it happened in the days of Noah, so it will be in the days of the Son of Man. They ate, they drank, they married and were given in marriage, until the day Noah entered the ark and the flood came and destroyed them all.

It was the same in the days of Lot. The people were carrying on all normal affairs until the day Lot went out from Sodom. On that day it rained fire and brimstone from heaven. That is the way it will be in the day that the Son of Man is revealed.

When that happens, if someone is on the housetop, and his possessions are in the house, let him not go down to get them. And the one who is in the field, let him not go back to the house. Remember Lot's wife.

Whoever seeks to gain his life will lose it, but whoever is willing to lose his life will preserve it. I tell you, in that night two men will be on one bed: one will be taken and the other left. Two women will be grinding grain: one will be taken and the other left.

Jesus' disciples asked, "Where will this happen, Lord?" To which Jesus replied: "Where the body is, that is where the vultures will be gathered."

NOTE:

This discussion in Luke 17:22-37 is similar in many ways to Jesus' conversation with the disciples in Matthew 24. It is best to understand the conversation as referring to the destruction of Jerusalem — especially in view of the warning not to go back into the house for one's possessions. Such a warning would have no application whatever to the second coming of Christ.

The expression "desire to see one of the days of the Son of Man" most likely refers to seeing a day when Christ would have the upper hand over His enemies. There will be many days when He will not seem to prevail. Then He foretells one of those occasions when He would show that He will ultimately prevail over all His enemies, and that is, when He would bring destruction upon Jerusalem (which was in A.D. 70).

It is ironic that, in the Jewish leaders' plans to *save* their nation by rejecting Jesus and killing Him, they were insuring that their nation would be destroyed by God.

Two parables on prayer: the unrighteous judge, and the Pharisee and the publican (Luke 18:1-14):

Jesus used an illustration to teach His disciples that they should always pray and not give up. "One time there was a judge who lived in a city. He did not care what anybody wanted, whether God or man. There was a widow in that city who came frequently to the judge, begging, 'Give me justice over my enemy.' But the judge was not interested, so he did nothing for a while. Finally, he said to himself, 'Though I do not fear God, or care what happens to any man, yet this widow keeps bothering me. So, to keep her from wearing me out by her continual coming, I am going to avenge her of her enemy.'"

Jesus said, "Listen to what this unrighteous judge says. Shall not God avenge His chosen ones, who cry to Him day and night? I tell you, He will avenge them speedily. Nevertheless, when the Son of Man comes, will He find faith on the earth?"

> NOTE:
>
> The comparison between the unrighteous judge and God is one of contrast. God is the *opposite* of the unjust judge. If the judge, who cares for no one, will see that justice is done for the widow just because she persists in her request, will not God, who loves His children, answer our prayers?

Jesus also told a parable to certain ones who were positive they were righteous and thought no one else was:

> Two men went up to the temple to pray. One was a Pharisee, and the other was a publican. The Pharisee said, "God, I thank you that I am not as other men: cheaters, unfair, adulterers, or even as this tax collector here. I fast twice every week; I give a tenth of all I get."
>
> But the publican, standing some distance away, would not even look up to heaven. Instead, he struck himself on the chest and said, "God, be merciful to me, a sinner."
>
> I tell you that this man is the one who went away to his house justified rather than the Pharisee, because everyone who lifts himself up will be humbled, but he who humbles himself will be exalted.

As Jesus travels from Galilee through Perea, He teaches concerning divorce (Mark 10:1-12; Matt. 19:1-12):

Jesus traveled down through Perea and came to the outskirts of Judea beyond the Jordan. There the multitudes came to Him, and as He was accustomed to do, He taught them and healed their sick.

The Pharisees came to see if they could catch Jesus in a mistake. They asked Him, "Is it lawful for a man to put away his wife for every reason?"

Jesus replied, "Have ye not read, that He who made everything from the beginning made them male and female and said, 'For this cause shall a man leave his father and mother, and shall cleave to his wife, and the two shall be one flesh' (Gen. 2:24)? So they are no longer two, but one. Therefore what God has joined together, let not man separate."

"Why then," they asked, "did Moses command that a man give his wife a certificate of divorce and send her away?"

Jesus answered, "Moses allowed you to divorce your wives because your hearts were hard, but it was not this way from the beginning. And I tell you that anyone who divorces his wife except for fornication, and marries another, commits adultery, and whoever marries the wife who is put away commits adultery."

A little later, in the house, Jesus' disciples asked Him further about this matter. They said, "If marriage is this way, it would be better not to marry!"

Jesus said, "My statement will not apply to all men. There are those who are born eunuchs, unable to beget children. There are men who have been made eunuchs by men, and there are eunuchs who made themselves eunuchs for the sake of the kingdom of heaven. Those to whom it does apply must pay attention to it."

NOTE:

These passages are vital for understanding the subject of marriage and divorce. There are several points the teacher needs to understand. These points need to be made to all ages from upper elementary to adults.

1. The passage cited by the Jews was Deuteronomy 24:1-4. They made the argument that Moses *authorized* them to divorce their wives by giving them a certificate of divorce; Jesus said Moses *permitted* them to do so. The passage in Deuteronomy does not address the reason for divorce, but rather makes the point that when a man divorces his wife, and she becomes the wife of another man, and then that second husband divorces her, or dies, her first husband cannot take her back. The Jews had used the passage to justify divorce for any cause.

2. Jesus and Moses were not in disagreement. Both were in harmony with God's arrangement in the beginning, which was that a man and a woman should marry and stay married (Gen. 2:24).

3. The wording of Genesis 2:24 shows that the laws of marriage were of general application and did not apply just to Adam and Eve.

4. When the disciples heard Jesus' teaching, they said, "If marriage is going to be that way, it would be better not to marry." Jesus did not back down at all. He replied, "The only ones to whom my words do not apply are those who do not get married." Note that He did not say, "My teaching applies only to believers," or that "those who are in the world are not bound by this teaching." He went back to the beginning, where God instituted marriage for the human family, for the basis of His own teaching on marriage. The only exception Christ made of those to whom His teaching would apply, was for those who would not marry. Therefore, this teaching of Jesus applies to *all* marriages.

Christ receives little children (Mark 10:13-16; Matt. 19:13-15; Luke 18:15-17):

At this time, parents came to Jesus bringing their little children for Him to touch them and pray for them. The disciples tried to keep them from bothering Jesus, reflecting the common idea that great men are too important to have time to deal with children.

Jesus was not that kind of great man, however. He was moved with indignation at the efforts of His disciples to keep the children and their parents away. He said, "Let the little children come to me. Do not tell them not to come, because the kingdom of God is made up of such. Whoever will not receive the kingdom of God as a little child, he will in no way enter into it."

Then Jesus took the children into His arms and blessed them.

> NOTE:
>
> You will see that from this point on, the three synoptic gospels (that is, Matthew, Mark, and Luke) will be parallel more frequently than they were even during the Great Galilean Ministry.

The rich young ruler; Peril of riches; Reward of following the Lord (Mark 10:17-31; Matt. 19:16-20:16; Luke 18:18-30):

As Jesus was going forth on His way, a certain young nobleman ran to Him and knelt before Him. The man said, "Good Teacher, what shall I do to inherit eternal life?"

Jesus said, "Why do you call me good? No one is good but God, but if you would enter into life, keep the commandments."

The ruler said, "Which ones?"

Jesus answered, "Do not kill; do not commit adultery; do not steal; do not bear false witness; do not cheat; honor your father and your mother; and love your neighbor as yourself."

Thrilled, the young man replied, "I have done all these things from the time I was a teenager. What else do I need to do?"

Jesus told him, "If you would be perfect, sell everything you have and give it to the poor, and you will have treasures in heaven."

The young man stared in shocked silence as he considered this commandment. Then he turned and went away with great sorrow because he was very rich.

Jesus loved the young man and hated to see him go away. He looked around at His disciples and said, "How difficult it is for a rich man to enter into the kingdom of heaven."

The disciples were amazed at His words. Jesus said, "Children, I tell you again, how hard it is for those who trust in riches to enter the kingdom of heaven. It is easier for a camel to go through a needle's eye, than for a rich man to enter the kingdom of God."

This statement astonished the disciples even more, so they said, "Who then can be saved?"

Jesus said, "With men it is impossible, but not with God, for all things are possible with Him."

Peter continued thinking about the rich, young ruler and the Lord's command to sell everything he had. So he said, "Look, we have left everything and followed you. What then will we have?"

Jesus considered this to be a fair question, so He answered it: "Really and truly, in the regeneration, when the Son of Man will sit on the throne of His glory, you also will sit upon twelve thrones, judging the twelve tribes of Israel. And everyone who has left houses, or brothers, or sisters, or father, or mother, or children, or lands, for the sake of my name and for the cause of the gospel, will receive a hundred times as much now, in this time: houses, and brothers, and sisters, and mothers, and children, and lands, although there will be persecutions as well; and then, in the world to come, eternal life. But many that are first will be last, and many that are last will be first."

Then Jesus told a story to answer Peter's question more fully:

The kingdom of heaven is like a landowner who went out early in the morning to hire men to work in his vineyard. Having agreed with them to pay a penny (a denarius, the wage for one day's common labor) each, he sent them into his vineyard.

About nine o'clock, he saw some other workers standing around in the market place with nothing to do. He said to them, "Go to my vineyard, and work for me, and I will pay you a fair wage." So they went to his vineyard.

At twelve noon, and at three o'clock in the afternoon, he went out and hired others with the same agreement.

Finally, about five o'clock in the afternoon, he saw some men standing around. He asked them, "Why are you standing here all day with nothing to do?"

The men answered, "Because no man has hired us." So the landowner told them also to go to work in his vineyard.

Evening came and the landowner called his overseer to him, and said, "Call the workers, and pay them their wages, beginning with the last down to the first."

Those who were hired last of all received a denarius. Those who had been hired first saw this, and they figured they would be paid extra when their turn came. But they, like all the rest, were paid a denarius. When they saw their wage, they complained and said, "These last workers only worked one hour. Yet you have treated them the same as us, who have worked all day and have endured the hottest time of the day."

The master said, "Friend, I have done you no wrong. Did you not agree with me to work for a denarius? Take what belongs to you and be on your way because it has been my will to give those who were hired last the same as I paid you. Is it not lawful for me to do what I want with my own possessions? Or is your attitude bad because I am good?"

In this way, the last will be first, and the first last.

NOTE:

Several points can be gleaned from this parable. It was told in direct answer to Peter's question about what they would receive since they had left all to follow Jesus. Notice that first Jesus gave a direct answer about what the apostles themselves would receive: they will sit on twelve thrones. Then the answer included all who are persecuted due to their service to God. They will receive many blessings here in this life: houses, brothers, mothers, etc. But then, Jesus came back to the original question: What do we receive for serving God? The bottom line is, God has promised the same wage to all who serve Him, that is, eternal life. The Father, in His mercy and in His wisdom, gives the same reward to those who were persecuted and underwent great tribulation as to those who lived their lives quietly in godliness and peace. The reward of eternal life is great beyond our comprehension, no matter what price it was necessary to pay in this life. But, the main point of the parable is that the Father has the right to pay as He wishes. Let that be our main point also.

Jesus again foretells His death and resurrection (Mark 10:32-34; Matt. 20:17-19):

As Jesus and His disciples were on their way to Jerusalem, the disciples were very upset and afraid. Jesus, therefore, took the twelve aside and told them the things which were about to happen to Him. "Listen to what I am saying. We are going up to Jerusalem, and the Son of Man will be delivered into the hands of the chief priests and the scribes. They will condemn Him to death and will deliver Him to the Gentiles who will mock Him and spit upon Him and scourge Him and crucify Him. And after three days He shall rise again."

But the apostles simply could not accept this awful news, so they did not understand what He said.

Jesus rebukes the selfish request of James and John (Mark 10:35-45; Matt. 20:20-28):

The mother of James and John came to Jesus and worshiped Him. She wanted to ask Jesus for something. So Jesus said, "What would you like me to do for you?"

She answered, "Command that these two sons of mine may sit, one on your right hand, and one on your left hand, in your kingdom."

But Jesus said, "You do not know what you are asking. Are you able to drink the cup I drink and to be baptized with the baptism that I am going to be baptized with?"

James and John said, "We are able."

Jesus said, "You will indeed drink the cup I drink, and you will be baptized with the same baptism I am to be baptized with, but to sit on my right hand or on my left hand is not mine to give. It is for them for whom it has been prepared by my Father."

> NOTE:
> Jesus was speaking of the suffering He would undergo when He used the expressions "drink the cup I drink," and, "be baptized with the baptism I am going to be baptized with."

When the other apostles heard what James and John had asked for (through their mother), they were angry with them. Jesus called them all to Him and said, "All of you know how those who rule among the Gentiles love to lord it over their subjects. They enjoy exercising their authority. But it will not be that way among you. Whoever would be great among you must be your servant, and whoever would be first among you will have to be everyone's slave. The Son of Man Himself did not come to the earth to be served, but to give His life as a ransom price for many."

The healing of Bartimaeus the blind man and his companion (Mark 10:46-52; Matt. 20:29-34; Luke 18:35-43):

After crossing the Jordan, Jesus drew near the city of Jericho. With Him were His disciples and a great multitude. Two blind men sat by the way. One of them was named Bartimaeus.

They cried out, "Jesus, son of David, have mercy on us." Many of those who went along with Jesus rebuked them, telling them to be quiet. But they only cried louder, saying, "Jesus, son of David, have mercy on us."

Jesus stood still and said, "Call him," probably referring to the more prominent one of the two.

The people told the blind men, "Cheer up! On your feet! He is calling for you." Immediately, they sprang up, leaving their cloaks behind, and went to Jesus.

Jesus asked, "What would you have me do for you?"

The blind men answered, "Lord, we wish you would open our eyes."

Jesus was moved with sympathy for them and He touched their eyes. Immediately they received their sight and followed Him, glorifying God. All the people, when they saw what had been done, also praised God.

Jesus meets Zacchaeus; Parable of the pounds (Luke 19:1-28):

While Jesus was going through Jericho, a rich tax collector named Zacchaeus decided he wanted to see Jesus, but he was so short he could not see over the crowds. So he ran before the crowds and climbed into a sycamore tree in order to be high enough to see Jesus.

Jesus, coming to the tree where Zacchaeus was, stopped and said, "Zacchaeus, hurry and come down, because today I am going to be staying at your house."

Zacchaeus quickly scrambled down the tree, thrilled to receive Jesus into his house. Everyone who saw it said, "He is gone to stay with a man who is a sinner."

But Zacchaeus said to the Lord, "Look, Lord, I give half of my possessions to the poor; and if I have wrongfully exacted anything from any man, I restore four times that much to him."

Jesus replied, "Today salvation has come to this house, because this man is also a son of Abraham. For the Son of Man came to seek and to save what is lost."

Jesus added a parable to His remarks because He was approaching Jerusalem, and because the people supposed that the kingdom of God would appear immediately when Jesus got to Jerusalem. He said:

A certain nobleman went away to a far country to receive a kingdom and to return. He called ten slaves that belonged to him and gave them ten pounds, one pound each (a mina — worth about three months' wages). He said, "Put this money to work till I get back."

The subjects of his kingdom hated him and sent a delegation to him to say, "We will not have this man to rule over us."

He was made king, nevertheless, and returned home. Then he sent for the servants to whom he had given the money to see what they had gained from it.

The first servant came and said, "Lord, your pound has gained ten pounds more."

The master said, "Well done, you good servant. Since you have been faithful in a very little, take charge of ten cities."

The second came and said, "Lord, your pound has gained five more."

His master answered, "You take charge of five cities."

Then another servant came and said, "Lord, look. Here is your pound which I have kept laid up in a cloth because I was afraid of you, knowing you are a hard man. You take out what you did not put in and reap what you did not sow."

The master said, "I will judge you out of your own mouth, you wicked servant. You knew that I am a hard man taking up what I did not lay down and reaping what I did not sow. If you thought that, why did you not at least put my money in the bank so that I could have gained interest from it?"

Then he said to his servants standing by, "Take the pound away from him and give it to the one who has ten pounds."

His servants replied, "Lord, he already has ten pounds."

The king answered, "To everyone who has, more will be given. But from him who has not, even that which he has will be taken away. But these enemies who would not have me reign over them, bring them here and put them to death."

When Jesus finished these words, He continued on His way toward Jerusalem, with His next stop at Bethany.

NOTE:

You have already looked on your map and followed this last journey that Jesus made before His death. Look once more and follow Him from Galilee, down through Perea, to Jericho, and now to Bethany just outside Jerusalem.

Life of Christ

Preparation
Beginning Ministry
Galilean Ministry
Retirement
Close of Ministry

*Last Week

 *Conflicts with Jews
 *Last Supper
 *Trial
 *Crucifixion

Resurrection
Exaltation

Look at the broad outline of Jesus' life one more time. Be sure you know the outline by now and can give a summary of what each period of His life includes. Be able to tell approximately how long each period lasted.

We call this section "The Last Week," and we all refer to the "last week of Jesus' life." Yet we must never forget that Jesus is unique. In reality His life never *began*, because He is as eternal as the Father. In the same way, His life never ended — but, of course, His life on earth had a distinct beginning when He took upon Himself a human form, and, He laid down that life at the cross. Even then, He was unique, because He arose from the dead, never to die again.

This part of the story has great significance to the scheme of redemption, because this is when Jesus offered Himself as the sacrifice for the world. He paid the price for sin.

Conflicts with the Jews

Jesus arrives in Bethany (John 11:55-12:11; Matt. 26:6-13; Mark 14:1-11):

Six days before the Passover, Jesus reached Bethany, the home of Lazarus and his sisters Mary and Martha.

CHRONOLOGICAL NOTE:
The journey from Jericho to Bethany was a very difficult one. It involved a continuous climb of about six hours' length from 840 feet below sea level at Jericho to a point over 2,500 feet above sea level. Faithful Jews would not have made such a trip on a sabbath day, because that day was a day of rest. Yet we know Jesus was in Bethany on that Saturday, because the feast we are about to describe took place on that evening. Therefore, Jesus likely arrived in Bethany on Friday, before sundown, when the Jewish sabbath officially began. Then, He and all the other Jews would

have rested during that day. It was evening when the following events took place.

A dinner was given in Jesus' honor. Martha helped serve the supper, and Lazarus was one of the guests who ate with the Lord. Mary was also present as we will see in a moment. Even though John mentions these three, yet the feast was not at their house, but at the home of a man called Simon the leper (Matt. 26:6; Mark 14:3).

NOTE:
   Simon was a leper who had been healed or who had recovered from his leprosy. Otherwise, this supper could not have taken place in his house as it did because lepers were counted as unclean. Almost certainly this is one Jesus had healed at some time, but we know nothing else about his story.

As the meal progressed, Mary came in with about a pint of pure nard, a very expensive perfume. She poured the nard on Jesus' head and feet and wiped His feet with her hair. The house was filled with the fragrant smell of the precious ointment.

Some of the disciples, particularly Judas Iscariot, said, "Why wasn't this perfume sold for three hundred days' wages and given to the poor?" Now Judas did not say this out of any concern for the poor, but because he was a thief, and because he carried the bag (for Jesus and His apostles) and stole what was placed in it.

Jesus replied, "Do not bother her, because she has done a good deed upon me. You will always have the poor with you, but you will not always have me. She has poured this ointment upon my body to prepare me for burial. And I tell you, wherever this gospel will be preached in the whole world, the thing this woman has done will be spoken of for a memorial of her."

The common people heard that Jesus was there and they came, not only to see Jesus, but to see Lazarus as well. But the chief priests took counsel to put Lazarus to death also, because so many Jews believed on Jesus because of him.

NOTE:
   The alabaster "box" was a flask, a tube-shaped bottle with a flange or wide lip around the top. The nard, or spikenard, was an aromatic perfume made from the Nardostachys Jatanransi, a member of the balsam family which grew on the Himalayan mountains. This nard was pure, that is, it was unmixed with cheaper and more common balsam.
   The nard was very expensive. It was worth three hundred denarii, or three hundred days' wages. Jewish women were very fond of precious perfumes. Even so, that Mary would have this perfume means that the family was fairly well off financially.

The story is a beautiful one. We have already learned that Mary would drop everything to hear Jesus teach (Luke 10:38-42). Also, when Lazarus was sick, the sisters sent immediate word to Jesus. Then when Jesus came, both sisters said, "Lord, if you had been here, our brother would not have died." Both sisters were deeply grieved over their brother's death. Then when Jesus raised Lazarus, their joy knew no bounds. Now Mary comes with her grateful heart, worshiping and adoring Jesus in silence — her heart too full for words.

Did Mary realize that Jesus was to be slain a few days hence? We cannot be certain. But Jesus accepted her gratitude and her worship, and He applied her gesture to His death and burial. He commanded that the story of her wonderful love be told in all the world as a memorial to her. Is it not thrilling, that two thousand years later, we are involved in carrying out Jesus' desire that we remember what Mary did?

From both Matthew's account and Mark's account, it would appear that this feast, and the story about Mary's deed, occurred later in the week, a little closer to the death of Jesus. Yet John is specific in saying it occurred six days before the Passover (which would be on Saturday evening before the death on the following Friday). Jesus' death was looming very near, so her act was especially appropriate. That is probably why Matthew and Mark tell the story later.

The triumphal entry (Mark 11:1-11; Matt. 21:1-11,14-17; Luke 19:29-44; John 12:12-19)

CHRONOLOGICAL NOTE:

Since Matthew, Mark, and Luke do not tell of Mary's anointing Jesus at this point, their narrative sounds as if Jesus made a continuous journey from Jericho to Jerusalem with only this brief pause at Bethany while the disciples went to get the donkey upon which Jesus rode into the city. From John's account, however, we know that Jesus was at Bethany from Friday evening until Sunday morning, which was the day of the triumphal entry.

As Jesus approached Jerusalem from Bethany, He sent two disciples into a nearby village (Bethphage), saying, "Go into this village and you will find a donkey tied and her colt, which has never been ridden. Bring them with you, and if anyone questions you about what you are doing, tell them that the Lord needs them."

The disciples went into the village and found the colt and its mother tied out in the street in front of the door of a house. They untied the colt and started to lead it away. Some people standing nearby said, "What are you doing? Why are you untying that colt?"

The disciples answered, "The Lord needs him," and they were allowed to take the donkey and her colt to Jesus.

When they got back to Jesus, the disciples laid some of their garments on the colt's back for padding, and Jesus sat upon it. Thus the prophecy was fulfilled which was spoken by the prophets (Isa. 62:11; Zech. 9:9): "Tell the daughter of Zion, 'Look, your king, coming to you meek, and riding upon a donkey, upon a colt the foal of a donkey.'"

The disciples did not see at the time the marvelous fulfillment of prophecy which this and other deeds of Jesus brought about, but when He was glorified, then they recalled that these things were written about Him, and that they had performed them for Him.

The core of the multitude that formed to accompany Jesus into Jerusalem was composed of those who had been with Him when He called Lazarus from the tomb. They had gone out to meet Jesus.

As the people went along with Jesus, they spread their cloaks before Him. Others took palm branches which they cut from the trees and laid them before Him. They accompanied Him from the top of the Mount of Olives to the city itself.

As they went along, the people cried out, "Hosanna to the son of David. Blessed is He who comes in the name of the Lord. Blessed is the kingdom which is coming, the kingdom of our father David. May there be peace in heaven, and glory in the highest. Hosanna in the highest."

NOTE:
"Hosanna" was a Hebrew and an Aramaic term which meant "help" or "save." (Arndt & Gingrich, p. 907.) It had come to be a cry of happiness and praise.

The Pharisees were very upset. They grumbled against each other saying, "See how futile your efforts are? Look, the whole world is gone after Him!" Moved with anger, they said to Jesus, "Teacher, rebuke your disciples and stop them from saying these things."

Jesus answered, "I tell you that if my disciples were to be quiet, the rocks on the ground would have to cry out."

As Jesus approached the city, He looked upon it and wept over it saying, "If you had known today the things that would bring you peace! But they are hidden from your eyes. The days will come when your enemies will cast up a rampart about you and will surround you. They will smash you to the ground and your children within you. They will not leave in you one stone upon another."

When Jesus reached the city, excitement ran throughout Jerusalem. People asked, "Who is this?" The multitudes said, "This is the prophet, Jesus, from Nazareth of Galilee." The blind and the lame came to Him in the temple, and He healed them.

When the chief priests and scribes saw His miracles, and heard the children shouting in the temple, "Hosanna to the Son of David," they were very angry. They asked Him, "Do you hear what these children are saying?"

Jesus said, "Yes. Have you never read, 'Out of the mouth of babes and infants have you raised up praise'(Ps. 8:2)?"

That evening, Jesus went back out to Bethany where He spent the night. It is the book of Mark (11:11) that tells that it was already late by the time Jesus was in the temple, so He went out to Bethany with the twelve.

The barren fig tree cursed (Mark 11:12-14; Matt. 21:18-19a):

As Jesus and His disciples were on their way from Bethany to Jerusalem the next morning, Jesus was hungry. Seeing a fig tree in full leaf ahead, He went over to see if He might find some figs. Instead, He found nothing but leaves because it was not the season for figs.

Jesus, therefore, said to the tree, "May no man eat fruit from you from now on forever." The disciples heard Him make the statement.

NOTE:
It was still in early spring. It was unusual for a tree to be in full foliage, though a tree placed to catch the utmost sunshine would put its leaves forth early. At this time of year, a fig tree would sometimes have a few of the old crop of figs still hanging on it. These were edible, so these were likely what Jesus was looking for. It

is a well-known fact, however, that in Palestine (as in other places), the fruit appears on a fig tree before the leaves. Therefore it was time for the new crop to be started. When Jesus came to the tree, there were neither old figs nor new green ones. This tree was barren.

Second cleansing of the temple (Mark 11:15-18; Matt. 21:12-13; Luke 19:45-48):

NOTE:
> Matthew and Luke tell of the cleansing of the temple topically with Jesus' triumphal entry. But, as Mark shows, it actually occurred on the next day which would be Monday (Mark 11:11-12).
> The cleansing of the temple was an application of Messianic authority. It took place once at the beginning of Jesus' public ministry (John 2:13-22) and now, again, at the close of His ministry.

Upon arriving in Jerusalem, Jesus went to the temple area. There He found merchants selling animals for sacrifices and money-changers exchanging shekels, which were required at the temple, for the Gentile money the people had.

Jesus drove the people out, overturning the tables of the money-changers and the benches of those selling doves. He would not allow them even to carry a vessel through the temple courts. He told them, "Is it not written, 'My house shall be called a house of prayer for all the nations'? But you have made it a den of robbers."

NOTE:
> It is interesting that on the occasion of the first cleansing, He rebuked the merchants and money-changers for making the house of prayer into a market place; but this time, He accuses them of dishonesty as well: "You have made it a den of robbers."

The chief priests and scribes heard what Jesus had done and they tried to find a way they could destroy Him. They were afraid just to seize Him in public because they feared His influence with the people, all of whom were astonished at His teaching.

Certain Greeks ask to see Jesus (John 12:20-50):

NOTE:
> This story could have happened on the day of the triumphal entry (Sunday) or on any one of the other days before the Passover. It is the only story John tells between the triumphal entry and the night when Jesus ate the Passover with His disciples. The entry into Jerusalem would certainly have gained Jesus the attention of these Greeks, but so would other events of the week. We have chosen to tell the story with Monday's events, but there is no evidence to prove which day it happened.
> This episode contains a tremendous lesson for Christians regarding life and death

as sacrifice. Be sure to think about it.

There were some Greeks among those who had come to Jerusalem to worship at the Feast. These Greeks were either proselytes (Gentiles who had accepted the whole law of Moses) or God-fearers (Gentiles who had accepted the God of the Jews, but not all the details of the law), since they had come to Jerusalem to take part in the Passover.

Somehow, these Greeks met Philip of Bethsaida, one of the twelve, and they said, "Sir, we would like to see Jesus." Philip went and told Andrew about the request, and, together, they went and told Jesus.

> NOTE:
>
> A discussion follows. There is no specific mention of the Greeks being in the group who heard Jesus, but since they had asked permission to see Him, it seems appropriate to assume they were there to hear Him.

Jesus answered:

The time has arrived for the Son of Man to be glorified. It is very much like a grain of wheat. Unless a grain falls upon the earth and dies, it remains as it is on and on. But if it dies, it bears much fruit. A man who loves his life too much to give it, loses it. The one who is willing to count his life as nothing in this world, will get to keep it for eternity. If any man plans to serve me (be he Greek or Jew), let him follow my example. Then he can be where I am and the Father will honor him.

Now my soul is very troubled, and what shall I say, "Father, save me from this hour"? But this hour is what I have come for. Father, glorify your name.

At that point, a voice spoke from heaven, saying, "I have glorified it and I will glorify it again." Some in the crowd said that it had thundered. Others said, "An angel has spoken to Him."

Jesus said, "This voice did not come for my sake, but for your sakes." He continued: "Now it is time for the judgment of this world. Now the prince of this world will be cast out."

> NOTE:
>
> In the mind of God and of Christ, this was climax of Jesus' work. Of all men, Jesus was the only one to realize that the most momentous event that had occurred since Satan triumphed in the Garden of Eden was about to happen. It was the climax long awaited, carefully planned, and brought about in the scheme of redemption. This was Jesus' greatest purpose for coming into the world: that is, to die for the sins of mankind.

Then Jesus added, "And I, if I be lifted up, will draw all men unto myself." By these words, He indicated the manner of His death.

The multitudes questioned Jesus: "We have heard from the law that the Christ remains forever. How then can you say, 'The Son of Man must be lifted up'? Who is this Son of Man?"

> NOTE:
>
> Jesus did not attempt to answer the question. The preaching had been done, the

134

signs given, and the life lived. He simply told them the importance of believing in Him.

Jesus replied, "The light is only going to be with you a little while. Walk while you have the light so you will not be caught and overcome by the darkness. One who walks in darkness does not know where he is going. While you have the light, believe on the light so that you may become children of light."

After saying these things, Jesus left and hid His presence from the crowd. It was obvious that in spite of so many signs which He had done, the people as a whole did not believe on Him. Thus the prophecy was fulfilled which Isaiah spoke: "Lord, who has believed our message? To whom has the arm of the Lord been shown (Isa. 53:1)." The reason why they did not believe was, as Isaiah said again, "He has blinded their eyes and hardened their hearts, lest they see with their eyes, and understand with their hearts, and repent, and He should heal them (Isa. 6:10)." Isaiah spoke these words because he saw the glory of Christ and spoke of Him.

Nevertheless, many of the rulers of the Jews believed in Christ, but because of the Pharisees, they did not confess it. They did not want to be put out of the synagogue, because they loved the glory of men more than the glory of God.

> NOTE:
> In Isaiah's prophecy we hear the anguish of all the spokesmen of God who have tried to teach God's word to their generation.
>
> God never hardens anyone before that one rejects His message. It is then that He hardens their hearts by sending His messengers to tell them to repent. They will not listen and actually intensify their determination to disobey.
>
> This passage is one of the proofs that Jesus existed before He came to earth. The glory which the rulers saw and rejected was the same glory which Isaiah saw over 700 years earlier (Isa. 6:1-3). The contrast between the rulers, who loved the glory of men more than the glory of God, and Isaiah, who saw the glory of Christ long before He came to earth, is vivid and fascinating. This means that the One whom Isaiah saw and by whom he was commissioned was the Lord, or Jesus, in His eternal identity.

Some time later, to another audience, Jesus cried out: "The one who believes on me does not ultimately believe on me, but on the One who sent me. Likewise, the one who beholds me beholds the One who sent me. I have come to be a light in the world so that whoever believes in me may not have to remain in darkness. If a man hears my sayings and does not keep them, I do not judge him, because I did not come to judge the world but to save it. The one who rejects me, and will not accept my words, does have something that *will* judge him, however, and that is the message that I have spoken. That is what will judge him in the last day. Because I did not bring you my own ideas. The Father who sent me gave me a commandment as to what I should say. I know that His commandment results in eternal life. That is why I speak the very things the Father gave me to say."

The barren fig tree found to be withered (Mark 11:19-25; Matt. 21:19b-22; Luke 21:37-38):

These were very full days. Every day Jesus taught in the temple, and every night He went out and stayed in the Mount of Olives. The next day (Tuesday) after Jesus had cursed the barren fig tree, He and His disciples returned to the city and passed by the tree. It had withered away from the roots up, from one morning until the next (the meaning of "immediately" in Matthew's account).

Peter and the other disciples were amazed. Peter said, "Rabbi, look, the fig tree which you cursed has already withered away."

Jesus told them, "Have faith in God. Really and truly I tell you: Whoever says to this mountain, 'Be lifted up and be cast into the sea,' and does not doubt in his heart, but believes that what he says will happen, he shall have it. So, I tell you, all things whatsoever you pray and ask for, believe that you have received them and you will have them. When you pray, though, remember to forgive anyone against whom you have a complaint, so that your Father in heaven will forgive you your mistakes."

The chief priests, scribes, and the Sanhedrin come to challenge Jesus' authority (Mark 11:27-12:12; Matt. 21:23-22:14; Luke 20:1-19):

When Jesus and His disciples reached the temple, He began preaching. A group of the chief priests, scribes, and elders came to Him and asked, "By what authority do you do all these things and who gave you this authority?"

> NOTE:
> Some think that this question referred to His cleansing of the temple while others think that, while the cleansing of the temple provoked this confrontation, the Jews were questioning Jesus about His authority to go about as a rabbi with disciples, and to do the various things He did.

Jesus answered the rulers saying, "I also will ask you a question. If you answer my question, then I will answer yours. The baptism of John, was it from heaven or from men? Which one?"

The Jewish leaders conferred among themselves and reasoned saying, "If we say from heaven, He will say, 'Why then did you not believe him?' But if we say from men, the people will stone us because they firmly believe John was a prophet."

They came back to Jesus and said, "We cannot tell which it was."

Jesus knew how they would answer. They refused to acknowledge John's authority from God. Therefore Jesus replied,

> Neither will I tell you by what authority I do these things. But let me see what you think about this situation:
> One time a man had two sons. He came to the first one and said, "Son, go work today in the vineyard." The son answered, "I will not," but afterward he changed his mind and went.
> The father came to the second son and said the same thing. This son said, "Yes sir, I will go," but he did not go. Now, which of the two did the will of his father?

The Jews replied the only way they could: "The first one."

Jesus said, "Truly, I tell you that the publicans and the harlots go into the kingdom before you. Because John came in the way of righteousness and you did not believe him, but the publicans and harlots believed him. And even when you saw this, you did not repent afterward so that you might believe him. Listen to another parable:

A certain man planted a vineyard and set out a hedge around it. He also dug a vat in the rock for a wine press, and built a tower in the vineyard. Then he put it into the hands of some vine-dressers and caretakers and went away into another country.

When the season came around for him to receive the profits from his vineyard, the man sent a servant to collect his harvest. The caretakers seized the servant and beat him and sent him away with nothing. The man sent another servant to whom they gave severe wounds and handled shamefully. He sent another servant; they killed him. The owner sent many other slaves. They beat some and killed others.

Finally, the owner said, "I will send my beloved son. Surely they will show him respect." But the husbandmen said, "Look, this is the heir. Let's kill him, then the inheritance will be ours." So they took the son and cast him out of the vineyard and killed him.

When the master of the vineyard does come, what do you think he will do to the caretakers?

Jesus' listeners were thoroughly involved in His story. Their wrath was stirred at the treatment the caretakers had given to the owner's slaves and to his son. They answered, "He will destroy those wretches and bring them to a miserable end. Then he will lease the vineyard to others who will give him his profits when they are due."

Jesus asked them, "Did you not ever read in the scriptures, 'The stone which the builders rejected, that very stone was chosen to be the chief cornerstone; this situation was from the Lord, and it is incredible in our eyes' (Ps. 118:22-23)? Therefore I am telling you that the kingdom of God will be taken away from you and will be given to a nation that will produce the fruits demanded. Everyone who falls over this stone will be broken into pieces. But upon whomsoever the stone falls, it will crush him and scatter him as dust."

By this time it dawned upon the chief priests and the Pharisees that Jesus was talking about them. But when they wanted to arrest Him, they were afraid to do so because they feared the people who accepted Him as a prophet.

Jesus spoke another parable:

The kingdom of heaven is like a king who prepared a marriage feast for his son. When it was ready, he sent his servants out to call the invited guests, but they refused to come. He sent other servants to tell the guests, "Look, I have prepared the feast: my fatted calves and oxen have been killed. Everything is ready; come to my feast." But the guests made fun of the feast and went about their business, one to his farm, another to his merchandise. Some of them seized the servants and killed them. This angered the king so that he took his army and destroyed the murderers and burned their cities.

The king then instructed his servants, saying, "The wedding is ready, but the ones who were invited have shown themselves to be unworthy. Go out to the crossroads and invite everyone you can find to the marriage feast."

The servants went out into the highways and invited as many as they could find, both good and bad. Soon the wedding was filled with guests. But when the king came in to look over the guests, he found a man who had not worn a wedding garment. He asked the man, "Friend, why did you come in here without wearing suitable clothing for a wedding feast?"

The man was speechless. Then the king told his servants, "Tie him up, hand and foot, and throw him out into the darkness outside." There will be weeping and grinding of teeth, because many are called but few are chosen.

NOTE:

This parable is a further development of an earlier parable told in Luke 14:15-24. In the earlier parable, the point was that the original guests will be rejected (the Jews) and new guests will be invited (Gentiles). Now Jesus makes that point, but also stresses that unless the newly invited guests prepare properly to attend the wedding to which they have been invited, they too, will be cast out.

In this parable, the idea is not that the guests were taken straight from the highway and were brought directly to the feast and expected to have on a wedding garment. Not many people walk about dressed like participants in a wedding party! But these new invited guests were supposed to prepare themselves to be at the feast. When this one man did not do so, he was thrown out. The point is that, yes, the Gentiles would be invited to enjoy the spiritual blessings of God, but not without their meeting the conditions God required.

Observe how Jesus meets the Pharisees, Sadducees, the chief priests, scribes, and others head-on this week. He does so publicly with no effort to defuse the situation as He had done so often before. Tuesday is the day on which the conflict between Jesus and the Jewish leaders reaches its climax.

The Pharisees and the Herodians seek to trap Jesus with a question about paying tribute to Caesar (Mark 12:13-17; Matt. 22:15-22; Luke 20:20-26):

The officials had been defeated when they approached Jesus directly in the story above. They left Him, frustrated because they knew He was talking about them in His parables, but afraid to take Him because of the people.

Later in the day, they sent some of their own disciples to act as spies on Jesus to see if they could catch Him in some mistake for which they could accuse Him before the Roman governor. Some of these spies went with the Herodians to set a trap for Him.

They said, "Teacher, we know that you do not hold back from saying the truth no matter who is involved. Truly you teach the way of God. Tell us, therefore, what you think: Is it lawful to give tribute to Caesar or not?"

NOTE:

Let us stop here for a moment, while everyone who has heard this question asked of Jesus ponders the answer. To see what a clever question it was, we need to note both the circumstances and the issues involved. First, the older, more mature Pharisees do not come themselves. They send some of their disciples, younger men who come pretending to be fresh, conscientious young men who really wonder about this matter. Second, they come *with* the Herodians, and it is the Herodians who take the lead in asking the question concerning tribute. It was more natural in some ways for them to ask this question than for the Pharisees. These factors were designed to take Jesus off guard.

Very little is known about the Herodians, either from the Bible or from historical sources. They are mentioned here as they join the Pharisees to try to trap Jesus, and they are mentioned in Mark 3:6 as joining with the Pharisees on a much earlier occasion to try to find a way to destroy Jesus. They may have been neither a religious sect nor an organized political party, but Jews who supported the rule of the Herodian family, and therefore, the rule of Rome. The Pharisees opposed the rule of the Herods and of Rome severely, so it was only their common hatred for Christ that would cause them to join the Herodians in a joint-effort of any kind.

Jesus was not deceived for even one moment. He perceived their wickedness and said, "Why do you try me, you hypocrites? Show me a denarius, the tribute money."

They brought a denarius and showed it to Him.

He asked, "Whose picture and title are these on the coin?"

They said, "Caesar's."

Jesus told them, "Then give to Caesar the things that belong to Caesar and give to God the things that are God's."

There was no way His enemies could dispute the answer before the people. They were amazed at His answer and they said nothing.

NOTE:

The question of paying tribute was a hot one among the Jews. There were some who argued that to pay taxes to Caesar was to admit that he was their king; but only Jehovah could be their king. Later, Judaism laid down the principle that the right of coinage implies the authority to levy taxes. Indeed, this is the force of Jesus' argument. It was Caesar's coinage that was possessed and used by the Jews. If they wanted to have the right to use his coins, then they should also submit to paying the taxes he demanded. Also, the fact that they were under Caesar's power meant that God had *given* them into that power. When that power was used to tax them, it must have been approved of God also.

What the Jews were counting on was that if Jesus answered saying, "No, it is not lawful for you to pay taxes," then He could be accused before the Romans. But if He said, "Yes, it is lawful," then He would anger many of the people and would be discredited in their eyes. His answer, however, prevented them from doing either one.

Remember Jesus' answer to this question. In spite of His answer, before the week is over the Jews will be accusing Him of forbidding them to pay tribute to Caesar in order to make Pilate agree for them to kill Him (Luke 23:2).

The Sadducees question Jesus about the resurrection (Mark 12:18-27; Matt. 22:23-33; Luke 20:27-40):

The Sadducees came next to take their turn. The Sadducees did not believe in a resurrection. They came with a question that, no doubt, was one of their stock questions to ask the Pharisees who did believe in a resurrection. So they tried it out on Jesus:

Teacher, Moses wrote that if a man die, having no children, then his brother should marry the dead brother's wife and raise up a child with the dead brother's name.

There were seven brothers. The first one took a wife, and died, leaving no children. The second brother took her for his wife, and he, likewise, died with no children. Every brother, in turn, married the woman and died. Finally the woman died also. Now in the resurrection, whose wife will she be? Because they all had her for a wife.

Jesus answered:

You have erred because you do not know the scriptures, nor the power of God. Those in this world marry and are given in marriage. But those who are counted worthy to reach the next age and to be raised from the dead will neither marry nor be given in marriage. Neither can they die any more for they will be equal to the angels and will be sons of God.

But that the dead are raised, have you never read in the book of Moses, in the passage concerning the burning bush that God said, "I *am* the God of Abraham, and the God of Isaac, and the God of Jacob"? God is not the God of the dead, but of the living, because everyone lives unto Him. You are badly mistaken!

The multitudes were astonished when they heard Jesus. Even the scribes said, "Teacher, you have answered well."

It seems the Sadducees had no further questions.

NOTE:

The argument Jesus made from the passage concerning the burning bush (Exod. 3:6) was simply this: When God spoke to Moses, Abraham, Isaac, and Jacob had been dead a long time. Yet God did not say, "I *used to be* the God of Abraham, Isaac, and Jacob." He said, "I *am* the God..." God is not the God of people that do not exist anymore. Therefore, somewhere Abraham, Isaac, and Jacob lived — and they lived with God. In other words, they exist and wait for the final resurrection.

A scribe questions Jesus: What is the greatest commandment? (Mark 12:28-34; Matt. 22:34-40):

When the Pharisees heard how Jesus had silenced the Sadducees, they gathered themselves together, and one of them, a lawyer, asked Jesus a question to put Him on the spot. "Teacher, which is the supreme commandment in the law?"

Jesus answered, "The first is: 'Hear, O Israel; the Lord our God is one, and you shall love the Lord your God with all your heart, and with all your soul, and with all your mind, and with all your strength' (Deut.6:4-5). The second commandment is similar to it: 'You shall love your neighbor as yourself' (Lev. 19:18). There is no other commandment greater than these. The whole law, and the prophets rest upon these two commandments."

The scribe said, "Teacher, truly you have answered well to say that He is one, and there is no other, and that to love Him with all one's heart, and understanding, and strength, and to love one's neighbor as himself, matters much more than all burnt offerings and sacrifices."

When Jesus saw how sensibly the scribe answered, He told him, "You are not far from the kingdom of God."

No one else dared to question Jesus.

Jesus poses a question to the scribes and Pharisees (Mark 12:35-37; Matt. 22:41-46; Luke 20:41-44):

While the Pharisees were still gathered together, Jesus asked them a question. "What do you think? Whose son is the Christ?"

They answered, "The son of David."

He replied, "Why then does David, guided by the Spirit, call Him Lord? David said, 'The Lord said unto my Lord, sit here on my right hand till I make your enemies the footstool of your feet' (Psa. 110:1). If the Christ is David's son, then in what sense can David call Him Lord?"

No one was able to answer His question. Neither dared anyone to ask Him any more questions.

Jesus denounces the scribes and Pharisees (Mark 12:38-40; Matt. 23:1-39; Luke 20:45-47):

NOTE:

All of Jesus' controversies with the Jews on this day took place in the temple (Mark 11:27; 12:35; 13:1; Matt. 21:23; Matt. 24:1). In these confrontations, Jesus showed that He was not afraid to meet the Jewish leaders in debate. On some earlier occasions, He had avoided them because He was not ready to die. The time had come now, so He met the Pharisees, the Sadducees, and the Herodians and put them all to silence. They were totally vanquished. Now He delivers a scathing condemnation to them, one which they had earned and richly deserved. Matthew has by far the fullest account of these "woes" against the Pharisees.

While the multitude was gathered around, Jesus spoke to them and to His followers, saying:

The scribes and the Pharisees sit in Moses' place. Therefore, whatever they tell you, be sure and do it, but do not follow after their ways because they tell others what to do, but they do not practice what they preach. O yes, they will load heavy burdens that are very hard to bear on the shoulders of others, and they will not lighten them at all.

They do all their works to make a show. They wear large phylacteries and enlarge the borders of their garments. They walk about in their robes, and they love the chief seats in the synagogues, and the greetings in the marketplace, and to have men call them rabbi. These are the same ones who take away widows' houses and for a show make long prayers. They shall receive greater condemnation. But you are not to be called rabbi because one is your teacher, and you are all brothers. And call no man on earth your father because you have one who is your Father, the One who is in heaven. Neither call one another master because one is your master, that is the Christ. The one who is greatest among you will be your servant. And anyone who lifts himself up will be put down; but whoever puts himself down will be lifted up.

NOTE:

Phylacteries were square leather boxes containing on small scrolls of parchment these four sections of the law: Exodus 13:1-10, 11-16; Deuteronomy 6:4-9; 11:13-21. These phylacteries (Tephillin) were fastened by long leather straps to the forehead, and around the left arm.

The "borders of their garments" refer to the fringes or tassels which the Jews were commanded to wear as a sign of their covenant with God (Num. 15:38). These were worn on the corners of a shawl which they used when praying. Elaborate rules had been established by the rabbis concerning the number of threads to be used and how they were to be tied. The law said to have these, but the Pharisees wanted to be sure that everyone noticed theirs.

Jesus continued:

But woe unto you, scribes and Pharisees, hypocrites! Because you shut up the kingdom of heaven against men. You will not enter it yourselves, and neither will you allow anyone else to do so.

Woe unto you, scribes and Pharisees, hypocrites! You will cover sea and land to make one convert, and when you have him, you make him twice as much a child of hell as you are.

Woe unto you, you blind guides. You say, "If anyone swears by the temple, it does not matter; but if anyone swears by the gold of the temple, he is obligated." You fools, you blind men — which is greater, the gold, or the temple that makes the gold special? You say, "If anyone swears by the altar, it does not matter; but if he swears by the gift that is on the altar, he is bound to keep the oath." You blind men — which is greater, the gift, or the altar that makes the gift special? Anyone who swears by the altar swears by it and by everything on it. If anyone swears by the temple, he swears by it and by the One who dwells in the temple. And the person who swears by heaven swears by the throne of God and by Him who sits upon it.

NOTE:

Since the Jews made a distinction between oaths which counted and those which did not, on the basis of trivial technicalities, their oaths were hypocritical and profane and really became an exercise in false swearing and lying.

Jesus continued:

Woe to you, scribes and Pharisees, hypocrites! Because you give a tenth of all your little potherbs (mint, anise, and cummin) and leave undone the more important matters of the law such as judgment, mercy, and faith. You ought to have done the little things, without leaving the other things undone. You blind guides, you strain at the gnat and go ahead and swallow the camel.

NOTE:

Mint, anise (or dill), and cummin were all small garden herbs. The "harvest" of these would have been tiny compared to wheat. Yet the Pharisees scrupulously gave a tenth of each handful of herbs.

Jesus continued:

Woe to you, scribes and Pharisees, hypocrites! Because you clean the outside of the cup and of the platter, but the inside remains full of cheating and selfishness. You blind Pharisees, clean first the inside of the cup, and of the platter, so that the outside can become clean also.

Woe to you, scribes and Pharisees, hypocrites! Because you build the burial vaults of the prophets, and decorate the tombs of the righteous. You say, "If we had lived in the days of our fathers, we would not have acted as they did." So I say listen to yourselves: you admit you are the sons of those who killed the prophets. Well, go ahead then, and act exactly the way your fathers did. You snakes! You children of vipers! How will you possibly escape the judgment of hell?

Therefore, look, I am sending to you prophets, and wise men, and scribes. Some you will kill and crucify; some you will whip in your synagogues, and persecute from city to city so that upon you may come all the righteous blood shed upon the earth, from Abel the righteous one to the blood of Zechariah the son of Barachiah whom you killed between the temple and the altar. I tell you truly that all this judgment will come upon this generation. (See information about Abel and Zechariah in the note on Luke 11:51, pages 103-104 of this material.)

Having delivered this stern message of condemnation to the Jews, Jesus suddenly changed His tone to one of sorrow and great regret. He said: "Oh Jerusalem, Jerusalem, who kills the prophets and stones those who are sent unto her! How many times I would have gathered your children together, just like a hen gathers her chicks beneath her wings, and you would not have it. Look! your house is left to you desolate. For I tell you, you will not see me from now on till you say, 'Blessed is the one who comes in the name of the Lord.'"

The widow's mite (Mark 12:41-44; Luke 21:1-4):

As Jesus went out of the temple, He came to the court of the women and He sat there watching those who came to bring their contributions.

NOTE:
To some, it seems a little strange that this story would come at this point. Matthew does not refer to it, but Mark and Luke do, and they tell it next. Probably the enemies of Jesus left hurriedly in the face of His fiery condemnation of them. The multitudes also may have turned away from His wrath. However it happened, we have here a moment of quietness and a valuable observation by Jesus before He goes out to the Mount of Olives with His disciples.

There were thirteen chests shaped like trumpets in the temple of Jesus' day. Into these were cast the religious and benevolent contributions of the multitude.

Jesus observed that many who were rich put a great deal of money into the chests. Then along came a poor widow who dropped in her pitifully small offering — two mites, which make one farthing. Jesus called His disciples and told them, "Truly I tell you, this poor widow has cast in more than everybody else because they are giving what they can so easily spare, but she has given all she has, the only thing she has to live on."

143

NOTE:

The widow gave two prutahs. The prutah was the very smallest coin in circulation. It was unlawful to drop in only one, so she gave two of them. The kind of coin she gave was also called a lepton. We have already learned that a denarius was a day's wages for a common laborer. Two Jewish leptons was worth one Roman quadran. Each denarius was worth sixty-four quadrans, so the widow gave one sixty-fourth of a denarius.

Jesus speaks of the destruction of Jerusalem and of His coming (Mark 13; Matt. 24; Luke 21:5-36):

NOTE:

The setting of this fascinating, private discussion between Jesus and His disciples was the Mount of Olives. The conversation began as they left the temple and proceeded east across the Kidron Valley and ascended the Mount of Olives. There they sat with a perfect, front-row seat to observe the city with its great wall and, above all, the snow-white expanse of the temple complex itself. Knowing that they all sat there, gazing across the valley at the magnificent, panoramic view of Jerusalem and of the temple, while Jesus told them of the utter destruction that was coming upon it, very much enhances the lesson.

As Jesus went forth from the temple, one of His disciples said to Him, "Master, look, what great stones and what kind of buildings."

Jesus said, "Do you see these great buildings? There will not be left of them one stone upon another."

NOTE:

The walls of the temple enclosure had single stone blocks which were up to twenty-four feet long. What might have provoked the disciples to talk to Jesus about the temple at this point is uncertain. This particular disciple may have noticed some especially beautiful stone that might have made him stop to look more carefully at the whole set of buildings. But Jesus' statement which He had already made: "Your house is left unto you desolate," plus His answer here: "There will not be left one stone upon another," definitely called forth the questions which came next. The disciples found it hard to imagine that such a great structure could be demolished.

As they arrived on the Mount of Olives, and Jesus sat down, Peter, Andrew, James, and John came and asked Him privately, "Tell us, when will these things happen, and what will be the sign that your coming and the end of the world are about to occur?"

NOTE:

It is beyond the scope of this book to make an exhaustive study of these passages, yet some view of them must be taken and presented. Here, before Jesus answers the disciples' questions, will be a good place to make a few comments about the speech.

The Last Week

We can dismiss the wild speculations of the pre-millennialists and narrow the choices of interpretation to two alternatives:

1. One position is that the entire discussion in Mark and Luke, and all of chapter 24 in Matthew, is about the destruction of Jerusalem and of the temple. Then, according to this position, Jesus deals with the end of the world and the final judgment in the judgment parables in chapter 25 of Matthew.
2. The second view is that the destruction of Jerusalem and of the temple is dealt with in Matthew 24:1-34, and the second coming of Christ and the end of the world is dealt with in Matthew 24:35-25:46.

The difference between the two views is not drastic. We encourage the teacher to study carefully and present the view he believes is true. To the older students, both views can be briefly and simply explained, but one primary view needs to be presented. They can wait until they are adults to study the matter in depth. The first view is the one we take in our presentation.

Mark and Luke record the disciples' questions as all relating to the destruction of the temple. Matthew also refers to Christ's coming and to the end of the world. We do not know how clear the disciples' thinking was as they asked the questions. It may be that they could not conceive of a destruction of the temple before the return of Christ in the final judgment. If that were their idea, then the two questions were combined as one in their minds. Also at this time, Jesus Himself did not know when His second coming would be (Mark 13:32).

For these reasons it is not surprising that Jesus' teaching concerning the destruction of Jerusalem and the end of all things is interwoven with language which fits with His final coming in judgment upon the world. Overall the best position on the chapter is probably that it concerns the destruction of Jerusalem and the end of the Jewish state. Yet there seem to be overtones of the final judgment discernible in His statements.

It was not uncommon for prophets to compress in one message things which would unfold in their own time and things which would come to pass in the future. Jesus Himself gave the limited commission to His apostles, and in that commission, He gave them instructions which did not apply until later, after the great commission was given (Matt. 10:18-22).

One more point before we look at Jesus' answer: Why would the destruction of Jerusalem and of the temple be important enough for Jesus to take this much time discussing it, and why would three of the gospel writers consider it important enough to record the discussion in such detail?

The Jewish people had been the covenant people of God since the days when He brought them out of Egyptian bondage (Exod. 19). Really, in promise, they had been His people since God first called Abraham out of Ur of the Chaldees, and promised to make a great nation of him (Gen. 12). Through the years, God shielded them; He guided them through the law, and then through inspired prophets who spoke His word to them. Jerusalem had been the city where God had placed His presence in the temple since the days of Solomon (1 Kings 8-9). Yet the Jews had a history of rejecting God. As punishment, God allowed that first temple of Solomon to be destroyed, and He allowed the people to be carried into captivity (2 Kings 25). After a time, God allowed the people to come home from captivity and to rebuild the temple (Ezra 1-6). The Jews learned some lessons from their punishment, but years had passed and now God had sent His Son into the world. In spite of all the prophecies and promises, in spite of all the blessings from God through the years, the Jewish nation as a whole was rejecting Jesus as the Christ. They were rejecting the greatest blessing God ever offered them.

It was necessary in the scheme of redemption that enough Jews reject Jesus for Him to be killed as our sacrifice, but there are enough wicked people in any generation for that to have been accomplished. The Jewish people as a whole could have accepted Jesus as the divine Messiah. But they did not. Therefore, destruction was inevitable! The destruction of the city of Jerusalem and of the temple was God's rejection of the Jews as His covenant people. There would be a totally new covenant people under the new law. Therefore, the fall of Jerusalem was a much sadder event in history than the fall of other cities. It was more than the fall of a city — it was the fall of a people — the fall of the people who had been more highly blessed than any other nation of people who have ever existed. They fell because they rejected God's greatest promise.

Jesus began: "Be careful not to let any man lead you astray. Many will come in my name, claiming, 'I am the Christ,' and will deceive many people. You will hear of wars and rumors of wars, but do not be alarmed by such things. Such things are going to happen, but the end is not yet. Nation will rise again nation, and there will be famines and earthquakes in various places. All these things are just the beginning of birth pains."

NOTE:
Remember this passage when someone shows up at your door to tell you that with all the wars and disasters going on, surely the end of the world is near. Jesus said that when His disciples heard of wars and rumors of wars, the end is *not* yet.

Then Jesus continued:

Be careful, because during this period, your enemies will bring you before councils, and you will be beaten in the synagogues and thrown into prisons. You will be brought before kings and governors to give your testimony for my cause. The gospel must be preached unto all the nations before destruction comes.

NOTE:
In a Jewish context, all the nations would not mean literally all the globe. It would refer to the nations of the Mediterranean world.
The persecutions predicted here were primarily those that would be faced in that first century.

The Last Week

Jesus continued:

When they lead you to judgment and deliver you up, do not worry about what to say. Do not think beforehand how to answer those who try you, because I will give you wisdom to know what to say through the Holy Spirit. Your enemies will not be able to answer you.

But a brother will turn his brother over to the authorities, and the father his child. The children will rise up against parents and will cause them to be put to death, and you will be hated of all men for my name's sake. Yet not a hair of your head will perish. In your steadfastness, you will preserve your souls.

Many false teachers will arise and will lead many people into error. And because of lawlessness, the love of many of God's children will grow cold. But the one who endures all the way to the end, he will be saved.

When you see the abomination of desolation, such as Daniel talked about, standing in the holy place, then let them that are in Judea flee into the mountains. Let him who is on the housetop not go down into his house to get anything. And let not the one who is in the field turn back to get his cloak. Let them flee, and let those who are in the midst of the city get out.

> NOTE:
> Daniel spoke of abominations that would make desolate in Daniel 9:27; 11:31; and 12:11. Daniel 9:27, and perhaps 12:11, seem to be the prophecy to which Jesus refers. The other passage in Daniel refers to the desecration of the Jewish temple by Antiochus IV in 168 B.C.
>
> There was more than one desecration of the temple in the years following this prediction by Jesus. The thing to which Jesus referred was something which would be a warning, which would afford an opportunity for those who wished to leave Jerusalem to do so before the Romans cut off all escape. In view of the parallel passage in Luke 21:20, likely He was referring to the coming of the Roman army itself.
>
> The Christians of Jerusalem heeded the warning of Christ and fled. Eusebius, a historian in the early church, says that the church in Jerusalem, following a revelation received by reliable men before the day, migrated to Pella in Perea.

Jesus continued:

These are the days of vengeance so that all the things which are written can be fulfilled. But woe to those who are pregnant, or who have small infants. And pray that it will not happen in the winter or on a sabbath, because those days will see great tribulation, such as has not been from the beginning of the world, nor ever shall be again. And if the time were not shortened, no one would be saved; all would perish. But because of the chosen ones, the days shall be shortened.

> NOTE:
> The chosen ones (or elect) are Christians; yet the Christians were not directly involved in the tribulations of Jerusalem. It was the Jews who would all have perished if the sufferings had not been abbreviated. What then does it mean that "because of

147

the chosen ones, the days shall be shortened"? The salvation in the context is deliverance from physical death and annihilation. There are two possible explanations deserving of consideration. One is that by the power of God, the Jews were kept from extinction and are preserved till this day as an example of those who reject God, and as an encouragement to the elect to remain faithful. "Because of the chosen ones" would mean that the Jews were spared as an example to the chosen ones. This explanation seems forced. The other explanation is that though Christians were not involved in the siege of Jerusalem itself, the longer the conflict went on the more it would involve all the inhabitants of Palestine, and that would include Christians. This is probably the true explanation.

Jesus continued:

There will be great distress upon the land and wrath upon the Jews. They will fall by the sword and will be led captive among the nations. Jerusalem will be taken over by the Gentiles until their times are fulfilled.

Then if any man says, "Here is the Christ," or someone else says, "Here He is," — do not believe them. There will be false Christs and false prophets who will show great signs and wonders so as to lead even the elect into error, if possible.

Now I have told you beforehand, so if anyone tells you, "Look, He is in the wilderness," do not go out to see. Or if one says, "Look, He is in this back room," do not believe it. Because as the lightning flashes in the east and is seen in the west, that is the way the coming of the Son of man will be. Wherever the carcass is, that is where the eagles will be gathered.

NOTE:

The word translated eagles is sometimes found as "vultures," but the reference here is likely to eagles. "Vultures" is used by some because of the reference to a carcass, but eagles also feed on dead animals. The dead, bloated animal which these eagles were going to pick and eat was Jerusalem. Jerusalem, as the headquarters of Judaism, was rejecting Christ. The Jews of Jerusalem would go from bad to worse until they would richly deserve to have the carcass of their sinful nation torn and devoured. Where such a job needed to be done, the eagles were sure to come — that is, the eagles of the Roman legions. The Roman flag poles were topped with eagles; moreover, the eagle was used by Rome on money and other things to such an extent that the eagle was readily associated with Rome. The prediction here was clearly the destruction of Jerusalem by the Roman legions.

Jesus continued:

In those days, after such tribulation, the sun will be darkened, the moon will not give her light, the stars will fall from heaven, and the powers in the heavens will be shaken. Then will appear the sign of the Son of Man in heaven. Then all of the tribes of the earth will mourn, and they will see the Son of Man coming on the clouds of heaven with power and great glory. He will send forth His angels with a loud blast of a trumpet, and they will gather together His chosen ones from the four winds, from one end of heaven to the other.

NOTE:

We must be careful to avoid bringing the false ideas of our own day to any passage we would try to understand. There are two ideas in this passage which may tempt us to do that. One is the reference to the sun, moon, and stars being darkened; the other is the reference to the coming of Christ.

It is commonly thought that the reference to the sun and moon must mean the final end of the world. The truth is, this very figure is used several times in the Bible to refer to judgment, but not necessarily the *final* judgment. Such figurative language is used by Isaiah about Babylon (Isa. 13:10), of the earth (Isa. 24:23); by Ezekiel of Egypt (Ezek. 32:7, 8); and by Joel of the same destruction of Jerusalem which Jesus prophesies (Joel 2:30-31; Acts 2:16-21). The language describes the upheaval of a society when it is destroyed.

The coming of the Son of Man in this context is to judge Jerusalem and the Jews. We have already discussed the idea of Jesus' coming in judgment in Matthew 16:27-28 and in Mark 8:38-9:1. All these passages probably apply to the destruction of Jerusalem, as does this one in Matthew 24. Yet the language may go beyond that destruction to receive its ultimate fulfillment in the final judgment. The very fact that the Son of Man would come in judgment upon the city, which had been the representation of God's covenant people, gives proof that He will someday come in judgment upon all mankind. Therefore, the judgment of Jerusalem foreshadows the final coming in judgment.

Jesus then used an illustration:

Consider the fig tree: when its branch begins to put forth buds, you know summer is near. In the same way, when you see the things I have warned you about, then know that the destruction I have predicted is near, even at the door. This generation will not pass away till all these things be done.

Heaven and earth will pass away, but my words will not pass away. But of that day and hour no one knows, not even the angels of heaven, neither the Son. Only the Father knows.

As it was in the days of Noah, so shall it be at the coming of the Son of Man. Just as in the days before the flood, people were eating and drinking and getting married right up until Noah entered the ark, so it will be at the coming of the Son of Man. Then two men will be in the field; one will be taken, the other left. Two women will be grinding; one will be taken, the other left.

NOTE:

In Luke 17:22-37 this same language is used to talk about the destruction of Jerusalem. Therefore we cannot assert that Matthew 24:34-44 is necessarily about the final judgment. It may concern the destruction of Jerusalem. In either case the chief lesson is that the judgment will not be according to whom you know or work with. Two men working closely in the field will be separated in the judgment, one being taken (to be saved), the other left (for the fire which will burn the chaff). Some of the figures here work out far better if their ultimate application is to the final judgment, while others seem to refer to the destruction of Jerusalem. Perhaps they refer to both in that the first destruction is a foreshadowing of the final day.

Jesus continued:

The thing you need to do is to watch and pray because you do not know when the Lord shall return. Be careful lest your hearts be filled with dissipation and drunkenness, and the cares of this life, and that day catch you by surprise like a trap.

It is as if a man went away to stay a while in another country. He left orders with the servants to do their work, and he commanded the guard at the door to watch. Therefore, be on guard, because you do not know when the master of the house will come back, whether in the evening, or at midnight, or at the dawn, or in the morning. If he comes suddenly, do not let him catch you sleeping. What I say to you, I say to everyone: Watch!

Realize that if the master of a house knew when the thief was coming, he would watch and would not allow his house to be ransacked. So you be ready, because in an hour when you do not expect Him, the Son of Man is coming.

Who is the trustworthy and prudent slave whom the master has set over his household to see after everything? Blessed is that servant whose lord finds him doing his job. He will then put him over everything he has.

But if the servant is evil and says to himself, "My master is not coming for a long time," and begins to beat his fellow-servants, and to party and get drunk, his master will come when he least expects him. The master will cut that servant off and will give him his fate with the hypocrites. There will be weeping and the grinding of teeth.

NOTE:
If all of these passages refer to the destruction of Jerusalem instead of the final judgment, of what value are they to us today? They serve as a grave warning to all of God's people, no matter what generation they live in. If God would destroy the city where He had placed His name and the nation which He had chosen as His own, because of their wickedness, then He will surely punish us if we do not keep our own covenant with Him. All judgments that God has brought against the wicked throughout history foreshadow the final judgment which will come at the last day. The lesson to us is to watch, to be prepared.

The first of three judgment parables: Ten virgins (Matt. 25:1-13):
In the first of the parables describing the final judgment, Jesus said:

At the judgment, the kingdom of God will be like ten virgins who took their lamps and went forth to meet the bridegroom. Five of these virgins were foolish because they took their lamps with them, but they carried no oil. The other five were wise because they not only took their lamps, they also took a supply of oil in a vessel. Reaching their position where they would await the procession, all ten virgins went to sleep.

NOTE:
According to the marriage customs of that day, the bridegroom would lead a procession to the house of his bride's father. There he would take his wife and return with her in procession to his own house.

About midnight there was a cry, "Look, the bridegroom! Come out to meet him!" The virgins all awoke and began getting their lamps ready to meet the procession. They lit their lamps, but the foolish virgins had no oil except the little that remained from their last use, and already their lamps were going out. So they asked the wise virgins, "Give us some of your oil because our lamps are going out."

But the wise virgins said, "We did not bring enough oil for us and for you. You need to go to those who sell oil and buy your own." The foolish virgins went away to buy oil. But while they were gone, the bridegroom came, and those who were ready went with him to the marriage feast. They went into the house, and the door was shut.

After a while, the foolish virgins returned and called out, "Sir, Sir, open up! Let us in." But he answered, "I tell you the truth. I do not know you people."

Watch therefore, because you do not know the day or the hour when the Son of Man comes.

NOTE:

In the interpretation of this parable, all the virgins would be at least nominal Christians because they were all invited guests. Five of them represent those who have the "form of godliness," but deny or repress "the power thereof" (2 Tim. 3:5). How foolish! The word translated "foolish" is the word from which we get our word moron. How utterly foolish for these virgins to have their lamps with them to go meet the bridegroom, but to carry no oil. How foolish it is for people to make some profession of Christianity and fail to develop the true character and essence of it in their lives.

The second judgment parable: The talents (Matt. 25:14-30):

Again Jesus said,

The kingdom of heaven at the judgment will be like a man who was going into a far-away country. He called his servants to him and gave his possessions into their care. To one he gave five talents, to another two, and to another one. He gave them money to handle according to their individual abilities. Then he went away on his journey.

Immediately the servant with the five talents went to work and used the money his master gave him to buy and sell. He made five more talents. Likewise the servant with the two talents gained two more. But the servant with one talent dug a hole in the earth and hid his master's money.

After a while, the master returned and called his servants in to receive a report on how they had done. The servant who had been given five talents came before his master and said, "Lord, you gave me five talents. Look, I have gained five more."

The master was pleased and said, "Good job! You are a good and faithful servant. You have been faithful in these few things; I will set you over many things. Enter into the joys your lord has provided."

The second one who had received two talents came and said, "Lord, you gave me two talents; look, I have gained two more."

The master told him also, "Good job! You are a good and faithful servant. You have been faithful in a few things; I will set you over many things. Enter into the joys your Lord has provided."

Finally the man who had received one talent came and said, "Master, I knew that you are a hard man, reaping where you did not plant, and gathering where you did not scatter. So I was afraid and hid your money in the earth. Look, here is your talent back."

But his master was angry and said, "You wicked, lazy servant! You knew that I reap where I do not plant, and gather where I do not scatter. Therefore you ought at least to have put my money in the bank so that I could get interest from it upon my return. Take away the talent from him, therefore, and give it to the one who has ten. Because to the one who has done well and who has been productive will be given more, and he will have plenty. But to the one who is lacking, even what little he has will be taken away. Cast this unprofitable servant into the darkness outside. There will weeping and the grinding of teeth."

NOTE:

The word "talent" in this story is not used at all in the sense we use the word. In English, we use the word primarily to mean an ability, something one can do well. But actually, even the English word has the meaning of a weight or a weighed amount of money. It is from the Latin word "talentum" and the Greek word "talanton." In Jesus' day, it was a unit of weight or money (the value of a talent's weight in silver or gold). Its weight varied widely in Greece, in Rome, and in the Near East, but the lowest weight for it was no less than fifty-six pounds, each pound having sixteen ounces. In today's values, even one talent of gold would be a vast amount of money (around three hundred thousand dollars).

In the parable, the talent represents simply a charge or responsibility. Each servant was given a charge which was suited to his own ability.

The third judgment parable: The sheep and the goats (Matt. 25:31-46):

Jesus continued with a third parable, still about the coming of the final judgment:

But when the Son of Man comes in His glory, with all His angels with Him, He will sit on the throne of His glory, and all the nations will be gathered before Him. He will separate the sheep from the goats. He will set the sheep on His right hand and the goats on His left.

Then the king will say to those on His right hand: "Come, you who are blessed of my Father. Inherit the kingdom prepared for you from the foundation of the world. Because I was hungry, and you fed me; I was thirsty, and you gave me drink; I was a stranger, and you let me live with you; in rags, and you gave me clothes to wear; sick, and you cared for me; I was in prison, and you came to me."

The righteous will answer Him saying: "Lord, when did we see you hungry and fed you, or thirsty and gave you something to drink? When did we see you a stranger and let you stay with us, or in rags and clothed you? And when did we see you sick and cared for you, or in prison and came to visit you?"

And the king will answer, "Truly, I tell you, each time you did one of these things for one of my brothers, even the least important one, you did it for me."

Then He will say to those on His left hand: "Get away from me, you who are cursed, into the eternal fire which is prepared for the devil and his angels. Because I was hungry, and you gave me no food; I was thirsty, and you gave me nothing to drink. I was a stranger, and you did not let me stay with you; I was in rags, and you gave me no clothes; sick, and in prison, and you did nothing to help me."

Then they also will answer, "Lord, when did we see you in any of these conditions and failed to help you?"

And He will answer, "When you failed to do such things for the least of my brothers, you did not do them for me." And these will go away into eternal punishment, but the righteous will go into eternal life.

NOTE:

There are many questions we might have about the second coming that are not answered in the scriptures. Notice that Jesus' answer to the disciples' question about His coming and the end of the world was that the time is unknown, but that it is not necessary for us to know the time. Our task on earth is to do the jobs set before us to the best of our abilities, and to watch for the coming of that great day. In this way, we will be prepared for the blessings of God — no matter when that day comes.

Jesus again predicts His crucifixion which would take place only two days later (Mark 14:1-2; Matt. 26:1-5; Luke 22:1-2):

When Jesus finished saying these things, He said to His disciples, "You know that the Passover is two days away, and the Son of Man will be handed over to be crucified."

Meanwhile the chief priests and the elders (the Sanhedrin) were meeting in the court of the high priest, Caiaphas, to try to figure out how they could take Jesus in some sly way and kill Him. They said, however, "We cannot kill Him during the feast lest we cause a riot among the people." This plan was changed when a startling development occurred.

CHRONOLOGICAL NOTE:

We have already shown that the story of Mary's anointing the feet of Jesus happened on Saturday evening at Bethany. We pointed out that Matthew and Mark put the episode later, because of its relationship to the prospect of Jesus' death and also to show why Judas was perhaps made angry enough to betray Jesus. We cannot *know* why Judas did such a thing, except that he wanted money.

Did Judas make his arrangement to betray Jesus on Sunday after Mary anointed Jesus' feet the night before, or did he wait until the middle of the week, on Tuesday or Wednesday? It seems to have been in the middle of the week, because the first intention of the Jews was to wait until *after* the Passover to kill Jesus. That still held true by Tuesday evening (Mark 14:1-2; Matt. 26:1-5), two days before the Passover. Also, the Jews were more prone to make their bargain after the events of Sunday, Monday, and especially Tuesday, the day of conflict. Therefore, it was almost certainly Tuesday evening or Wednesday when Judas made his deal with the Jews.

Judas bargains with the rulers to betray Jesus (Mark 14:10-11; Matt. 26:14-16; Luke 22:3-6):

Judas left the company of Jesus' apostles and went to the chief priests to bargain with them to betray Jesus. He asked, "What are you willing to give me to deliver Him to you?" (The point was that Judas would know where the enemies could find Jesus away from the crowds who might object to His being taken.)

The Jews were glad to have this opportunity and they made an agreement to pay Judas thirty pieces of silver. From that time on, Judas began to seek an opportunity to deliver Jesus into the hands of His enemies.

CHRONOLOGICAL NOTE:

Not one event is recorded as happening on Wednesday. After Tuesday, there was no further need for Jesus to meet the Jews in debate, so He likely spent that Wednesday in solitude with His apostles.

We need to point out, however, that there are enough questions about the chronology of the last week that we should not be dogmatic about which day a particular event happened. The chronology of the last week is not as important as the events themselves. Do not get preoccupied with the subject.

See Appendix 1 at the end of the material for more details about the chronology of the week.

Preparation for the last Passover (Mark 14:12-16; Matt. 26:17-19; Luke 22:7-13):

On the first day of unleavened bread, when the Passover was sacrificed, Jesus' disciples came to Him and asked, "Where would you have us prepare to eat the Passover?"

Jesus said, "Go into the city, and you will meet a man carrying a pitcher of water; follow him. Whatever house he goes into, you say to the owner of the house, 'The Master says: Where is my guest-room, where I shall eat the Passover with my disciples?' He will show you a large, upper room furnished and ready for use. There you can make preparations for us." The disciples went into the city and found things exactly as Jesus had said, and there they made ready for the feast.

NOTE:

Remember that the Passover was the feast ordained to commemorate Israel's deliverance from the plague of the firstborn and, consequently, from Egypt (Exod. 12:1-28; 13:3-10). In the record found in Exodus, it is clear that the Israelites were also to eat unleavened bread for seven days. Therefore, the feast of Passover was associated with the days of unleavened bread. Note the reference to the "first day of unleavened bread, when they sacrificed the Passover" (Mark 14:12).

The Last Supper

Strife among the apostles; Jesus washes their feet (Mark 14:17; Matt. 26:20; Luke 22:14-16; John 13:1-17):

As Jesus sat to eat with His disciples that evening, He said, "I have eagerly desired to eat this Passover with you before I suffer, because I tell you I will not eat it again with you until it is fulfilled in the kingdom of God."

> NOTE:
>
> As we combine the four accounts of this last supper, it is impossible to be sure exactly which event or which discussion came first. At some point in the evening, strife arose between the apostles about which would be reckoned as the greatest. No servant had been available to wash their feet and not one of them would volunteer to wash the others' feet. They were all too interested in their status and their "rights" to do such a thing. It is best to connect Luke's statements about this strife with John's record of Jesus' washing the disciples' feet. This event seems to have taken place early in the evening, with the institution of the Lord's Supper coming later, probably after Judas left, yet before the meal was completely finished because both Matthew and Mark use the expression "...while they were eating" to introduce the Lord's Supper (Mt. 26:26; Mark 14:22).

A quarrel began among the apostles about who was estimated to be the greatest. As usual, they would have wanted their quarrel kept quiet so that the Lord would not hear them. Imagine their surprise when Jesus, knowing that the Father had given all things into His hand, and that He came forth from God and would return unto God, arose from the supper and laid aside His outer garments. Saying nothing, He fastened a towel about Him. Then He poured water into a bowl and began to wash the disciples' feet and to wipe them with the towel. What humility in Jesus the Lord! What pain, what shame in the hearts of the apostles, as Jesus did what they would not think of doing for one another! But Jesus, who loved His disciples all along, loved them unto the last.

When Jesus came to Peter, Peter said, "Lord, are you thinking you will wash my feet?"

Jesus answered, "You do not know now what I am doing, but later you will understand."

Peter was very upset. He said, "You will never wash my feet." Peter was horrified to think of Jesus performing such a menial task for him.

Quietly, Jesus said, "If I do not wash you, you have no part with me."

Peter answered, "Lord, then please do not just wash my feet, but wash my hands and my head also!" Oh, Peter did not want to be cut off from the Lord!

Jesus said, "One that is bathed does not need to wash anything but his feet, and then he will be clean all over; and you are clean, but not all of you." Jesus added that last phrase because He knew that one would betray Him.

When Jesus had finished, He sat back down and said:

> Do you realize what I have done for you? You call me Master and Lord, and you do so correctly for that is what I am. If I then, your Lord and Master, have washed your feet, you also ought to wash one another's feet. You see, I have given you an example, that you also should do as I have done.

You know that the kings of the Gentiles exercise lordship over them, but it must not be so among you. He that is greatest among you, let him serve. Because who is greater, the one who sits at meat, or the one who serves? Is it not the one who sits to eat? Nevertheless, I am in your midst as one who serves. You will be blessed if you do these things.

You are the ones who have gone through all of my trials and I appoint unto you a kingdom, even as my Father has appointed unto me, that you may eat and drink at my table in my kingdom. And you will sit on thrones judging the twelve tribes of Israel.

NOTE:

This was an evening charged with the most intense emotion. We must feel the aching hearts, the puzzled minds; we must see the quiet searching of one another's eyes and hear the words, now calm, now tremulous with emotion, in order even to begin to appreciate the events of the evening.

Jesus was not instituting a ceremony of foot-washing that was due to be performed in worship services. Rather He was teaching a lesson on humility as He had done several times before; for example, like the time He put the little child in their midst and told the disciples they must become as a little child in order to enter the kingdom of heaven (Matt. 18:1-3).

Jesus points out Judas as the betrayer (Mark 14:18-21; Matt. 26:21-25; Luke 22:21-23; John 13:18-30):

Jesus said, "I do not refer to you all. I know whom I have chosen, but it was necessary that the scripture be fulfilled which says, 'He that eats my bread lifted up his heel against me' (Psa. 41:9). I have told you before it comes to pass so that when it has happened, you may believe. Really and truly, I tell you that he who receives anyone I send, receives me, and he who receives me receives Him that sent me."

After He had said these things, Jesus was troubled and said, "One of you who eats with me shall betray me. And the Son of Man indeed must go, as it has been planned, but woe to that man through whom He is betrayed. It would be better if that man had never been born."

This news created great distress among the apostles. They stared at one another and were sorrowful. They began to say, one by one, "Is it I, Lord?"

Even Judas said, "Surely not I, Rabbi?"

Jesus answered, "Yes, it is you."

John was leaning back on the shoulder of Jesus. Simon Peter motioned to him and said, "Tell us who it is He is talking about."

John quietly asked Jesus, "Lord, who is it?"

Jesus replied, "It is the one for whom I will dip this piece of bread and to whom I give it." So when He had dipped the bread, He gave it to Judas the son of Simon Iscariot.

After the bread was given to Judas, Satan entered into him. Therefore, Jesus said to him, "What you are about to do, do quickly."

No one at the table knew what Jesus meant. Some thought that because Judas had the money bag, Jesus was telling him to: "Buy the things we need for the feast," or that he should give something to the poor.

So Judas left. By now it was night.

NOTE:

Plenty had been said to let the disciples know that Judas was the one who would betray Jesus, but the enormity of Judas' deed was apparently beyond the apostles' power to accept. Just as they could not conceive of Judas' wicked plan, they could not conceive that Jesus would really be taken and killed as He had been warning them for months now.

Before we continue, stop to think how many times Jesus has warned these men about His approaching death and how clearly He has told them what will happen. He has told them of the sorrow to come and He has also told them of the joy to come afterward when He will be raised from the dead. He will continue to tell them information during this last evening together. But they do not understand.

Jesus warns all the disciples (Peter in particular) against desertion (Mark 14:27-31; Matt. 26:31-35; Luke 22:31-38; John 13:31-38):

When Judas was gone, Jesus said, "Now the Son of Man is glorified and God is glorified in Him. God will glorify the Son in Himself, and He will do so quickly.

"Little children, I am going to be with you only a little while now. You will seek me, but as I told the Jews, 'where I go, you cannot come.' That is, you cannot come at the present. I want to give you a new commandment: that you love one another even as I have loved you. By this all men will be able to tell that you are my followers, if you love one another."

Peter asked, "Lord, where are you going?"

Jesus answered, "Where I am going you cannot follow me now, but later you will follow me."

Then Jesus shocked His disciples by telling them, "All of you will turn away from me because it is written: 'I will strike the shepherd, and the sheep will be scattered' (Zech. 13:7). Nevertheless, after I am raised, I will go before you into Galilee."

Peter protested, "Lord, why can I not follow you even now? I will lay down my life for you! Moreover, all the rest may turn away from you, but I will never be ashamed or turn away from you."

Jesus answered, "Simon, Simon, look! Satan asked to have you so he could sift you like wheat, but I prayed for you and made request for you that your faith not fail you. And when you are recovered, you establish your fellow disciples."

Peter said, "Lord, I am ready to go with you to prison, and to death."

Jesus replied, "Will you lay down your life for me? I tell you, Peter, the rooster will not crow twice this coming day before you have denied three times that you even know me. Before the cock crowing time, you will have done this."

But Peter denied the Lord's warning vehemently: "I will not deny you!" All the disciples declared they would not deny Him.

Turning to a different subject, Jesus said, "When I sent you forth without money, or knapsack, or extra shoes, did you lack anything?"

"Not a thing," they replied.

"Now, however, I am telling you differently," Jesus said. "If you have a billfold, take it, and a backpack too. If you do not have a sword, sell your cloak and buy one. Because I tell you, that the word which is written must be fulfilled in me: 'And he was reckoned with transgressors' (Isa. 53:12), because that which concerns me is about to be fulfilled."

The disciples said, "Lord, look, we have two swords."
Jesus said, "That is enough."

NOTE:

Jesus' point was that the limited commission was a unique situation to help train the apostles, to teach them that they could rely upon God. Now, as Jesus is about to be treated as a transgressor (to be killed as a criminal), He wanted them to approach their coming work differently. He wanted them to make normal preparations: take along supplies, money, food, and a sword. These were all things that someone going on a journey might carry with him. The disciples did not understand what He meant. They thought He wanted a sword for whatever approaching evil He kept talking about. Jesus did not try to enlighten them. They would have to wait until later before they would understand.

It is impossible to know beyond doubt the exact procedure for the feast in Jesus' day, but a few things are interesting and helpful to observe.

The Passover feast observed by the Jews of Jesus' day was different from the observance of the first one in the book of Exodus in several ways. The participants in the original feast ate the Passover lamb hurriedly, with unleavened bread, and bitter herbs. They were to be standing with their robes gathered up for walking and with shoes on their feet. That was because God had told them to be prepared to leave Egypt as soon as the word came from Pharaoh (Exod. 12:7-11). This has continued to be the way the Samaritans celebrate the Passover on Mt. Gerizim.

In Jerusalem, the feast began by filling a cup for each guest with the fruit of the vine (grape juice). Then it was blessed by the host. After this, hands were washed in a basin of water, and a table was brought in on which were placed bitter herbs, unleavened bread, a dip made of dates, raisins, and vinegar (others mention nuts, raisins, apples, and almonds), the Passover lamb, and an additional sacrifice called the chagigah, which provided additional meat in case the lamb was not enough to satisfy everyone's hunger. It would be eaten as the lamb was eaten.

The fruit of the vine was the red grape juice of Palestine. It was mixed with water, one part of grape juice to two parts of water. Four times during the evening, cups were filled with the fruit of the vine. The cup mentioned by Luke before the Lord's Supper was one of the earlier cups, perhaps the first.

The "sop" such as Jesus handed to Judas usually consisted of some of the meat of the Passover Lamb, a piece of unleavened bread, and bitter herbs wrapped together.

Interestingly, after the Passover lamb was eaten, nothing else was to be eaten according to Jewish tradition, but Jesus, realizing that this was the last Passover with the force of law, after the supper instituted a new supper that should be eaten in memory of Him.

It is also significant that the first Passover was instituted immediately before Israel was delivered from bondage and before they became the people of God. So, here, the Lord's Supper was instituted before the people of God from all nations were delivered from sin and before they became that "royal priesthood" and that "holy nation" (1 Pet. 2:9).

It would be erroneous to think that Jesus adapted the Passover to the Lord's Supper. His feast was a brand new one. Two elements used in the Passover were used by the Lord: unleavened bread and the fruit of the vine, but Jesus Himself is our Passover sacrifice.

Jesus institutes the Lord's Supper (Mark 14:22-25; Matt. 26:26-29: Luke 22:17-20; cf. 1 Cor. 11:23-26):

NOTE:
  Mark and Matthew are virtually identical in their accounts while Luke's account is very similar to that of Paul's in 1 Corinthians 11.

According to Luke, Jesus took a cup of the fruit of the vine early in the evening and said, "Take this and divide it among you. For I tell you I will not drink again of the fruit of the vine until the kingdom of God comes."

Then later in the evening, but while they were still eating, Jesus took bread and blessed it and broke it and gave it to the disciples and said, "Take this and eat it, for it is my body which is broken for you. Do this in remembrance of me."

In the same way, after supper (likely the fourth and last cup of the Passover) Jesus took a cup of grape juice, and having given thanks, He said, "This cup is the blood of the new covenant which is shed for many in order to secure the removal of sins. I tell you I will not drink of this fruit of the vine from now on until I drink it anew with you in my Father's kingdom."

NOTE:
  The expression "blood of the covenant" found in Matthew 26:28 is identical to the one used by Moses at Mt. Sinai many years earlier as the Israelites sealed their covenant with God. On that occasion they promised to do all that God had commanded so that they might enter into a covenant relationship with Him, so that He would be their God and they could be His people (Exod. 24; see particularly v. 8).

  In the same way, the sacrifice of Christ enables us to have a covenant relationship with God. He is our Father and we are His children. Therefore, as we remember this sacrifice of Christ in observing the Lord's Supper, we should also remember that the sacrifice enables us to have the enormous blessing of forgiveness and the hope of heaven.

  The Israelites wanted the blessings that came from God, but they were quick to forget they had obligations on their side of the covenant. Let us learn the lesson from their example and remember to keep our side of our covenant with God. As we take the Lord's Supper and remember His death, let us examine ourselves to be sure we are each one keeping our promise to God that we made when we were baptized and became a part of the family of God.

The farewell discourse in the upper room (John 14):

Jesus continued talking to His disciples: "Do not let your hearts be troubled. You trust in God, believe in me also. In my Father's estate there are many dwelling places. If it were not so, I would have told you. I am going to prepare a place for you. And if I go to prepare a place for you, I will come and take you to be with me so that you can be where I am. And you know the way to the place where I am going."

Thomas said, "Lord, we do not know where you are going. How should we know the way?"

Jesus replied, "I am the way, and the truth, and the life. No one can come to the Father but by me. If you had really known me, you would have known my Father also. From now on, you know Him and have seen Him."

Philip seemed to feel that he had missed seeing the Father, so he said to Jesus, "Lord, show us the Father, and that will be all we could ever wish."

Jesus answered:

Have I been with you all this time, and yet you do not know me, Philip? When you see me, you have seen the Father. How can you say, "Show us the Father"? Do you not believe that I am in the Father and the Father in me? The words I tell you, I do not get from myself, but the Father who is always in me is doing His works. Believe me when I say I am in the Father and the Father is in me. Or, at least, believe me because of the works you have seen.

Truly, I tell you, he who believes on me, the works which I do, he will do also. And even greater works he will do, because I go to the Father. And whatever you ask in my name, I will do, so that the Father may be glorified in the Son. If you ask for anything in my name, I will do it. If you love me you will keep my commandments.

I will ask the Father, and He will give you another helper so that He may be with you forever, even the Spirit of truth. The world cannot receive Him because it does not behold Him, nor does it know Him, but He will abide in you, and will be in you. I will not leave you abandoned; I will help you.

Just a little while, and the world will behold me no more; but you behold me. Because I live, you will live also. In that day you will know that I am in my Father, and you in me, and I in you. The one who has my commandments, and keeps them, he is the one who loves me. And the one who loves me will be loved by my Father. And I will love him and show myself to him.

Judas, not Iscariot, (probably the one we usually call Thaddaeus, see Luke 6:16) said, "Lord, what is going to happen that you will show yourself to us, and not to the world?"

Jesus answered and said:

If a man love me, he will keep my word, and my Father will love him. We will come to him, and reside in him. He who does not love me, does not keep my word. And the words you hear are not mine, but the Father's who sent me.

I have told you these things while I still remain with you, but the Helper, even the Holy Spirit, whom the Father will send in my name, He will teach you all things and will cause you to remember everything I have told you. I am leaving peace with you. I mean *my* peace, not that of the world. Do not let your heart be troubled, neither be afraid. You heard how I said, "I go away," and "I am coming to you." If you loved me, you would have rejoiced because

I am going to the Father, because the Father is greater than I. Now I have told you before it happens, so that when it happens, you will believe. I will not speak much more to you because the prince of this world is coming to make his move. He has no use for me, but in order that the world may know that I love the Father, and as the Father gave me commandment, so I do.

It is time, let us go.

NOTE:

Notice that in John 14:31, Jesus says, "Rise up and let us go forth." This probably indicates that Jesus and His apostles left the upper room at the close of chapter 14 and were on their way out to the Garden of Gethsemane as Jesus continued the message recorded in John 15-17. Or, He may be saying that the time for His death is growing ever closer, and this is an admonition to be ready. We cannot be sure.

If Jesus did not speak these things as they were on their way to Gethsemane, then John 14:31 is a puzzle. Certainly the conversation between Jesus and His apostles on that journey would have been sober and yet beautiful, just as the chapters of John are. Nevertheless, the chronology is not the essence of our lesson. It is a minor consideration. Be sure and keep it minor as you teach your students.

Jesus and His disciples depart from the upper room (Mark 14:26; Matt. 26:30):

Jesus and His disciples sang a hymn, probably one of the Psalms, as they rose to leave the upper room. Then they prepared to go out to the Mount of Olives where they had spent the other nights during this week (see Luke 21:37).

Discourse on the way to Gethsemane (John 15-16):

Jesus said:

I am the true vine, and my Father is the vinedresser. Every branch in me which does not bear fruit, He prunes away. And every branch that bears fruit, He trims it so that it may bear more fruit. Already you are trimmed because of the word I have told you. Remain in me, and I will remain in you. As a branch cannot bear fruit of itself, unless it remains attached to the vine, so neither can you bear fruit unless you abide in me.

I am the vine; you are the branches. The one who remains in me and I in him, that one will bear much fruit, because apart from me, he can do nothing. If he does not remain in me, he will be cast forth as a branch which withers. They gather the dead branches and cast them into the fire, and they are burned. If you remain in me, and my words remain in you, ask whatsoever you will, and it will be done to you. This is the way my Father will be glorified, that is, that you bear much fruit. In this way you will be my disciples.

Just as my Father has loved me, I also have loved you. Remain in my love. The way for you to do that is to keep my commandments, just as I have kept my Father's commandments and have remained in His love.

These things I have told you, that my joy may be in you and that your joy may be fulfilled. This is my commandment to you, that you love one another, even as I have loved you. No man can have greater love than this, that he would lay down his life for his friends. You are my friends if you do the things I command you.

No longer do I call you bond-servants because a bond-servant is not told what his lord is doing. No, I am calling you friends, because everything I have heard from the Father, I have made known to you.

You did not choose me, but I chose you, and appointed you to go and bear fruit; and that your fruit should last, so that whatever you ask of the Father in my name, He may give it to you.

These things I command you, that you may love one another. If the world hates you, realize that it hated me before it hated you. If you were of the world, the world would love its own. But because you are not of the world, but I chose you and took you out of the world, therefore the world hates you. Remember what I told you: "A servant is not greater than his lord." If they persecuted me, they will also persecute you. If they keep my word, they will keep yours also. But all these things they do to you for my name's sake, they will do because they do not know God.

If I had not come and told them, they would not be responsible, but now they have no excuse for their sins. (This refers to the particular sin of rejecting Jesus as the Christ.) He that hates me hates my Father also. If I had not done among them the works that no other man did, they would not have sin (would not be responsible for not believing), but now they have both seen and hated both me and my Father. But this has happened to fulfill the word written in their law: "They hated me without a cause" (Psa. 35:19; 69:4).

But when the Helper comes, whom I will send to you from the Father, even the Spirit of truth, which goes forth from the Father, He will bear witness of me. You will also bear witness because you have been with me from the beginning.

Chapter 16: Jesus continues:

I have told you these things so that you will not be caused to stumble. You will be put out of synagogues. Indeed, the hour will come when whoever kills you will think he is serving God. These things they will do because they have known neither the Father, nor me. I did not tell you earlier because I was with you. But now I am going back to the One who sent me, and none of you is asking me, "Where are you going?" But because I have told you these things, sorrow has filled your hearts. Nevertheless, I tell the truth. It is good for you that I go away, because if I do not go away, the Helper will not come to you. But if I go, I will send Him unto you. And He, when He has come, will convict the world in respect of sin, and of righteousness, and of judgment: of sin, because they do not believe on me; of righteousness, because I go to the Father, and you will look upon me no more; of judgment, because the prince of this world has been judged.

I have yet many things to say to you, but you cannot deal with them now. However, when the Spirit of truth is come, He will guide you into all the truth because He will not speak from Himself, but whatever He hears, these things He will speak. He will announce unto you the things that are to come. He will glorify me, because He will take of mine, and will announce it to you. All things the Father has are mine. That is why I said that He takes of mine and will announce it to you. A little while, and you will look upon me no more; and again after a little while, you will see me.

The disciples were puzzled. They began to ask among themselves, "What does He mean by saying, 'A little while and you will see me no more, and again a little while and you will see me,' and 'because I go to the Father'? We do not understand what He is talking about."

Jesus knew they wanted to ask Him about His statements, so He said:

Are you wondering among yourselves what I mean by my statement about your not seeing me after a while, and then a little later seeing me again? I tell you truly that you will weep and be sorry, but the world will rejoice. You will be sorrowful, but your sorrow will be turned into joy. It is like a woman giving birth; she has sorrow at the time of delivery, but when she has her baby, she does not remember the anguish any more for the joy that a man is born into the world. You, therefore, have sorrow now, but I will see you again, and your hearts will rejoice, and no one will be able to take away your joy. In that day, you will have no questions to ask me. I tell you, truly, if you ask anything of the Father, He will give it to you in my name. Up until now you have asked for nothing in my name; ask and receive so that your joy may be made complete.

I have spoken to you in parables, but the time is coming when I will not speak any more in figures, but will tell you plainly from the Father. In that day you will ask in my name, although I do not mean that I will have to ask the Father for you, because He Himself loves you because you have loved me and have believed that I came forth from the Father. I came from the Father into the world; now I leave the world and go again unto the Father.

Jesus' disciples said, "Now you speak plainly and not in figures. Now we know that you know all things, and there is no need for any man to ask you questions. By this we believe that you are come from God."

Jesus answered them: "Do you believe? Consider this: the hour is coming, in fact it is now time, that you will be scattered, everyone of you, and you will abandon me. Yet I will not be abandoned because the Father is with me. I have told you these things so that in me you can have peace. In this world you will have tribulation, but take courage, for I have overcome the world."

Jesus' prayer to the Father (John 17):

Having completed His words to the apostles, Jesus looked up to the heavens and said:

Father, the hour has come. Glorify your Son, that your Son may glorify you, even as you gave Him authority over all flesh, so that to all those you have given Him, He may give eternal life. And this is life eternal that they should know you, the only true God, and that they should know the One you have sent, Jesus Christ. I glorified you on earth since I have accomplished the work you sent me to do.

And now, O Father, glorify me in company with yourself with the glory I shared with you even before the world was. I showed your name to the men you gave me out of the world. They were yours and you gave them to me, and they kept your word. Now they know that every single thing you have given me is from you, because the words you gave me, I have given them. They received them and knew that it was indeed true that I came forth from you, and they believed you sent me.

I pray for them. I do not pray for the world, but for those whom you have given me,

163

because they are yours. All things that are mine are yours, and I am glorified in them. And I am to be no more in the world, but these will continue in the world, and I am coming to you. Holy Father, keep them which you have given me in your name, so that they may be one, even as we are.

While I was with them, I kept them which you gave me in your name. I guarded them, and not one of them perished, except the son of destruction and ruin. He fell so that the scripture might be fulfilled.

But now I am coming to you, and I speak these things while I am still in the world, so that they might have the full measure of my joy in them. I have given them your word; and the world hated them, because they are not of the world, just as I am not of the world. I do not pray that you would take them from the world, but that you should keep them from the evil one. Make them special by the use of truth. Your word is truth.

As you sent me into the world, even so I send them into the world. And for their sakes I dedicate myself (as a sacrifice) that they themselves may also be set apart as special by the use of the truth.

Neither do I pray for these alone, but also for those that believe on me through their word, that they all may be one. May they be one even as you, Father, are in me, and I in you, that they also may be in us, so that the world may believe that you sent me.

And the glory that you have given me, I have given them, that they may be one, even as we are one: I in them, and you in me. May they be brought to complete unity to let the world know that you sent me and have loved them even as you have loved me.

Father, I will that those you have given me, will be with me where I am so that they can behold my glory, which you have given me, because you loved me before the foundation of the world. O righteous Father, the world knew you not, but I knew you, and these know that you did send me. And I have made your reputation and character known to them, and will continue to make it known, so that the love with which you loved me may be among them, and I among them.

NOTE:

In this prayer to God, there is a distance between Jesus and His apostles, a distance between the human beings of the world, who were helpless to do anything to save themselves, and the Divine Man, who alone could do what had to be done. Jesus had taught and nurtured His disciples for over three years. Now He faces His greatest trial. He has come to the turning point of all eternity. Though His disciples are on His mind, even during His suffering, yet now He rises above humanity to that point between heaven and earth where He, both Man and God, must do the task no other in Heaven or upon the earth could do.

Jesus enters Gethsemane and prays in agony (Mark 14:32-42; Matt. 26:36-46; Luke 22:39-46; John 18:1):

Jesus and the disciples crossed the dark Kidron Valley over to the Mount of Olives where there was an enclosed garden called Gethsemane (an olive grove). He told His apostles, "Sit here while I pray, and you need to pray that you do not come into temptation."

Then He took Peter, James, and John with Him a little further into the garden. The Lord became very troubled. He told the three men with Him, "My soul is extremely sorrowful, even unto death. Stay here and watch with me."

Then He went forward a little more, fell on His face, and prayed: "O my Father, if it be possible, let this cup pass away from me; nevertheless let it not be as I want but as you want."

Jesus returned to find His apostles asleep. He said to Peter, "Simon, are you asleep? Could you not watch with me one hour? Watch and pray that you do not enter into temptation. The spirit is indeed willing, but the flesh is weak."

Again Jesus returned to pray. At some point before He finished praying, an angel appeared to Him, strengthening Him. Being in agony, He prayed more earnestly, and His sweat became as it were great drops of blood falling upon the ground. This second time, He prayed, "O my Father, if this cup cannot pass away, unless I drink it, your will be done."

He came again and found His disciples still asleep, because their eyes were heavy, and they did not know what to say. Luke adds the comment that they were "sleeping for sorrow" or, as we might say it, exhausted from sorrow.

A third time, Jesus went away and prayed. Then He came back to the disciples and said, "Do you sleep now and take your rest? It is enough. The time has come for the Son of Man to be betrayed into the hands of sinners. Get up and let us go because the one who betrays me is near."

The Trial

The arrest of Jesus (Mark 14:43-52; Matt. 26:47-56; Luke 22:47-53; John 18:2-12):

Judas was familiar with the garden of Gethsemane because Jesus often went there with His disciples. So, having gathered soldiers and officers from the chief priests and the Pharisees, Judas led them there. They were armed with lanterns, torches, and weapons. A great mob came to the entrance to the garden.

> NOTE:
> The soldiers included Roman soldiers as well as Jewish temple guards. The term "sword" in Matthew 26:47, and the references to the "band" (John 18:3,12), and to the "chief captain" (John 18:12), show that Romans were there. The sword was the Roman short-sword, the band was the Roman cohort, and the chief captain was the military tribune or chiliarch. The officers and captains of the temple (John 18:3,12,18,22) were Jewish temple guards. It was a very strong force that came out to seize Jesus. There is, however, not one iota of evidence that Pilate was in on the plot at this point in the story. Indeed, evidence points to the contrary.

The noise of the multitude interrupted Jesus even as He spoke to His sleeping disciples. Jesus, knowing everything that was coming upon Him, went out to meet the mob. Now Judas had given the multitude a sign that he would use to point out which one Jesus was, as if he expected Jesus to be difficult to find. The sign was a kiss. Jesus did not, however, wait for Judas to identify Him. He approached the crowd and said, "Whom do you seek?"

They replied, "Jesus of Nazareth."

Jesus said, "I am He."

Judas was standing with the leaders of the multitude. When Jesus spoke, the multitude went backward and fell to the ground. (Was this not the man who had power to raise the dead and still the storms at sea? They were afraid of Him.)

Jesus asked again, "Whom do you seek?"

Again they replied, "Jesus of Nazareth."

Jesus said, "I have told you I am He. If you seek me, then let these who are with me go," so that the scripture would be fulfilled which said, "of those whom you gave me, I did not lose one" (John 17:12).

Judas came forward at that moment and said, "Rabbi," and kissed Jesus (perhaps to show the multitude it was safe to approach Him).

Jesus said, "Judas, do you betray the Son of Man with a kiss?" Then He said, "Friend, do what you have come to do."

Jesus' disciples, seeing what was about to happen, said, "Lord, do you want us to fight with the sword?"

NOTE:
What courage, that eleven men with two swords would take on a mob of armed Roman soldiers and temple guards! They had the courage to fight, but not the courage to submit to death, as we shall see.

Before anything else could be said or done, Peter drew his sword and struck a servant of the high priest, cutting off his ear. The servant's name was Malchus.

Jesus said, "No more of this," and He touched the servant's ear and healed him. Then He said to Peter, "Put your sword back into its sheath because all those who take the sword shall die by the sword. Do you not realize that I could ask my Father, and He would send me twelve legions of angels? Shall I not drink the cup which my Father has given me? How would the scriptures be fulfilled which state that it must be so?"

NOTE:
The mob did not take Jesus until Jesus was ready to be taken. He *gave* His life; it was not *taken* from Him (see John 10:17-18). There is a significant difference.

The soldiers seized Jesus and bound Him. He asked them, "Why have you come out with swords and clubs to take me prisoner, as if you were taking a thief into custody? Every day I was with you in the temple teaching; you did not take me then. But this is your hour, and the power of darkness. All of this is happening so that the writings of the prophets may be fulfilled."

Jesus' disciples, seeing Him taken captive, scattered and fled. One young man who had followed along with Jesus and the disciples had a linen garment wrapped around him. Apparently he had come hurriedly, because he had no other clothes on. When soldiers seized him, he left the linen cloth and fled naked.

NOTE:
Mark is the only writer that mentions this young man. This has led many to assume he was Mark. No one knows for sure.

Jesus before Annas (John 18:12-14, 19-23):

The multitude, having seized Jesus, and having bound Him, took Him to Annas first. Annas was father-in-law to Caiaphas who was the high priest that year. Annas had been high priest before Caiaphas and was still referred to as high priest as an honorary title.

Annas asked Jesus about His disciples and about His teaching. Jesus answered, "I have spoken openly to the world. I always taught in the synagogues, and in the temple, where all Jews gather together. I spoke nothing in secret. Why do you ask me? Ask those who heard me what I said. They know the things I said."

When He said this, one of the officers standing by struck Jesus with his open hand, saying, "Do you answer the high priest in such a way?"

Jesus responded, "If I have spoken evil, tell me what I said wrong; but if I said only what was proper, then why do you hit me?"

Jesus is condemned and mistreated by the Sanhedrin (Mark 14:53,55-65; Matt. 26:59-68; Luke 22:54,63-65; John 18:24):

Annas sent Jesus on, still bound, to the house of Caiaphas. It was still night, but all the chief priests, scribes, and the elders (Sanhedrin, the Jewish council) were gathered together.

> NOTE:
> The council's meeting in the night for trial was illegal. They also gave Jesus no opportunity to prepare a defense or to call witnesses to testify for Him. Instead, they tried to find witnesses who would condemn Him. The whole procedure was illegal and wicked from start to finish.

The council sought witnesses to condemn Jesus. Many witnesses testified, but they were false witnesses, and even their testimony did not agree. Finally two men said, "This man said, 'I am able to destroy the temple of God, and to build it in three days.'" Even their testimony did not fully agree.

The high priest stood up and asked Jesus, "Do you have nothing to say? What is this thing which has been testified concerning you?" But Jesus made no reply.

The high priest pressed Him: "I put you under oath to the living God to tell us the truth: are you the Christ, the Son of God?"

Jesus answered, "I am, and the time will come when you will see the Son of Man sitting at the right hand of Power (God), and coming with the clouds of heaven."

The high priest tore his clothes and said, "He has spoken blasphemy! What further need do we have for witnesses? Look, you yourselves heard Him blaspheme. What is your decision?"

Everyone said, "He is worthy to die." As they condemned Him, their anger knew no bounds. They spat on Him; they blindfolded Him and slapped Him and said, "Prophesy, O you Christ, who just hit you?" They reviled Him in many ways and mistreated Him.

Peter denies Christ three times (Mark 14:54,66-72; Matt. 26:58,69-75; Luke 22:54-62; John 18:15-18,25-27):

Two of the disciples followed Jesus: one followed fairly closely, the other, who was Peter, followed afar off.

NOTE:

Almost certainly, the one who followed Jesus closely was John because he is the one who tells that part of the story, and he never calls his own name in his book.

This unnamed disciple was known to the high priest and entered with Jesus into the courtyard. Peter stood outside. So the other disciple went to the woman who was keeping the door and had her let Peter in. She continued, however, to watch Peter.

It was cold that night, and the servants and officers had built a fire of charcoal and were warming themselves. Peter joined them at the fire and waited to see what would happen. The maid who kept the door looked very carefully at Peter in the light of the fire and asked, "Are you also one of this man's followers?"

Peter answered, "No, I am not." Then he moved away from the fire to another part of the court — and a rooster crowed! It was still before dawn, not the usual time for the rooster to crow. That time was called "cock crow."

After a while, someone else saw Peter and said, "This man also was with Jesus the Nazarene." But Peter denied with an oath and said, "I do not know the man."

About an hour passed by and someone said, "You really are one of them. I can tell by your speech that you are a Galilean."

One of the servants of the high priest, a kinsman of Malchus whose ear Peter had cut off, said, "Did I not see you in the garden with Him?"

Peter began to curse and to swear, "I do not know this man, I tell you." Immediately, the rooster crowed a second time! It was cock crow. Dawn's light was beginning to show.

The Lord turned and looked straight at Peter. Then Peter remembered that Jesus had told him that before the cock crow, or before the rooster crowed twice, he would deny Him three times. Peter went out from the court, and, realizing what he had done, wept bitterly.

After dawn, Jesus is formally condemned by the Sanhedrin (Mark 15:1; Matt. 27:1; Luke 22:66-71):

As soon as it was day, Jesus was taken before the council (Sanhedrin) a second time. Their strategy had already been worked out during the night. They said to Jesus, "If you are the Son of God, tell us."

But He said, "If I tell you, you will not believe, and if I ask you, you will not answer. But hereafter you will see the Son of Man seated on the right hand of the power of God."

They all replied, "Are you then the Son of God?"

Jesus answered, "I am."

The council members said, "What further need do we have of testimony? We ourselves have heard from His own mouth what He says."

NOTE:

This farce of a second trial was an effort to make the action they had already taken legal, but no ratification of wrong can make it right.

Judas Iscariot commits suicide (Matt. 27:3-10; Acts 1:18-19):

When Judas saw that Jesus was condemned to death, he deeply regretted what he had done. He brought the thirty pieces of silver back to the chief priests and elders and said, "I have sinned because I betrayed innocent blood."

They said, "What do we care? That is your problem!"

Judas threw the money down into the temple and fled. He went out and hanged himself. Either immediately, or perhaps a little later, the thing upon which he hanged himself, or the rope, broke and Judas' body fell into a field which was purchased with the money he had been paid to betray Jesus.

Meanwhile, the chief priests picked up the money which had been thrown down and said, "It is against the law to put this money into the treasury, since it is blood money." (Is it not ironic that they could callously kill an innocent man and pay for his betrayal, but they objected to putting that same money into the treasury?)

They decided to buy a potter's field in which to bury strangers. Therefore the field was called Akeldama, which means "field of blood." Then was fulfilled the statement spoken by Jeremiah saying, "And they took the thirty pieces of silver, the price put upon the head of the one whom the children of Israel priced, and they gave them for the potter's field, as the Lord appointed me."

> NOTE:
>
> This quotation is from Zechariah 11:13. Matthew may have said Jeremiah because of his references to buying a field (Jer. 32:6-15). Sometimes a writer of the New Testament would combine elements from two different prophets and refer to the more prominent one as his source.

Jesus is brought to Pilate for the first time (Mark 15:1-5; Matt. 27:2,11-14; Luke 23:1-7; John 18:28-38):

Jesus was bound and taken by the Jews to the praetorium which was in the Tower of Antonia just northwest of the temple enclosure. It was still very early in the morning. The Jews were putting an innocent man to death, but they would not enter into the judgment hall lest they should be defiled and not be able to eat the Passover.

> NOTE:
>
> Some have been very confused by the statement that they should not be able to eat the Passover (John 18:28). Some reason, therefore, that Jesus did not actually eat the Passover on the night before His betrayal. Yet the scriptures unequivocally state that He did (Matt. 26:17-19; Mark 14:12-16; Luke 22:1,7-15).
>
> The Passover referred to in John 18:28 could not have referred to the eating of the Passover lamb anyway, because uncleanness from entering a place of the Gentiles only lasted until sunset, and the Passover lamb was eaten in the evening. So defilement early in the day on Friday would not have prevented the Jews from eating the Passover lamb Friday night.
>
> The truth is that the whole week of Unleavened Bread was called Passover (Luke 22:1) and that the term Passover was applied not only to the Passover lamb, but also to all sacrifices offered during the whole week. The day following the eating of the

Passover lamb was the first festive day of the week of Unleavened Bread. The offering for that day was offered immediately after the morning services, and was eaten on that same day. It was *this* Passover offering which the Jews did not want to miss because of defilement.

Obligingly, Pilate went out to meet the Jews. He asked, "What accusation do you bring against this man?"

They answered, "If this man were not an evil-doer, we would not have brought Him to you."

Pilate said, "Take Him yourselves, and judge Him according to your law."

NOTE:

It appeared at this point that the Jews hoped Pilate would take their word for Jesus' guilt and just go ahead and execute Him. Then Pilate may have been taunting them as he told them to take Him and judge Him by their own law. There was no love lost between Pilate and the Jews.

The Jews replied, "It is not legal for us to put any man to death. But we have found this man leading our nation astray, and forbidding to pay taxes to Caesar, and saying that He Himself is Christ, a king."

NOTE:

It is true that it was illegal for the Jews to put anyone to death, but the next two statements were audacious lies. Nevertheless, they got the attention of Pilate. While the Jews, from their viewpoint, might have convinced themselves that Jesus was leading the nation astray, there was no way they could have thought that He forbade paying taxes to Caesar. Only three days earlier, He had gone on public record saying that it *was* lawful to pay tribute to Caesar.

Observe that they are accusing Jesus of being the very kind of king they had wanted the Messiah to be. If Jesus had come as the conquering, military king who would lead an army against Rome, the Jews would have been glad to accept Him. Now, they make this accusation because they know this is the one that will get the attention of a Roman official most quickly.

Pilate entered the judgment hall and had Jesus brought to him. He asked, "Are you the king of the Jews?"

Jesus answered, "Is this your question, or do you ask it just because of what you have heard?"

Pilate was offended. "Am I a Jew? Your own nation has delivered you to me. What have you done?"

Jesus replied, "My kingdom is not of this world. If it were, then my servants would fight to keep me from being delivered up. But my kingdom is not of this world."

Pilate asked, "Then are you a king?"

Jesus answered, "Yes. For this purpose I was born, and to this end I have come into the world, that I should tell men what the truth is. Everyone who wants the truth listens to me."

Pilate replied, "What is truth?" Then he turned and went back out to the Jews and said, "I find no crime in this man."

But the chief priests and elders were rabid in accusing Jesus. Having been brought back out, Jesus stood quietly, saying nothing. Pilate was amazed at Him. "Listen to all these accusations! Do you have nothing to say?" But Jesus continued in silence.

The Jews, however, kept on clamoring, saying, "He has stirred up the people, teaching throughout all Judea. He began in Galilee and has continued His teaching even to this place."

Pilate's ears perked up when they said "Galilee." He thought he saw a way out for himself. "Is He a Galilean?"

When they assured him that Jesus was indeed a Galilean and, therefore, under the jurisdiction of Herod, Pilate sent Him to Antipas who was in Jerusalem for the feast.

Jesus before Herod Antipas (Luke 23:6-12):

When Herod saw Jesus, he was very glad because he had wanted to see Him for a long time. He had heard much about Jesus and hoped he would get to see Him do a miracle.

Herod asked Jesus many questions, but Jesus made no response whatever. The chief priests and elders kept up their torrent of accusations which Jesus ignored also.

So Herod and his soldiers mocked Jesus. They dressed Him in gorgeous apparel, as a joke, for, after all, was He not the king of the Jews? Then Herod sent Jesus back to Pilate.

From that day on, Herod and Pilate were friends. Before this, they had been enemies.

> HISTORICAL NOTE:
> Perhaps this would be a good time to take a look at Pontius Pilate. We know very little about him outside of what the Bible tells us. In 1961, a stone slab was found at Caesarea with his name on it. The Roman historian Tacitus says that Jesus Christ "suffered under the procurator Pontius Pilate." He is also mentioned by two Jewish writers, Josephus and Philo, who tell us several incidents in which Pilate came into conflict with the Jews.
>
> He was appointed procurator of Judea in A.D. 26 and ruled until A.D. 36. Due to problems he had with the Jews, Pilate was finally deposed by the Roman governor of Syria, Vitellius. Pilate is described as a harsh, spiteful, and brutal man. One reason why he may have given in to the Jews as he did on this occasion was his fear of causing another tumult. Eusebius recorded that Pilate committed suicide after returning to Rome.

Jesus before Pilate the second time (Mark 15:6-14; Matt. 27:15-23; Luke 23:13-22; John 18:39-40):

Pilate called the chief priests, the rulers, and the people together and told them, "You brought this man to me as one who leads the people astray. Having examined His case thoroughly, I find no fault in Him regarding the accusations you have made. Neither does Herod because he sent Him back having found that He has done nothing worthy of death. I will therefore scourge Him and release Him."

At some point, while Pilate sat on the judgment seat, his wife sent him a message saying, "Do not have anything to do with that righteous man, because I have suffered many things today because of a dream I had about Him."

At the Passover, it was customary for some prisoner held captive by the Romans to be released. There was a prisoner named Barabbas in custody. He was a terrorist and had committed murder in his activities as an insurrectionist.

Pilate, therefore, said to the Jews, "Whom would you like for me to release to you, Barabbas, or Jesus, which is called the Christ, the king of the Jews?"

According to Matthew's account, the Jewish leaders had anticipated somehow that this choice might be given and had made plans to see that it would not be Jesus who was released. They had persuaded the multitude to ask for the release of Barabbas. Therefore the crowd shouted, "Take this fellow away and release unto us Barabbas."

Pilate taunted them: "What then shall I do with Him whom you call king of the Jews?"

"Crucify Him!" the multitude replied.

> NOTE:
>
> Notice that Matthew and Mark both say that Pilate gave Jesus over to be scourged and crucified, as if the scourging immediately preceded the crucifixion, but John gives one more conversation between Pilate and the Jews before sentence was given. John does not relate the statement of the Jews that "His blood be upon us and upon our children." As they have done in other circumstances, Matthew and Mark simply group the scourging and the crucifixion together without giving details about the scourging. John gives the more detailed account of the order of the scourging and sentencing. It is impossible to tell exactly which taunting statement from Pilate came first and which of the shouts from the Jews came first in this portion. We have tried to include all the details as best we can, but we cannot be certain of the exact order of each thing.

Jesus is scourged and mocked by the Roman soldiers (Mark 15:16-19; Matt. 27:27-31; John 19:1-3):

At this point, Pilate sent Jesus away to be scourged.

> NOTE:
>
> How simply the statement is made that Pilate scourged Jesus. But how excruciating was the reality of scourging! The scourge was a whip with a handle (or stock) and several lashes. Bits of metal and bone were often embedded in the lashes. The results of a whipping by such an instrument were gruesome. It was quite easy for someone to be scourged to death. The scourging would not leave mere welts upon the skin, but would tear gashes in the flesh through which internal organs might be exposed. We are not told how severe Jesus' beating was, but it was only part of the ordeal He suffered. It was due in great part to this scourging that Jesus was too weak to carry His own cross only a short time later and that He died after only six hours on the cross.

After Jesus was scourged, the soldiers who had led Him away called the whole company of soldiers around Jesus and began to mock Him. They plaited a crown of thorns and put it on His head. They draped Him with a purple robe and placed a reed in His hand for a scepter to mock His claim to be king. They came to Jesus and bowed before Him saying, "Hail, King of the Jews." They spat on Him and struck Him on the head repeatedly.

> NOTE:
> To these wicked Roman soldiers, it was only a joke that such a man in this condition could be king of anything. If only they had known!

Pilate gives in to the Jews and sentences Jesus to be crucified (Mark 15:12-15; Matt. 27:22-26; Luke 23:20-25; John 19:4-16):

It is the book of John that tells us that after the scourging, the soldiers took Jesus back to Pilate who brought Him out to the Jews and said, "Look, I am bringing Him out before you so that you may know that I find Him guilty of no crime." Jesus was still wearing the crown of thorns and the purple garment as a cruel parody of royalty. Pilate said, "Look at the man!"

> NOTE:
> Was Pilate seeking to gain sympathy for Jesus or to show that any pretension He made to be king of the Jews was absurd so that he could release Him? Perhaps so, because it seems he did want to release Him by this time, but he did not have the moral courage to do so.

When the crowd shouted, "Crucify, crucify," Pilate said, "You take Him and crucify Him, because I find no crime in Him."

> NOTE:
> This was the petulant, frustrated reply of a man who knew what he should do, but realized he was going to allow himself to be persuaded by what the crowd wanted. He knew the Jews did not have the power to crucify.

The Jews replied, "We have a law, and by that law He ought to die, because He made Himself the Son of God."

When he heard this, Pilate was even more afraid. He took Jesus back into the judgment hall and said, "Where are you from?" Jesus did not answer.

Pilate said, "Are you not going to speak to me? Don't you realize that I have power to release you and power to crucify you?"

Jesus answered, "You would have no power against me, except that it was given to you from above. Therefore, he who delivered me to you has the greater sin."

Pilate continued to try to release Jesus, but the Jews used their most potent argument on Pilate: "If you release this man, you are not Caesar's friend. Everyone who sets himself up as a king opposes Caesar."

When Pilate heard this, he brought Jesus out to give his decision. He could not refrain from taunting the Jews as he said, "Look, it is your king!"

In anger, they cried, "Take Him away; crucify Him!"

Pilate said, "You would not have me crucify your king!"

The chief priests said, "We have no king but Caesar."

When Pilate saw that he was getting nowhere and that a riot was building, he took water and washed his hands before the multitude, saying, "I am innocent of the blood of this righteous man. It is your responsibility."

All the people answered, "Let His blood be upon us and upon our children."

Then in order to please the crowd, Pilate gave the sentence for Jesus to be crucified and released Barabbas unto them.

NOTE:

The Jews gladly accepted the responsibility of Jesus' death, but they had no idea of the enormity of what they were saying. They reached the peak of their wickedness when they rejected the Son of God, the Messiah they had been promised for so long. They were glad to accept the consequences of Jesus' death at this point when they thought there would be no consequences, but we will see how quickly they forgot their words (Acts 5:28).

The Crucifixion

Jesus is led away to be crucified (Mark 15:20-23; Matt. 27:31-34; Luke 23:26-32; John 19:16-17):

Jesus' own garments were put back on Him and He was led away to be crucified. The soldiers placed the cross on Jesus' back forcing Him to carry it, but He was too weak to hold it. Therefore, the soldiers compelled a man named Simon of Cyrene, who was a passer-by, to carry the cross for Jesus.

NOTE:

Mark's account says that Simon was the father of Alexander and Rufus. Since these names are given to help identify Simon, it is believed that these men were well known to the readers of Mark's account, hence Christians. This is all we know about Simon.

A great multitude of the people followed Jesus. There were women in the group weeping and wailing, but Jesus turned to them and said, "Daughters of Jerusalem, do not weep for me; weep for yourselves and for your children. Because the days are coming when people will say, 'Blessed are those who could never have children.' Then they will begin to say to the mountains, 'Fall on us,' and to the hills, 'Cover us.' Because if they do these things when the tree is green, what will they do when it is dead?"

NOTE:

Jesus meant that if all the multitude saw was an innocent man being led away to be put to death, then they were not seeing the true situation. Because of this event, judgment would come upon the nation of Israel. If now, while the tree of Judaism was still alive and green, the Jews were capable of cursing their Savior and putting Him to death, what frenzies of madness would they commit when the tree of Judaism was dead and rotten?

Two criminals were led out with Jesus to be put to death also. So, they brought Him to Golgotha which in the Aramaic language means "the place of the skull." Calvary is the Latin word which means the same thing.

NOTE:

The scriptures do not refer to the "hill of Calvary," but to the "place" of Calvary or Golgotha. Why it was called the place of the skull is not known. The two main explanations are: first, that it was a place associated with skulls (executions); but much more likely, that it was a hill shaped like a skull. No one knows the exact spot where Jesus was crucified.

Before the crucifixion, Jesus was offered wine mixed with gall (myrrh). When Jesus tasted it, He would have none of it.

NOTE:

This substance had a stupefying effect on the victim. We are not told who offered the wine, whether the soldiers or, as some authorities have suggested, the women of Jerusalem. It was offered as an act of kindness, but Jesus would not take it. He intended to face death clear-headed, to take the pain of the cross undiminished. Jesus' work was not yet finished.

NOTE ABOUT CRUCIFIXION:

None of the writers give a graphic account of the crucifixion. For one thing, the gruesome horror of crucifixion was very familiar in the Roman world. For a second thing, the gospel writers wrote under the guidance of the Spirit. There is a divine restraint and elegance in their accounts which make their stories the more poignant and beautiful because of their understatement.

Information about crucifixion is very easy to find. Some of it seems to conflict, but that is only when someone tries to affirm that there was only one kind of cross, only one way to crucify. It is not to be expected that the exact same method was used every time and in every place one was nailed to a cross. We are simply not told all the details of Jesus' crucifixion.

Crosses were shaped either like an X, like a T, or like a   . Most writers agree that there was a wooden peg or block upon which the sufferer painfully sat. The best evidence indicates that all clothing was removed, a part of the dreadful humiliation. Was the victim nailed to the cross before it was stood up? Sometimes. On other occasions, the victim was seated on the peg and his arms and legs were tied. Then nails were driven through his hands and feet. Some (the Egyptians are mentioned in particular — Farrar, *Life of Christ,* p. 639) merely bound the victim to the cross, where he died of thirst and starvation. We do know that Jesus was nailed because of the mention of the wounds in His hands (John 20:25, 27).

At least many times, if not most, the nails were driven through the wrists between the radius and ulna. In this way, the nail would not tear through the flesh as was possible if the nail were driven through the palms. Nails were also driven through the feet. Ancient writers speak especially of the large spikes which were used. It is stated by some that the heads of the spikes were bent over so that they could not be pulled through the flesh.

The crosses were not very high. A stalk of hyssop was only about eighteen inches long, and a sponge stuck on the end of the stalk reached Jesus' mouth, so His feet were probably no more than a yard off the ground.

The agony of crucifixion has been abundantly described by various witnesses from ancient times. There was even a man who was crucified and then released. One of his statements was, "On the cross every second is an eternity." There was simply no escape from the pain except when death came. Due to the nails pulling at the wounds, the cramped muscles, the physical shock, the dehydration, and slow asphyxiation, the agony multiplied by the moment. It was a relief to know that death would come by the end of the day. Sometimes death did not come for three or four days.

Do not dwell morbidly on all the aspects of crucifixion in your class. The best practice to follow is to answer the questions your students raise and then go on with the class. This information is provided for those who may not have access to it otherwise. Remember that authorities differ a good bit over details, as well as over the origin of crucifixion.

It is more important to remember the significance of this occasion. There have been many other men who died gruesome deaths. There have even been many other innocent men who were killed unjustly. Why the significance this time? This was Deity dying on a cross; this was the Creator of the universe being put to death by His creatures; this was the promised Messiah being killed by His chosen people. But even more important, it was Deity willingly dying as a sacrifice for the sins of the world! The world was not *taking* His life from Him; He was *giving* His life for their sins. Let us take time to look at the suffering He underwent so that we can appreciate the sacrifice He made, but let us never lose sight of the larger picture of what was happening.

Be sure to note that the crucifixion fulfills the prophecy in Psalm 22:1-18. There was the shame and reproach and the taunts (22:6-8); Jesus was given into the hands of His enemies (22:12-16); His hands and feet were pierced (22:16); His body was contorted in agony (22:17).

Jesus on the cross; From nine o'clock until twelve o'clock noon (Mark 15:24-32; Matt. 27:35-44; Luke 23:33-43; John 19:18-27):

When the soldiers had crucified Jesus between the two thieves, Jesus said, "Father, forgive them, for they do not realize what they are doing."

NOTE:

That Jesus was crucified with two thieves branded Him as a criminal in the eyes of the world. Therefore, He was "numbered with the transgressors" (Isa. 53:12). The earlier part of Isaiah 53 tells of the oppression of the Christ, the Servant of God. It describes how He was condemned. As Jesus hung upon the cross, the question Isaiah asked is particularly appropriate: "Who considered that He was cut off out of the land of the living for the transgression of my people who were due to receive the blow themselves?" (Isa. 53:9).

The soldiers divided Jesus' garments into four parts. Jesus also had an inner garment, the tunic, which was woven together so that there was no seam in it. The soldiers said to one another, "Let's not tear this to divide it. Instead, let us cast dice for it to see who will win it."

NOTE:

This act of the soldiers fulfilled yet another prophecy found in Psalms 22: "They parted my garments among them, and upon my vesture did they cast lots" (22:18).

The garments of convicted men were divided among the soldiers as part of their spoils, because the owner would never need them again since he was dying. It is ironic that this particular One dying would need clothes again — because He did not remain dead!

A plaque (usually a wooden tablet with gypsum daubed on it) was placed above Jesus' head. On it was written in black letters: "This is the king of the Jews." The writing was in the three most common languages in that part of the world: Latin, Greek, and Aramaic. The place of crucifixion was near the city and, therefore, many of the Jews passed by and read the title.

The chief priests went to Pilate and said, "Do not write, 'King of the Jews,' but that He said, 'I am king of the Jews.'"

Pilate answered, "What I have written, stays written!"

NOTE:

Pilate would have the last laugh! The Jews meant Jesus' crucifixion to insult Him, but Pilate turned it into an insult to them.

There are seven statements Jesus made while on the cross. These are sometimes called the "Seven Words" of Jesus. We cannot be precisely sure what the order of these statements is, and the order is not vital to our understanding of the meaning of the things said. There are good reasons, though not conclusive, for the order in which we will present these sayings. We have already heard the first: "Father, forgive them, for they know not what they do."

Those who passed by made fun of Jesus and taunted Him, shaking their heads (see Psa. 22:7) and saying, "Ha! You were the one who could destroy the temple and build it again in three days. Save yourself if you are the Son of God."

The chief priests and the elders also joined in the mockery: "He saved others; Himself He cannot save! He is the king of Israel. Let Him come down from the cross now and we will believe Him. He trusted in God; let God deliver Him if He wants to, because He said, 'I am the Son of God.'"

The Roman soldiers also continued to mock Jesus. They offered Him wine vinegar (a sour wine) to drink and said, "If you are the king of the Jews, save yourself." At first, even the two thieves on either side of Him cast reproach upon Him.

NOTE:

Surely one of the terrible things about Jesus' suffering was the callous and flippant attitude His enemies exhibited. Remember that the cross was not high above the ground so Jesus could hear the rude comments being made.

It is more reasonable to suppose that Jesus' next statement concerned His mother and not the thief because both thieves cast reproach upon Him at first. There had to be time for one of the thieves to hear enough and to think enough to change his mind. Therefore, we put Jesus' statement to His mother next.

Jesus' mother, her sister Mary the wife of Cleopas, and Mary Magdalene all stood by the cross of Jesus. No doubt Mary remembered at this point the prophecy of old Simeon some thirty-three years before that "a sword shall pierce through thine own soul" (Luke 2:35). The disciple whom Jesus loved was also standing by. (Most students consider that disciple to be John. As we have indicated before, John never uses his own name in his book.)

When Jesus saw them, He said to His mother, "Woman, look, your son," meaning John. Then He said to John, "Son, look, your mother." From that hour, John took Mary into his own home to care for her as her "son." By this second statement on the cross, Jesus saw that His mother was provided for by the disciple whom He loved.

NOTE:

The gospel writers do not take time to tell of the agony those who loved Jesus were feeling at this time. The location of only these three women and this one disciple is given at this point. At the moment of His death, a few more women are mentioned (Mark 15:40-41; Matt. 27:55-56). Where were the others? All of the disciples had fled in terror when Jesus was arrested in the Garden of Gethsemane. John knew the high priest and was able to enter the court there. Peter had followed afar off until he, too, was allowed to enter the gates at the request of John (John 18:15-16). But then Peter left after he realized he had denied his Lord. We do not know where any of the rest of the apostles or other disciples were during that dreadful night and now on this dreadful day.

Even though Jesus had told them exactly what was going to happen to Him, they did not understand. He had also told them that their grief would soon be turned to joy, but they did not comprehend. They firmly believed He was the promised Messiah, that He was indeed the Son of God as He claimed to be — yet here He was dying! Their grief must have known no bounds.

One of the criminals crucified with Jesus said, "Aren't you supposed to be the Christ? Save yourself and us."

But the other thief had a change of heart (see Mark 15:32; Matt. 27:44). He rebuked the first thief, saying, "Do you not even fear God, seeing you are under the same sentence of death? And we, indeed justly, because we are getting what we deserve, but this man has done nothing wrong at all." Then he said, "Jesus, remember me when you come in your kingdom."

Jesus answered, "Truly I tell you, today you will be with me in Paradise."

NOTE:

The thief was saved by Jesus because he believed on Him and demonstrated that faith by defending Him. He also called upon Jesus to "remember" him. Before Jesus died, His will or testament had not taken effect. Therefore, He could save a person under any conditions He chose. Now that He has died and has risen from the dead, He saves men by the terms of His new testament.

But notice further the degree of this man's faith. We have just noted above that Jesus' closest disciples had fled in terror and grief. Jesus had prepared them for His death and had told them of the final victory that would come — but they had not understood and now felt defeated. Yet, this thief, who had not walked daily with the Lord, could see that this occasion did not mark the defeat of Jesus' plan. He could see that Jesus, though dying, would yet "come in His kingdom"! How remarkable!

Jesus on the cross; From twelve noon until three o'clock in the afternoon (Mark 15:33-37; Matt. 27:45-50; Luke 23:44-46; John 19:28-30):

At the sixth hour (which was twelve noon as it is given in the books of Matthew, Mark, and Luke) a darkness came over the whole land, until three o'clock in the afternoon. Very near to 3:00 (the ninth hour), Jesus cried out in a loud voice: "Eli, Eli, lama sabachthani," which means, "My God, my God, why have you forsaken me?"

NOTE:
On the meaning of this question, see Appendix 2.

About this time also, Jesus, knowing that everything was now finished, and so that the scriptures might be fulfilled, said, "I am thirsty."

Nearby was a vessel containing the sour wine commonly drunk by Roman soldiers. Someone put a sponge on the end of a stalk of hyssop and dipped it into the vinegar and lifted it to the lips of Jesus, fulfilling the prophecy of Psalm 69:21: "They gave me also gall for my meat; and in my thirst they gave me vinegar to drink."

Some standing nearby thought He had called for Elijah, so they said, "Leave Him alone. Let's see if Elijah comes to take Him down."

Once again Jesus cried out in a loud voice. This time He said, "It is finished." Then He said, "Father, into your hands I give my spirit," and He bowed His head and died. The work He had come into the world to do was now completed.

NOTE:
Notice that Jesus refused to drink the wine mixed with gall (or myrrh) that He was offered when He was first nailed to the cross (Matt. 27:34; Mark 15:23). That would have dulled His senses. But later, the soldiers offered Him wine vinegar even while they were taunting Him (Luke 23:36-37). He may have drunk it at that time. Now, here just before His death, He asked for something to drink. Thirst was one of the agonies of crucifixion. Jesus knew He needed to make some very important statements before He drew His last breath and He had to have His throat moistened to be able to speak aloud.

Note that these last statements are not those of a helpless victim. They are the statements of One who had deliberately given Himself. It was a deliberate task that

Jesus had come to perform and now the task was finished. He *delivered* His spirit into the hands of His Father.

Miracles accompanying the death of Christ (Mark 15:38-41; Matt. 27:51-56; Luke 23:45,47-49):

The priests were busy at the temple at 3:00 in the afternoon preparing the evening sacrifice and the offering of incense. All at once, they saw the great veil of the temple tear from top to bottom. The torn pieces of this magnificent curtain exposed the Most Holy Place.

The earth shook and rocks were split. Tombs were opened and many bodies of holy ones from the past were raised. Coming forth out of their tombs, after the resurrection of Christ, they entered into Jerusalem and appeared unto many.

The Roman centurion who had been in charge of the guard detail at the crucifixion site, when he saw that Jesus had died, and beheld the earthquake, was very afraid. He cried out, "Truly this was the Son of God."

The multitude, observing these things, went away striking themselves on the chest. Those who had known Him and had loved Him stood a long way off and watched all these things. The women who had ministered to His needs since the time of His Galilean ministry are particularly mentioned in this group.

NOTE:

It was an awesome occasion, truly one of the saddest moments of history — if this were the end of the story. Instead, it is the first part of the climax of the whole Bible. Here we need not just a note, but a song, a whole lesson, many lessons! Because by the deed we have just studied, all things were accomplished. At this moment it looked as if Satan had won — as if he were victorious — but Satan had only bruised the heel of the Savior as predicted in the very first promise ever made (Gen. 3:15). But the story does not end here. Christ will soon crush the head of Satan as that same promise foretold. His apparent defeat will be turned into a glorious victory!

Indeed, by this death, redemption has been purchased. Jesus has nailed to the cross the bond written in ordinances — in other words, He has paid off the promissory note left by every sin which had ever been committed and then repented of up until that date (Col. 2:14). By His death, He has put away sin (Heb. 9:26). He has tasted of death for every man — the very purpose for which He was made a man (Heb. 2:9). He redeemed us from the curse of the law by becoming a curse for us (Gal. 3:13). The humiliation of Jesus is now past, the task is finished, and the time for His exaltation is approaching (Phil. 2:5-8). When He arises from the dead on the third day hence, He will no longer be subject to the will of men. He will be glorified, He will be seated on the right hand of the Father, to rule upon the throne of David throughout the entire gospel age (Phil. 2:9-11; Eph. 1:20-23).

The death of Christ on the cross is the culmination of all ages. It was a plan that only God could have thought of. It was hidden from the world — the mystery of God — until it was done (1 Cor. 2:6-8). Even Satan did not know. He played right into God's hands. By carrying out his own wicked plan, thinking he was defeating God by killing His Son, he sealed his own doom, because by that death Jesus paid the sacrifice for sin and made it possible for men to be released from the power of Satan (Heb. 2:14-15).

Yet, remember, if the story ended here at the death of Christ, it would not be a story of victory. Satan would indeed have won. It would be of no more significance than the story of any other innocent man who was put to death unjustly. But the story continues!

The burial of Jesus' body in the tomb of Joseph of Arimathea (Mark 15:42-46; Matt. 27:57-60; Luke 23:50-54; John 19:31-42):

Since the sabbath was about to begin, the Jews wanted to be sure that the sufferers were dead and their bodies removed from their crosses before sunset. Since this sabbath occurred during the Passover, it was a special sabbath. The Jews, therefore, went to Pilate and asked that the legs of the dying men be broken to hasten their deaths.

Pilate sent soldiers to do the Jews' bidding. They came to the first thief and broke his legs and then on to the other thief and did the same. But when they came to Jesus and saw that He was already dead, they did not break His legs. One of the soldiers took his spear and thrust it into the side of Jesus. Blood and water came gushing out. The point of the soldier's deed was that it was his duty to be sure Jesus was dead.

John, who saw all this, testified that these things were true so that we might believe. The matter worked out this way so that the scripture might be fulfilled which says, "Not a bone of Him shall be broken" (Psa. 34:20), and "They shall look on Him whom they pierced" (Zech. 12:10).

Because the sabbath was about to begin, a man named Joseph from Arimathea went to Pilate and asked for the body of Jesus that he might bury it. Joseph was a rich man who was a member of the Council (Sanhedrin). He was a good and righteous man who was himself a disciple of Jesus and he waited for the kingdom of God. He had become a disciple secretly for fear of the Jews, but he had not consented to their decision and action against Jesus. Now we see him boldly come forward as a disciple and take this step.

Pilate was surprised to hear that Jesus was already dead, so he called the centurion to him and asked if Jesus were indeed dead. When he learned that He was, he gave Joseph permission to take the body away for burial.

So Joseph bought clean linen cloth, and Nicodemus, who had come to Jesus by night early in His ministry, joined Joseph to help. Nicodemus came bringing about seventy-five pounds of spices, myrrh and aloes, worth a fortune. Together, they laid the body in the spices and wrapped it in the linen cloth. Tenderly they took Jesus' body to a garden near the place of crucifixion and there, in Joseph's own new tomb where no one had been laid, they laid the body of Jesus. The tomb was cut from stone, and they rolled a great stone over its door and left. Some of the women observed these things and noted the sepulchre where His body was laid.

NOTE:

It has been said Jesus died like a criminal and was buried like a king. Isaiah foretold that "they made His grave with the wicked, and with a rich man in his death" (Isa. 53:9).

The watch over the sabbath (Mark 15:47; Matt. 27:61-66; Luke 23:55-56):

Mary Magdalene and Mary the mother of Joses sat near the sepulchre and saw how He was laid. Then they went home and prepared more spices and perfume for the burial. But they rested on the Sabbath in obedience to the commandment.

NOTE:

What thoughts must have gone through their minds. The Man who had transformed their lives and who had become the center of their existence was now gone. A great, empty chasm was left in their hearts and lives. Their hope lay buried in a tomb, and, though He had on numerous occasions predicted His resurrection, none of them displayed the slightest faith that He would live again. In the absence of that faith, their lives had come to a sudden halt; they were paralyzed. That is the way they would have continued, too, if something had not happened to change them. Only gradually would they have begun to take up the reins of their existence once more. They would have drifted back into their old ways and would never have forgotten the Man whose life they had shared for three years — but they would have been forever perplexed about what the whole experience had meant. Of course, this is not what happened, as we shall see.

On the sabbath day, the chief priests and Pharisees went to Pilate and said, "Sir, we remember that this imposter said, while He was still alive, 'After three days I will rise again.' Command therefore that the tomb be secured until the third day, so that His disciples will not come and steal Him away, and then say to the people that He is risen from the dead. Such an error would be worse than the first."

Pilate said, "Take a detail of soldiers; go and make the tomb as secure as you can." The Jews went to the tomb and placed the Roman seal on it and left the guard to watch.

NOTE:

It is evident that the Jews anticipated one of the very things suggested by unbelievers today as an explanation for Jesus' resurrection: that is, His disciples might steal the body. The Roman seal and the Roman guard saw to it that such a thing would not happen. Besides, the psychology is all wrong. Not one scrap of evidence indicates that such an idea even occurred to the disciples. They were still numb by the third day. In the nature of false causes, one could imagine how in a month or two, some fanatic might come up with the idea of stealing the body of Jesus in order to start a cause of his own, but this situation would be over one way or another by the third day. No disciple of Jesus would have been psychologically inclined to do such a thing as stealing His body within that period of time. This theory has to be false.

The Resurrection and Exaltation

(Matt. 28:1-20; Mark 16:1-20; Luke 24:1-51; John 20:1-21:25; Acts 1:1-12; 1 Cor. 15:5-7; Rev. 4-5)

The Resurrection

The entire Bible story has been building toward this moment. Mankind had been wicked, but God's love caused Him to send His Son into the world (John 3:16). But they rejected Him, declared Him to be an imposter, and crucified Him. But God declares Him to be the genuine Son of God by the resurrection. No wonder this is the moment we celebrate by worshiping God each first day of the week.

The resurrection (Matt. 28:2-4):

Suddenly, there was a violent earthquake, for an angel of the Lord came down from heaven and, going to the tomb, rolled back the stone and sat upon it. His appearance was like lightning, and his clothes were white as snow. When the Roman guards saw him, they trembled and fainted dead away.

> NOTE:
> No writer gives a detailed account of the process of the resurrection. Matthew is the only writer who describes the resurrection itself at all. It was apparently instantaneous and with an outpouring of great power (see Eph. 1:19-20) which not only raised Jesus but also caused the stone to be rolled away, and made the Roman guards faint from fear. What a sight it must have been!

Visit of the women to the tomb to finish burying Christ (Mark 16:2-8; Matt. 28:1-8; Luke 24:1-8; John 20:1):

Very early on the first day of the week, at dawn, Mary Magdalene, Mary the mother of James (probably the same as

Mary the mother of James and Joses, Mark 15:40), Salome, Joanna, and other women as well (see Luke 24:10), came bringing spices to anoint the body of Jesus. The time of their arrival was as it was beginning to dawn, in that twilight of early morning, which at one moment is still dark but getting lighter, and in the next moment, "the sun is risen."

NOTE:

The first day of the week was the first opportunity they had to do any more for Jesus' burial. Decomposition of a body would be very rapid under such circumstances, so this explains why they came to the tomb so early.

As they went along, the women were saying, "Who will roll the stone away for us?" because it was very large.

NOTE:

Almost certainly, they did not know that a detachment of Roman soldiers had been set to guard the tomb or that a Roman seal had been placed to forbid its removal. The only thing they were worried about was the weight of the stone over the entrance. Some of them had watched the burial, but they left before the guard was set.

The "swoon theory" that unbelievers offer to deny the resurrection says that Jesus fainted upon the cross and later revived. Think of it, however: Here was a man who was mistreated all night. He was scourged, then crucified for six hours. He was already too weak to carry His cross even before He arrived at the place of crucifixion. When the soldiers came to see if He were dead, they thought He was, but made sure by thrusting a spear into His body. When Joseph and Nicodemus prepared His body for burial, they were convinced He was dead. They placed Him in the tomb and there He remained from shortly before sunset Friday evening until sometime before daylight on Sunday morning without food or drink. When He "revived," He must have cast away the large stone at the entrance by Himself. Several women were wondering how they were going to manage to roll that stone from the tomb because it was "exceeding great" (Mark 16:4). Then He must have fought and defeated the Roman guards who were stationed there. The swoon theory cannot be true.

But when the women got to the tomb, there were no Roman guards, and the stone had been rolled back. In fact, the book of John says it was "taken away," indicating more than merely being rolled in its track. It had been violently rolled away and was probably lying flat because an angel sat upon it at the moment of the resurrection (Matt. 28:2).

At this point, it seems that Mary Magdalene left the party of women. Horrified, she rushed to find some of the apostles.

While Mary Magdalene was on her way to find the disciples, the other women went into the tomb and found it empty. The body of Jesus was gone! Instead, to their amazement, they found two men in dazzling garments. At first, one of these young men was sitting on the right side of the tomb (Mark 16:5). The women were frightened and bowed low.

One of the men spoke and said, "Do not be afraid. You seek Jesus the Nazarene, who was crucified. Why do you seek the living among the dead? He is risen; He is not here. See the place where He was laid. Remember how He talked to you while He was still in Galilee saying that the Son of Man must be given into the hands of sinful men, and be crucified, and the third day rise again."

Then the women recalled Jesus' words.

The angel continued: "Now, go and tell His disciples and Peter that He is going before you into Galilee. There you will see Him, as He told you earlier."

The women left the tomb and fled because they were filled with fear and astonishment. At first they were so overcome by their fear and awe they could do nothing.

Mary Magdalene tells Peter and John about the empty tomb (John 20:2-10; Luke 24:12):

> NOTE:
>
> All four writers agree on the time the women came to the tomb. It was about dawn. John says Mary Magdalene came to the tomb while it was still dark. He does not mention the other women because his emphasis is on the message Mary took to Peter and John which brought them to the tomb.
>
> There is, however, no way Mary Magdalene could have made an early trip to the tomb by herself and then a later one with the other women, because, on the trip with the other women, they were wondering who was going to roll the stone back (Mark 16:1-3). If Mary Magdalene had already been to the tomb as John describes (John 20:1-2), she could have not only told them they did not need to worry about the stone, she could have saved them the whole trip. So the visit of Mary Magdalene recorded by John is the same one recorded by the other writers in connection with the other women — John just does not say there were others with her.

Meanwhile, Mary Magdalene ran until she found Peter and John and told them, "They have taken the Lord out of the tomb, and we do not know where they have laid Him!"

At this shocking news, the two disciples raced to the tomb. John outran Peter and got there first. He did not go in, but he looked inside and saw the strips of linen cloth lying where the body had been. When Simon Peter got there, he went on into the tomb. He also saw the linen cloths. The napkin which had covered Jesus' head was not lying with the cloths, but was rolled up in a place by itself. Then John also went into the tomb, and he saw and believed.

Even to this point, they had not realized the message of the scripture, that Jesus would arise from the dead (Psa. 16:10). They then left, each going to his own home. Luke says Peter went home "wondering in himself" what had happened.

The Appearances of Jesus

Five appearances of Jesus are described on this first day of the week, the day He arose from the dead. The five appearances on this first day were:

(1) to Mary Magdalene (see Mark 16:9)

(2) to the other women
(3) to the two men going to Emmaus
(4) to Simon Peter
(5) to ten apostles and others with them

Appearance of Jesus to Mary Magdalene (Mark 16:9-11; John 20:11-18):

After telling Peter and John about the empty tomb, Mary Magdalene returned to the tomb. When she arrived, the two disciples had already gone to their separate places. She stood outside, weeping. As she wept, she stooped down and looked into the tomb. Once again, the angels were there. They were dressed in white, one sitting at the head and the other at the feet, where the body of Jesus had been. They said to Mary, "Woman, why are you crying?"

She said, "Because they have taken away my Lord, and I do not know where they have put Him."

Having said these words, she turned around and beheld Jesus, but she was so upset she did not recognize Him. Jesus said to her, "Woman, why are you crying? Whom are you looking for?"

Mary, supposing Him to be the gardener, said to Him, "Sir, if you have carried Him away from here, tell me where you have put Him, and I will take Him away." No doubt, these words were spoken in a beseeching manner.

Jesus said, "Mary."

She turned back to Him and said in Hebrew, "Rabboni," which means, "My Master!"

> NOTE:
> These were words of recognition and astonishment spoken when she realized that the One whom she thought held the very meaning of life in His hands, and whom she was sure was dead, was now indisputably alive.

Jesus said to her, "Do not cling to me, for I have not yet ascended to the Father. Go instead to my brethren and tell them that I am going to my Father and your Father, to my God and your God."

> NOTE:
> Understandably, Mary was in ecstasy. She seized Him and did not want to let Him go. Jesus' words were to assure her that He would be around for a while.

Mary went her way and told the disciples, "I have seen the Lord." She also told them the words Jesus had said.

The book of Mark specifically says that Mary Magdalene, out of whom the Lord had cast seven demons, was the first to see the Lord alive.

Appearance of Jesus to the other women (Matt. 28:9-10):

As the other women hurried away from the tomb, afraid and uncertain, Jesus met them and said, "Greetings to everyone." (To put it in our expression, He said, "Hello, everybody," as if there were nothing unusual in His greeting.)

They were astonished and came and fell at His feet, worshiping Him. Jesus told them, "Do not be afraid. Go tell my brothers that they are to go into Galilee, and they will see me there."

Now their fear turned to joy, and they ran to take the word to Jesus' disciples.

NOTE:

This account indicates that Jesus appeared to the other women when Mary Magdalene was not with them, before they got to the disciples to tell them what the angels had said. We cannot afford to be dogmatic about the exact sequence of all these events.

Though women were not chosen as apostles, and though they were not leaders in His cause, it is clear they were among Jesus' most faithful and devoted disciples. It was the women who first saw the angels, and it was to women that Jesus first appeared after His resurrection.

The women report their findings to the other disciples (Luke 24:9-12):

Not long after Mary Magdalene had found Peter and John, the other women came with their news to the rest of the apostles and other disciples with them. They heard the words of the women, but they did not believe, because their words seemed to them like nonsense.

The guards report to the Jewish rulers (Matt. 28:11-15):

Meanwhile, the Roman guards who had been set to watch the tomb hurried into the city and told the chief priests all the things that had happened. The chief priests met with the Sanhedrin and agreed to pay a large sum of money to the guards. They told them, "We want you to say, 'His disciples came by night, and stole the body away while we slept.' And, if word comes to the governor's ears, we will persuade him. You will not need to worry about him."

So, the soldiers took the money and did as they were told. Their tale was spread among the Jews and continues to this day.

NOTE:

It was not a great concern of the Romans whether the disciples stole a dead body or not. Roman soldiers guarding a dead man's tomb would not be at jeopardy should they lose their prisoner as they would have been if they had been guarding a live man. Feeling that it was a matter for the Jews to handle, the guards went to them. We do not know precisely when they went to the Jews, but reason would indicate that they would go soon after the event happened. Matthew says it was while the women were going to find Jesus' brethren. Therefore, they were making their trip into the city while the events we have described above have been happening.

By this tale that the Roman guards spread, they painted themselves as complete dullards. They slept on duty, for which they *could* have been in serious trouble. But what sleepers they were! The disciples could come and throw the stone back without waking them! Yet they knew and could tell exactly what happened! The story was foolish, but the Jews had no better explanation, and they continued in their unbelief.

Appearance of Jesus to two disciples on their way to Emmaus (Mark 16:12-13; Luke 24:13-32):

Later on that same first day, two disciples left Jerusalem and walked to the village of Emmaus, about eight miles away. As they walked along, they were talking about the things which had happened. Suddenly, Jesus Himself drew near and began walking with them. Their eyes were kept from recognizing Him at this point.

Jesus said to them, "What are these things you are talking about as you walk along and are so sad?"

The two men looked at Him in astonishment, and one of them, who was named Cleopas, said, "Are you the only one staying in Jerusalem who does not know the things that have happened in the last few days?"

Jesus said, "What things?"

They replied: "The things concerning Jesus of Nazareth, who was a prophet mighty in deed and in word before God and all the people; and how the chief priest and our rulers delivered Him to be condemned to death, and crucified Him. We had hoped that He was the one who would redeem Israel. Yes, and besides all this, it is now the third day since these things happened and some of the women from our group have amazed us. They went to the tomb early this morning, and when they did not find His body, they came to us saying they had seen a vision of angels, who said He was alive. Some from our number went to the tomb and found that the women were telling the truth, but they did not see Jesus."

Then Jesus said to them, "O foolish men! How slow you are to believe in your hearts all that the prophets have spoken! Was not the Christ supposed to suffer these things, and to enter into His glory?" Then beginning from Moses, He went through all the prophets, interpreting all that the scriptures said concerning Himself.

When they reached the village where they were going, Jesus made as if He would go further. But the men insisted that He stop with them, saying, "Stay with us because it is getting dark." So He went to stay with them.

After a while, when they sat down to eat, Jesus took the bread, and blessed it, and broke it, and gave it to them. As He did so, their eyes were opened, and they recognized Him. Then He vanished out of their sight.

The men were astonished and they said to one another, "Were not our hearts burning inside us, while He spoke to us on the road, while He explained to us the scriptures?"

Appearance of Jesus to Peter (Mark 16:13; Luke 24:33-35; 1 Cor. 15:5):

Then, even though it was evening and they had just come from the city, the two men got up immediately and hurried back to Jerusalem. There they found the apostles gathered together, with other disciples as well.

Before they told their own news, the assembled group told them, "The Lord really has risen and has appeared to Simon (Peter)."

Then the two men told of the things that had happened to them on their way to Emmaus and how they had recognized Him during the breaking of the bread. According to the book of Mark, the news was still too astounding for the disciples to believe their words.

NOTE:

The stage has now been set for Jesus to appear to the whole company of disciples who were gathered together.

The appearance of Jesus to the disciples who were gathered together (Mark 16:14; Luke 24:36-43; John 20:19-23):

According to Luke, as the two men spoke with the disciples, Jesus stood in the midst of them. Mark says it was as they were eating their meal. The doors were shut for fear of the Jews, and, though Jesus had tried to prepare them, when He suddenly appeared in their midst, they were terrified. They thought they were seeing a ghost.

But Jesus said, "Everything is all right. Why are you troubled? Why do questions arise in your minds? See my hands and my feet, see that it is really I myself. Handle me and see for yourselves that it is not a ghost. A spirit does not have flesh and bones as you see me having."

Having said these words, He showed them His hands and His feet with the nail scars in plain view. While they still thought the news was too good to be true (unable to believe for joy), He said, "Do you have anything here to eat?" They gave Him a piece of broiled fish and a piece of honeycomb. He took them and ate before them. This was further proof that He was indeed alive, because a ghost (spirit) would have had no need for food.

Mark describes Jesus' comments to His disciples as "upbraiding" them because of their unbelief and hardness of heart. He told them they should have believed the evidence that had been brought to them from those who had already seen Him alive.

Finally the disciples accepted the marvelous fact that Jesus was really alive. He said, "May you have peace. As the Father has sent me, I am sending you." When He had said this, He breathed on them and said, "Receive the Holy Spirit. The sins of whomsoever you forgive, they are forgiven, and the sins of whomsoever you retain, they are retained."

NOTE:

These last words were part of the final instructions Christ gave to the apostles. This was not the outpouring of the Holy Spirit in baptismal form. The actual outpouring of the Spirit came on the day of Pentecost as we will soon study (Acts 1:8; 2:33). This was a further promise of that occasion to come.

Thomas was absent (John 20:24-25):

Thomas, who was one of the twelve, called Didymus (twin), was not with the rest when Jesus came. The other disciples told him, "We have seen the Lord."

But Thomas said to them, "Unless I see the print of the nails in His hands, and put my finger into those prints, and put my hand into His side where He was pierced, I will not believe."

NOTE:

Thomas was not with the assembled group, yet Luke says that Cleopas and his companion found the "eleven" gathered together. We have already noted from Mark that it says Jesus came "while they sat at meat." Therefore, it is possible that the term "eleven" was used to apply to the whole group of apostles as a unit even though

189

every single member was not present. Or, possibly, enough time had passed since Cleopas had arrived for him to tell his news, for a meal to have been finished, and for Thomas to have left during that interval. Luke says it was while they were discussing the matters of the day, but with it so much on their minds, they would have discussed very little else that evening.

Thomas has been severely criticized for not believing at this point, but remember that the others had not believed either until they were shown the evidence by the Lord Himself. Continue following the story of Thomas before making your final judgment.

The appearances of Jesus during the rest of the forty days:

By now we have looked at the five appearances of Jesus that are recorded on that first day of the week when He arose. Now let us look at the ones that came in the next few weeks (40 days). During this interval, He appeared to:

(1) the apostles a week later,
(2) seven disciples by the Sea of Galilee,
(3) above 500 brethren at once,
(4) James,
(5) the apostles on the occasion of the great commission according to Mark,
(6) the apostles on the occasion of the great commission according to Matthew,
(7) the apostles on the occasion of the great commission according to Luke, and the ascension.

There is no way we can be sure of the exact order of the appearances during these forty days or exactly where they took place each time. The appearance to the apostles when Jesus convinced Thomas that He had arisen from the dead was a week after the resurrection (John 20:26) and was likely while they were still in Jerusalem. The appearance told in John 21 was some time later, and the disciples had returned to Galilee. The accounts of other appearances, scattered in Mark, Matthew, Luke, and referred to in 1 Corinthians 15:5-6, are impossible to fix with certainty as to time or place.

The account in Mark of the great commission is appended to what seems to be the occasion when Christ convinced Thomas that He was alive (Mark 16:14-18). The account of the great commission in Matthew was clearly after the disciples returned to Galilee (Matt. 28:16-20). Then, Paul refers to the appearance of the Lord to above five hundred brethren at one time and a separate appearance to James (probably the brother of the Lord) (1 Cor. 15:6-7). Luke gives an account of the great commission and indicates that it occurred immediately before the ascension of Jesus (Luke 24:50-53; Acts 1:9-12).

There is really no way to be sure exactly how many separate times are recorded in which He came to them and talked with them after the resurrection. We are just told that He showed Himself alive after His resurrection by "many infallible proofs" (Acts 1:3).

The appearance to the disciples a week after the resurrection and the convincing of Thomas (John 20:26-31):

Eight days later, the disciples were again shut up in a room, and this time Thomas was with them. Once again, Jesus suddenly stood in their midst in spite of the closed door. He said, "Peace unto you."

Then He turned to Thomas and said, "Stretch forth your finger and see my hands. Stretch forth your hand and put it into my side. Do not be without faith, but believe."

Thomas answered and said, "My Lord and my God!"

Jesus said, "Because you have seen me, you have believed. Blessed are they who have *not* seen, and yet have believed."

Jesus did many other signs in the presence of His disciples which are not written in the book of John, or in any of the other gospels, but these were written so we may believe that Jesus is the Christ, the Son of God, and that by believing, we may have life through His name.

> NOTE:
>
> Thomas' belief is one of the strongest testimonies to the resurrection. Like all the rest of the disciples, he did not accept the first reports that some had seen the Lord alive. He even declared that he would not believe until he could actually touch the wounds in the Lord's body. Yet, when he did see Jesus, he declared, "My Lord and my God," which was the strongest kind of affirmation of faith in Jesus and in His true identity.
>
> These were not men who were plotting how they could formulate an elaborate story to deceive the multitudes. These were men who were so grieved they thought all their hopes were gone. These were men who were too shocked to believe the news as they began hearing evidence. These were men who required strong evidence to convince them Jesus was alive — but they received that strong evidence! There was no question left in their minds when they saw Jesus. We can believe their testimony.

Appearance to seven disciples beside the Sea of Galilee; Miraculous catch of fish (John 21):

> NOTE:
>
> There is no way to know exactly when this appearance occurred except that it was obviously at least a few days after the resurrection and before the ascension. Notice the disciples are no longer in Jerusalem; they are back in Galilee.

After these early events, Jesus showed Himself to some disciples at the Sea of Galilee (called Tiberias in this passage). Simon Peter, Thomas, Nathanael, James, John, and two other disciples were together.

Peter said, "I am going fishing."

The others said, "We will go with you." So, they entered a boat and fished all night, but they caught nothing.

When it was daybreak, Jesus stood on the beach, but the disciples did not know it was He. He called to them, "Children, do you have anything to eat?"

They answered, "No."

He called back to them, "Cast the net on the right side of the boat and you will find what you are seeking."

They cast the net as Jesus had said, and when they tried to pull it in, they could not do so for the load of fish they had caught. John said to Peter, "It is the Lord."

When Peter heard this, he wrapped his coat about him (because he was naked, that is, he had on just his under-tunic) and dived into the sea to swim to shore. The other disciples brought the boat in because they were only a hundred yards or so from shore. They dragged the net full of fish beside them as they came.

When they reached shore, they saw a bed of coals with fish and bread already baking on it. Jesus said, "Bring some of the fish which you have caught."

Peter, therefore, went and drew the net to land. It was full of large fish, 153 of them to be exact, and yet the net was not torn.

Jesus said, "Come and break your fast," (or as we would say, "Come eat your breakfast"). None of the disciples ventured to ask, "Who are you?" because they knew it was the Lord.

Jesus took the bread and the fish and gave it to them to eat. This was the third time He had shown Himself to the disciples after He was risen from the dead.

NOTE:

Now follows a very poignant and painful conversation between Jesus and Peter. The conversation was essential because Peter had denied the Lord on the night of His trial. Peter's denial is the key to understanding the episode. Our understanding of the conversation is greatly enhanced if we see the play on the different words used for "love." Observe that Jesus does not call him by the name He Himself had given Simon — Peter — which means "rock" (John 1:42). Notice also that Peter had denied the Lord three times, so the Lord questions him about his love three times.

When the disciples had eaten, Jesus said to Simon Peter, "Simon, son of John, do you greatly admire and appreciate me more than these do?" This question recalled to Peter's mind the boast he had made just before the dreadful events of the betrayal and arrest that, "Though all forsake thee, I will not" (Mark 14:29).

Peter answered, "Yes, Lord. You know that I have warm affection for you."

Jesus said, "Feed my lambs." Then a second time, Jesus said, "Simon, son of John, do you greatly admire and appreciate me?"

Again Peter answered, "Yes, Lord. You know that I have warm affection for you."

Jesus replied, "Tend my sheep." The third time, Jesus asked, "Simon, son of John, do you have warm affection for me?"

Now Peter was grieved, because this time Jesus had said, "Do you have warm affection for me?" Peter answered, "Lord, you know all things. You know that I have warm affection for you."

Jesus replied, "Feed my sheep. Truly I tell you that when you were young, you dressed yourself and went wherever you wished. But when you become old, you will stretch forth your hands, and another will dress you and lead you where you do not want to go." Jesus said this to indicate the death by which Peter would glorify God. Then He said to him, "Follow me."

At that point, Peter turned and saw John, the one who had leaned on the Lord's chest during the Passover supper, and he said, "Lord, what will happen to this man?"

Jesus answered, "If I want him to stay here till I come again, what business is that of yours? You follow me."

From this exchange, the saying went out that John would not die, but would live until Jesus returns. But Jesus did not say that John would not die, but rather He asked Peter what business it was of *his* if the Lord wanted John to tarry until He comes again.

Then the writer of the book (John) states: "This is the disciple which testifieth of these things, and wrote these things." John included this story in his account in order to stop the false rumors that had gone out about the conversation between Jesus and Peter.

Then John wrote: "There are many other things which Jesus did, which if all of them were written, I suppose that even the world itself could not contain the books which could be written."

> NOTE:
>
> It is from these last verses of the book of John that we learn that the "disciple whom Jesus loved" is the apostle John. Scholars are agreed that the book we call the gospel of John was written by the apostle John. And here, in 21:24, he declares that it is the writer of the book who is referred to throughout the book as "the disciple whom Jesus loved" (see 21:20).

Appearance to above five hundred brethren at once and to James (1 Cor. 15:6-7):

Paul, by the inspiration of the Spirit, says: "After that, He was seen of above five hundred brethren at once," and that most of those were still alive to give their testimony in the days when Paul wrote of the event.

Then Paul says that Jesus appeared unto James. Verse 5 of that chapter tells of the appearance to Peter (Cephas) which we have already mentioned, which occurred on the day Jesus arose (see Luke 24:34).

We know nothing else about these appearances. There is no mention of them in the gospel accounts. These are some of those things that Jesus did which are not recorded for us in the gospel accounts (see John 20:30-31; 21:25).

> NOTE:
>
> There is no way to be certain which James is the one mentioned here. Among the apostles, there was James the brother of John and James the son of Alphaeus (Matt. 10;2-3). James, the brother of John, was killed by Herod Agrippa I not many years after the church was established (Acts 12:1-2). We do not have any information about where James, the son of Alphaeus, preached. In addition to these two men, there was another James who was very prominent in the early church in Jerusalem (Acts 12:17; 15:13; 21:18; Gal. 2:9). This James was the brother of Jesus (see Gal. 1:19). It is thought it was this James who wrote the epistle of James. Since this James was so prominent in the early church, and since Paul did not feel the need to identify this James more than by his name alone, almost certainly it was to James, the Lord's brother, that Jesus appeared to give evidence He was alive.

NOTE ABOUT THE RESURRECTION:

All the theories seeking to avoid the resurrection are foolish and completely without foundation or proof. Some try to say that all the appearances of Jesus to His disciples after the third day were mere hallucinations. But if so, they all had the same hallucination, even when they were not expecting to see any such thing (John 20:19-20). The Roman guards must have had a similar hallucination (Matt. 28:2-4). And one of the bitterest enemies Christ ever had, Saul of Tarsus, must have seen this same hallucination on the road to Damascus (Acts 9:3-6,17). In fact, more than 500 brethren must have had the same hallucination at once (1 Cor. 15:6).

This theory could not be true because Jesus went to a great deal of effort to prove to His disciples He was not an hallucination (Luke 24:36-43). He ate with them; He showed them His wounds; He even told them to feel the wounds (John 20:27).

Thus we can see that no one can suggest a logical theory to explain away the resurrection without denying every fact given in the gospel accounts. One then wonders why the enemies of Christ do not just deny the whole story and leave it at that. It is because *something happened*. The body was not in the tomb on the first day of the week. In spite of all Jewish and Roman efforts to guard the tomb, Jesus was no longer there! He arose! There is no other logical explanation.

Go Tell the Good News

Do you see we have reached the climax of the whole Bible story? God's plan for the redemption of mankind is nearing completion. From the day of the first sin in the Garden of Eden, God has been preparing for the coming of His Son to win the victory over Satan (Gen. 3:15), and to provide for the salvation of mankind. Now, Christ has come; He has lived before men and shown what God is like and how God wants men to live; He has allowed Himself to be taken and killed by wicked men; but He has been proven to be God's Only Begotten Son because He did not remain dead, but arose never to die again. Now He has revealed Himself to His disciples and has convinced them that He is indeed alive.

Before Jesus goes back to heaven, He gives a charge to His apostles to carry this good news (gospel) concerning the Savior all over the world. It is now time to tell the world what God's mystery had been. It is no longer a mystery; it has been revealed. Therefore, go tell the good news (the gospel) to the whole world. The ultimate sacrifice has been made for sin. Tell the story to every individual so that all who hear and accept the terms of salvation can be saved.

It seems that each time He was with them during this last period of forty days, Jesus reminded the apostles of this charge, which we call the great commission, because it was a commission that covered the whole world. He told them things concerning the kingdom that was about to begin. Obviously, none of these accounts is complete by itself. We must put all the various accounts together to get a complete picture.

As we move from the study of the life of Christ into the study of the book of Acts and of the rest of the New Testament, we will be watching as the apostles and other faithful disciples go about carrying out this charge of telling the good news about Jesus and the plan of God. Let us take renewed zeal in our own hearts after studying the story of Christ and try harder to do our part in carrying out this continuing charge to tell the world of our day the good news about our Savior.

The great commission according to Mark (Mark 16:14-18):

While the eleven were eating, Jesus showed Himself to them and said: "Go into all the world and preach the gospel to every person. He who believes and is baptized shall be saved, but he who does not believe will be condemned."

Then Jesus promised them that they would be able to confirm their message by the signs which they would be able to do: "And these signs shall accompany them who believe: in my name they will cast out demons, and they will speak with new tongues. They will take up serpents, and if they drink any poison, it will not hurt them in any way. They will lay hands on the sick, and they will recover."

> NOTE:
>
> There have been many questions about these signs that would accompany the believers. Were these signs due to accompany believers through all generations to come? Or, were they given for a unique purpose which would be accomplished within a definite period of time? In view of all other passages on the subject, the answer is that, though Christ is with His disciples through all the ages of time, the miraculous signs were for that generation alone. That generation of disciples stood in a unique position. They were about to go into the world and proclaim an amazing message of a Savior that had come into the world to bring salvation. Yet, they had no written proof for their message. Therefore, they were given the Holy Spirit to guide them into knowing the truth to proclaim and to give them ability to do miracles to prove that they were speaking with the approval of God. As part of their work, they wrote their message down by the inspiration of that same Spirit so that all succeeding generations could have the complete story of the plan of God. We now have that written record (the Bible) and we do not need miraculous proof that the message is true.

The great commission according to Matthew (Matt. 28:16-20):

This appearance took place in Galilee upon a mountain where Jesus had appointed that the eleven apostles go. When they saw Him, some doubted. They were still trying to grasp the fact that He had been raised from the dead.

Jesus came to them and said: "All authority has been given to me in heaven and earth. Go, therefore, and make disciples from all the nations, baptizing them into the name of the Father, and of the Son, and of the Holy Ghost. Then teach those new disciples to keep all the things which I have commanded you. And, lo, I am with you always, even to the end of the world."

The great commission according to Luke (Luke 24:44-49):

This account is parallel to some degree with Acts 1:4-8. Since Luke wrote both accounts, the two books overlap at this point. Although this passage follows immediately after Luke's record of Jesus' appearance to the apostles on that first resurrection day, it is obvious from the subject matter (particularly v. 49) that this episode occurred immediately before Jesus' ascension.

Jesus told the disciples: "These things which have happened are the things I told you about while I was yet with you. The things I told you about had to be fulfilled: the things written in the law of Moses, and in the prophets, and the psalms, concerning me."

Then Jesus opened their minds so that they could understand the scriptures. He said to them, "Thus it is written that the Christ should suffer, and rise again from the dead on the third day, and that repentance and remission of sins should be preached in His name unto all nations, beginning from Jerusalem. You are witnesses of these things. Look, I am sending the promise from the Father upon you (the Holy Spirit). But you are to wait in the city of Jerusalem until you are clothed with power from on high."

The Exaltation of Christ

The Ascension (Mark 16:19-20; Luke 24:50-53; Acts 1:9-12):

Jesus led His disciples out to the Mount of Olives to a place near Bethany. He lifted up His hands and blessed them. Then, as they watched, He was taken up into the sky where a cloud hid Him from their sight.

While they continued to stare into the sky in amazement, two men stood by them in white clothing. They said, "You men of Galilee, why do you stand here gazing into heaven? This same Jesus, who was received up from you into heaven, shall return in the same way you saw Him going into heaven."

Then the disciples returned to Jerusalem to wait for the Spirit to come upon them, just as Jesus had commanded. Luke says that they worshiped Him and returned to Jerusalem with great joy and continued in the temple, praising and blessing God. Mark ends his book by summarizing the work the apostles did in the days and years ahead by saying, "And they went forth, and preached every where, the Lord working with them, and confirming the word with signs following." We will be observing that work as we move into the study of the book of Acts.

The Coronation of Jesus (Revelation 4-5):

Mark says that Jesus was received into heaven and "sat on the right hand of God" (Mark 16:19). In the next book we will study Acts 2 and see Peter preaching the first gospel sermon to the Jews in Jerusalem. In that sermon, Peter declared that the same Jesus whom the Jewish officials had crucified had been raised to sit on the throne, exalted at the right hand of God. He quoted David's prediction that the Lord would be told, "Sit thou on my right hand, until I make thy foes thy footstool" (Acts 2:30-36). The book of Philippians declares that after Jesus became obedient to death, He was highly exalted by God and was given a name above every name: "That at the name of Jesus every knee should bow, of things in heaven, and things in earth, and things under the earth; and that every tongue should confess that Jesus Christ is Lord, to the glory of God the Father" (Phil. 2:9-11).

The gospel accounts do not tell any details of that exaltation, but years later, the apostle John was shown a vision which took him behind that cloud that hid Jesus on the day of the ascension and showed him the throne scene of Jehovah and the coronation of the Lamb of God which had been offered as the sacrifice of mankind. Let us go to Revelation 4 and 5 and see that coronation:

Resurrection and Exaltation

The scene opens with John seeing a door opened into heaven. Then a voice spoke and told John, "Come up here, and I will show you things which must be hereafter."

Immediately, John was in the spirit and was transported into the throne room of God Himself. Looking at the One sitting upon the throne was like looking at a jasper or a sardius stone and there was an emerald rainbow around the throne. Twenty-four elders were sitting upon seats surrounding the throne. They were dressed in white raiment and had crowns of gold upon their heads. Out of the throne came forth lightnings and thunderings and voices. Immediately before the throne, there were seven lamps which are the seven Spirits of God. And before the throne, there was a sea of glass like crystal. In the midst of the throne and around the throne were four beasts full of eyes before and behind. The first beast was like a lion; the second like a calf; the third had the face of a man; and the fourth was like a flying eagle. Each beast had six wings and they were full of eyes. They continually praised God, saying, "Holy, holy, holy, Lord God Almighty, which was, and is, and is to come." As the beasts praised God, the twenty-four elders also fell before Him and worshiped, casting their crowns before Him. They said, "Thou art worthy, O Lord, to receive glory and honor and power: for thou hast created all things, and for thy pleasure they are and were created."

But then, as the vision continued, John saw that the One on the throne was holding a book in His right hand. The book was written upon inside and out and it was sealed with seven seals. Just then, a strong angel cried out in a loud voice, "Who is worthy to open the book, and to loose the seals of it?" But there was no one in all of heaven or earth able to take the book and open it and read it.

John began to weep because no one worthy was found to open the book, but one of the elders spoke to him and said, "Do not weep, because, look, the Lion of the tribe of Judah, the Root of David, has prevailed to open the book and to loose the seven seals of it."

John looked, and there in the midst of the throne and of the beasts and of the twenty-four elders, there stood a Lamb that had been slain. It had seven horns and seven eyes which are the seven Spirits of God sent forth into all the earth. As John watched, the Lamb went forward and took the book out of the right hand of the One upon the throne. And when He had taken the book, the four beasts and the twenty-four elders fell down before the Lamb, each having harps and golden vials of incense which are the prayers of the saints. Then they sang a new song, saying, "Thou art worthy to take the book, and to open the seals upon it: for you were slain, and have redeemed us to God by your blood out of every kindred, and tongue, and people, and nation; and have made us kings and priests unto our God; and we shall reign on the earth."

John continued to watch as thousands upon thousands of angels around the throne joined in the worship of the Lamb, saying, "Worthy is the Lamb that was slain to receive power, and riches, and wisdom, and strength, and honor, and glory, and blessing." And every creature in existence joined the celebration by saying, "Blessing, and honor, and glory, and power, be unto Him that sitteth upon the throne, and unto the Lamb forever and ever." The four beasts said, "Amen," and the twenty-four elders fell down and worshiped the Lamb who lives forever.

Thus the glorious plan of God is complete. Deity came to earth in human form and performed the task that had been planned from eternity — He died to pay the sacrifice for sin so that men might be forgiven for their sins, and then He returned to Heaven to sit upon David's throne to reign at the right hand of God. Now, as we go through the rest of the New Testament, we will watch as the apostles take the message to the whole world of their day. They will tell the wonderful story of God's plan, and they will tell the terms of salvation so that men may partake of the blessings available. As we watch them go out, we should grow in our own realization of the blessings we have available and grow in our determination to tell the story more effectively to our generation. It is the greatest story that has ever been told.

Refresh your memory:

Review one more time where the story of Jesus fits into the overall story of the Bible. The next book in the series will cover the history of the early church and the epistles that were written.

Creation Stories
The Flood
Scattering of the People
The Patriarchs
The Exodus
Wandering in the Wilderness
Conquest of the Land
Judges
United Kingdom
Divided Kingdom
Judah Alone
Captivity
Return
Years of Silence

*Life of Christ

Early Church
Letters to Christians

Appendix Number 1

Chronology of the Last Week

We have emphasized throughout the study of the life of Christ that chronology is a matter of secondary importance. Nevertheless, it does need some attention.

We approach the effort to determine the order of events in the last week of Jesus' life with the same awareness of difficulties as we have had in dealing with chronology throughout His ministry. Some points of chronology in this last week are bitterly disputed, especially by those who teach we should worship on Saturday, the seventh day (sabbatarians). We are not, however, concerned with suiting anyone's presumptions. We seek only the truth. The following chronology is as well-founded as any other you may find. We have tried to establish every point by the scripture. It is easier to begin with the crucifixion and resurrection and work backwards, so that is the way we will proceed.

All four gospel writers identify the "preparation" as the day on which Jesus died and was buried (Matt. 27:50-62; Mark 15:42-44; Luke 23:52-54; John 19:31-42). According to Mark, the preparation is specifically said to be the day before the sabbath (Mark 15:42). The sabbath was Saturday, the seventh day of the week. The preparation was the day before, thus Friday. Therefore, Jesus died on Friday. Luke says, "It was the day of the preparation, and the sabbath drew on" (23:54). Then he says, "And on the sabbath they rested according to the commandment" (23:56). Finally, "But on the first day of the week, at early dawn, they came unto the tomb, bringing the spices which they had prepared. And they found the stone rolled away from the tomb. And they entered in, and found not the body of the Lord Jesus" (24:1-3).

Luke thus accounts for every single day of Jesus' death and burial, mentioning each one of them specifically. All of the accounts are clear on this. Therefore we can confidently say Jesus was raised from the dead on the first day of the week, Sunday. He lay in the tomb over the sabbath. He was crucified on Friday, the day of preparation. He ate the Passover and was betrayed the night before the crucifixion, which was, therefore, Thursday night. It was during the day Thursday that the Passover was prepared (Matt. 26:17).

None of the gospels tell anything that can definitely be fixed on Wednesday. The fact that nothing specific is mentioned for the day Wednesday gives rise to some questions about which night Jesus partook of the Passover and was betrayed, and then which day He was crucified. Yet, from the above passages cited, the evidence is clear that He was crucified and buried on the day immediately before the sabbath (thus Friday).

Wednesday might have been the day when Judas made his deal with the Jews. There is good evidence that he had not made any such deal before Tuesday. Going backward from Thursday, the next day specifically mentioned is two days before the Passover (Matt. 26:1-2; Mark 14:1-2). This would bring us to Tuesday. The things recorded in Matthew 21-25 and in Mark 11:20-13:37 obviously occurred not later than the time mentioned in Matthew 26:1-2 and Mark 14:1-2, which was two days before the Passover, Tuesday. Yet that day began with the discovery that the fig tree Jesus had cursed the day before was withered away (Mark 11:20). So all the events described in Matthew 21-25 and Mark 11:20-13:37 occurred on Tuesday. Jesus cursed the fig tree on Monday (Mark 11:12-13; Matt. 21:18-19) and cleansed the temple on that same day (Mark 11:12-18). The triumphal entry was the preceding day, hence Sunday (Matt. 21:1-18; Mark 11:1-14).

A feast was made for Jesus at Bethany on the day before the triumphal entry (John 12:1-12). Since the triumphal entry was on Sunday, the day before that was the sabbath, or Saturday. The feast eaten at the house of Simon the leper would have been eaten in the evening (supper, John 12:2) after the sabbath had ended. John clearly shows this feast occurred the night before the triumphal entry (John 12:2-12).

Jesus arrived at Bethany, not during the sabbath, but on Friday evening just before the sabbath began. No faithful Jew would have made the arduous six hour journey from Jericho to Bethany on the sabbath, so Jesus arrived just as the sabbath began, six days before the Passover (John 12:1).

One other point needs to be mentioned. Jesus used Jonah as a sign for that generation and said that as Jonah was in the belly of the whale for three days and three nights, so the Son of Man would be in the heart of the earth three days and three nights (Matt. 12:38-40). Understandably, people would like to get three full days and nights to match up with the prophecy.

Obviously, if Jesus died on Friday, and was buried that afternoon, and was raised on the first day of the week, Sunday, then He was in the grave parts of three days and two nights. Even then, the three days can only be attained by counting parts of Friday and Sunday, plus the whole day Saturday.

Therefore, some people try to have Jesus crucified and buried Thursday and raised on the first day. This way, He was in the grave Thursday night, Friday night, and Saturday night, three nights. Yes, but then one must count the partial day Thursday, the whole days of Friday and Saturday, and the partial day of Sunday. Then you have four days and three nights.

Though it seems strange to us, the expression three days and three nights did not mean three complete days and three complete nights. Jesus Himself, after giving the "sign of Jonah," repeatedly predicted He would be raised *on the third day.* There is no way one could get three full days and three full nights out of a period due to end *on the third* day. Westerners are the only ones who have had problems with this. Neither Jesus, nor His disciples, nor even His enemies had any problem understanding that Jesus did not mean three literal full days and three literal full nights (Luke 24:21; Matt. 27:64).

APPENDIX NUMBER 2

"My God, My God, Why Hast Thou Forsaken Me?"

One of the seven statements that Jesus uttered while on the cross was, "My God, My God, why hast thou forsaken me?" (Matt. 27:46; Mark 15:34). The statement is a quote of the first verse of the twenty-second psalm.

There are two thoughts which are brought to our minds by His question: (1) God must have forsaken Jesus while He was on the cross; (2) Jesus did not know why God had forsaken Him. If we take the question at face value and conclude that God really did forsake Jesus, then we will have to conclude also that Jesus did not know why He was forsaken.

During the Protestant Reformation, Martin Luther used this passage, along with some others, to teach the imputed righteousness of Christ. Then and now, men will start with 2 Corinthians 5:21: "Him who knew no sin He made to be sin on our behalf; that we might become the righteousness of God in Him." From this point, the idea goes like this: God took our sins and placed them upon Jesus so that those sins became the sins of Jesus — He actually became guilty of them. This transfer made it possible for God to be just in transferring the righteousness of Christ upon us so that His righteousness becomes our righteousness, just as our sins became His sins. Therefore, the reason why Jesus asked why God had forsaken Him was that when He took our sins upon Himself, He became a sinner, guilty of our sins, and in that moment, God turned His back on Jesus, so that for the first time ever in all eternity, Jesus was separated from God, and this is what moved Him to ask why God had forsaken Him. This awful experience is then used to explain why Jesus underwent such agony in the Garden of Gethsemane. It was not that He was merely dreading the ordeal of crucifixion. Many have faced similar pain and suffering without the dread Jesus showed. Therefore, He was facing that moment of separation when God would abandon Him to bear the sins of the world alone.

The position appears to be a logical one. It seems to hold together well — except there are some fallacies which show up upon more thorough investigation. Any Bible student must be willing to evaluate honestly the evidence on both sides of every position if he wants to arrive at truth.

Consider these questions: Where does the Bible say God turned His back on Jesus, that, for this moment, God abandoned Jesus? It is assumed that this is what happened, since Jesus asked His question as He did. But, as we will see, Jesus' question may not have meant what it appears to mean at first glance. Neither can 2 Corinthians 5:21 be cited as the reference because though the passage clearly says Christ was "made to be sin," it does not at all tell *how* He was made to be sin. We must be very careful not to assume a meaning, but to let scripture interpret scripture.

There is no passage which teaches that God literally turned His back on Jesus and literally separated Himself from Jesus so that the bond of consciousness and fellowship which had always existed between them was broken.   Furthermore, does it not seem strange, almost unfair, for God to send His Son into the world to do what He did on the cross (John 3:16; Rom. 3:25; 1 Pet. 1:18-20), and then turn His back on Him while He did it? Here Jesus comes to do the will of the Father (Heb. 10:7), to obey the Father even unto death (Phil. 2:8), to prove His love for the Father as a Son (Heb. 5:8-9; John 14:31), and yet when He does exactly what the Father wanted Him to do, God turns His back on Him and severs the bond which had always existed between them.

Another thing which is strange is that Jesus would ask, "*Why* hast thou forsaken me?" It cannot be answered that He did not know it was going to happen until the moment it did, so that in shock and astonishment, reeling from the spiritual pain, Jesus cried out His question. Remember that according to the doctrine presented above, it was this precise thing which He was dreading in the Garden. He asked the Father to let the cup pass from Him, "Nevertheless, Father, not my will be done, but thine." Moreover, Jesus knew that He came to give His life a ransom for many (Matt. 20:28). The quotation of Psalm 40:6-8 by the Hebrew writer (10:5-8) should prove that the Christ knew what He had come to do. In the face of these undeniable facts, why did Jesus say, "Why have you forsaken me?"

If the traditional explanation is true, then so be it. But is it true? Or is there a better explanation? There *is* a better explanation, one which takes everything into account.

First, let us examine verses which will help us to understand *how* Christ was made to be sin on our behalf (2 Cor. 5:21). He was not literally and actually made guilty of our sins because Paul says that *we* were under the curse of sin (Gal. 3:10). This curse is also called the curse of the law (Gal. 3:13a). Jesus redeemed us, not by taking the actual curse we were under upon Himself, but by taking another curse: "Cursed is every one that hangeth upon a tree" (Gal. 3:13b). We who were under the curse of sin deserved to be there. Jesus did not deserve to be under the curse He came under. The curse pronounced upon Jesus was a curse based upon the presumption of guilt on the part of anyone publicly executed by hanging on a tree, but Jesus only *appeared* to be a wrong-doer. Thus He did not deserve to be hanged upon a tree. By His taking a curse upon Himself (hanging on the tree) which He did not deserve, He made it possible for God to remove the curse (transgression) which was upon us.

The Bible teaches that Jesus became sin only in that He took the *punishment* of sin. He was punished, executed as an evil-doer, even though He was not guilty of sin. Listen to Isaiah: "He hath borne *our* griefs, and carried *our* sorrows: yet we did esteem Him stricken, smitten of God, and afflicted. He was wounded for *our* transgressions, He was bruised for *our* iniquities; the chastisement of *our* peace was upon Him; and with His stripes we are healed. All we like sheep have gone astray; we have turned every one to his own way; and the Lord hath laid on Him the iniquity of us all" (Isa. 53:4-6). Surely it can be seen that the point is that as our sacrifice, our substitute, Jesus took the *punishment* we deserved for our iniquities, not the literal guilt of sin.

Appendix

Look at other statements in this chapter of Isaiah: "Who among them considered that He was cut off out of the land of the living for the transgression of my people to whom the stroke was due?" (Isa. 53:8). "Yet it pleased the Lord to bruise Him; He hath put Him to grief: when thou shalt make His soul an *offering for sin*, He shall see His seed, He shall prolong His days, and the pleasure of the Lord will prosper in His hand. He shall see of the travail of His soul, and shall be satisfied" (53:10-11a). "And He shall bear their iniquities [as a sacrifice]. Therefore will I divide Him a portion with the great, and He shall divide the spoil with the strong; because He poured out His soul unto death, and was numbered with the transgressors: yet He bare the sin of many, and made intercession for the transgressors" (53:11b-12).

Jesus was not, neither at any point did He become, a transgressor. Nor did He ever become literally *guilty* of the transgressions of men. He bore them as a sacrifice by receiving the punishment due them. Let us not forget the nature of a sacrifice, as it was so carefully taught during the Old Testament. A sacrifice was a *substitute*, and the sacrifice was never guilty of the sins it bore. It bore them only in that it took the punishment for sin.

What Jesus did is referred to an as act of righteousness (Rom. 5:18). God sent His own Son in the likeness of sinful flesh and for sin (Rom. 8:3). The book of Hebrews is filled with statements having to do with Jesus' sacrifice (7:26-28; 9:11-14; 9:26; 10:4-18). Nowhere do the scriptures teach that Jesus took the guilt of our sins upon Himself so that, since He was sin-laden for that moment, God turned away from His Son, and a separation came between them for a time.

So what did His question mean? Let us go back to 2 Corinthians 5:21 where we began, and let us see what that passage *does* mean in the light of all the verses we have studied. Then, we will look back to Jesus' question and see what He meant.

"Him who knew no sin He made to be sin on our behalf; that we might become the righteousness of God in Him" (2 Cor. 5:21). Either Jesus became sin in that He literally took our sins to be His own so that we could take His righteousness to be our own, or Jesus took the *punishment* due our sins so that we could be *forgiven* by God and by that forgiveness be righteous. Which explanation is true? The one for which innumerable passages can be cited, the latter. By His stripes we are healed so that we can be *forgiven*, and thus be righteous.

At this point, though, all we have done is to remove one of the main pillars upon which the traditional explanation of Jesus' question is based. We have not explained the question itself. If it does not mean that God literally and actually turned His back on Jesus to let Him bear the brunt of sin alone, what does it mean?

Jesus was the Christ. He was the Servant of God (Isa. 52:13). He was the One concerning whom God gave His angels charge that they should bear Him up lest He dash His foot against a stone (Psa. 91:11-12). Jesus came into the world claiming to be the Son of God, claiming to be the Messiah. Yet, when everything came to a showdown, His enemies seized Him, convicted Him falsely, and crucified Him. Where were the angels? Where was God? Why did He forsake Him? The explanation should be obvious. It was *before men* that Jesus appeared forsaken by God. It was in the eyes and minds of men that God forsook Christ. He did not literally and actually forsake Him. Jesus could have called for twelve legions of angels (Matt. 26:53). *No one* took His life from Him. He laid it down of

Himself (John 10:17-18).

As Isaiah said, "We *esteemed*" or "counted" Him as one smitten of God (Isa. 53:4). He was not really smitten of God; He was wounded for *our* transgressions (Isa. 53:5).

The twenty-second psalm, from which Jesus quoted the question, is often overlooked as a key to understanding the question. The psalm is Messianic from start to finish. Listen to the words of the Christ a thousand years before He was born: "I am a worm, and no man; a reproach of men, and despised of the people. All that see me laugh me to scorn: they shoot out the lip, they shake the head, saying, 'Commit thyself unto Jehovah; let Him deliver Him: let Him rescue Him, seeing He delighteth in Him'" (Psa. 22:6-8). What the people did not know was that Christ *did* commit Himself to Jehovah. He put everything into His Father's hand. The people did not know that Jehovah *did* delight in His Son because His Son was doing exactly what the Father wanted and what He had planned. The Father abandoned Jesus to the evil will of the multitude so that the sacrifice could be made. He did not intervene, but it was not because He and the Son were separated. It was because by this marvelous gift and sacrifice, God would save men. This sacrifice required that Jesus die. Therefore, God had to *let* Him die. But during that awful time when Jesus appeared deserted, when only He and God knew what was being done, I believe the bond between them was stronger than ever.

Why then did Jesus ask, "My God, my God, why hast thou forsaken me?" Jesus knew exactly why He was dying. He knew all that it involved beforehand. His question was certainly not to *find out* something He did not know. Look again at the psalm. In Psalm 22, we find the Christ speaking of how He has been abandoned to evil men, surrounded by bulls of Bashan. Yet His hope is God. Hear Him: "Thou art He that took me out of the womb; thou didst make me trust when I was upon my mother's breasts. I was cast upon thee from the womb; thou art my God since my mother bare me. Be not far from me; for trouble is near; for there is none to help" (22:9-11). Again He cries, "But be not thou far off, O Lord: O thou my succor, haste thee to help me. Deliver my soul from the sword, my darling from the power of the dog. Save me from the lion's mouth; yea, from the horns of the wild-oxen thou hast answered me" (22:19-21).

The psalm is not a puzzled, plaintive request for an explanation; it is a poignant cry for deliverance. Compare this psalm with other psalms which follow a similar pattern (Psalms 10:1; 13:1-4).

In quoting these words of the first verse, Jesus was appropriating the cry of the psalm for Himself. The psalm was His, penned by His ancestor David a thousand years before. It became His cry for deliverance upon the cross. Shortly after He said these words, He died. His task as a sacrifice was finished.

One other question remains: if Jesus were not separated from the Father by the sin which He took as His own, what did He agonize over in the Garden? In the first place, one cannot support a position on the basis of a question which is not specifically answered in the Bible. The Bible does not specify all that Jesus dreaded. This silence does not by any means permit us to invent a theory which is entirely unsupported by any scripture.

Appendix

Jesus agonized over the shame and the pain of the cross. He had known it was there all His life. He knew more graphically what it would mean to be crucified than anyone else could have known who had not been crucified. The righteous heart and sensitive mind of Jesus would recoil in horror at the entire ordeal. He also dreaded the appearance of being a transgressor, being counted as a wrong-doer, forsaken in this manner. If all these things were not enough to make Him sweat great drops of blood, then we know not what it was, but that does not give us permission to come up with an unfounded explanation, especially an explanation which would place God in the extremely reprehensible position of literally and actually turning His back on His Son when He was only doing what the Father had willed Him to do.

Bibliography

Aharoni, Yohanan, and Avi-Yonah, Michael. *The Macmillan Bible Atlas.* Rev. ed. New York: Macmillan Publishing Company, 1977.

Arndt, William F., and Gingrich, F. Wilbur. *A Greek-English Lexicon of the New Testament.* Chicago: University of Chicago Press, 1957.

Edersheim, Alfred. *The Life and Times of Jesus the Messiah.* n.a.: MacDonald Publishing Company, n.d.

Edersheim, Alfred. *The Temple.* Grand Rapids: Wm. B. Eerdmans Publishing Company, 1976.

Farrar, Frederic W. *The Life of Christ.* Second American Edition. Albany, N.Y.: Rufus Wendell, 1876.

Foster, R.C. *Introduction and Early Ministry.* Grand Rapids: Baker Book House, 1966.

Foster, R.C. *The Final Week.* Grand Rapids: Baker Book House, 1962.

Foster, R.C. *The Middle Period.* Grand Rapids: Baker Book House, 1968.

Ganzfried, Solomon. *Code of Jewish Law.* Trans. Hyman E. Goldin. New York: Hebrew Publishing Company, 1927.

Gardner, Joseph L., ed. *Reader's Digest Atlas of the Bible.* Pleasantville, New York: Reader's Digest Association, Inc., 1981.

Josephus, Flavius. *Antiquities of the Jews.* Trans. William Whiston. Grand Rapids: Associated Publishers and Authors, Inc., n.d.

Lenski, R.C.H. *Interpretation of St. Matthew's Gospel.* Columbus, Ohio: Wartburg Press, 1943.

Lenski, R.C.H. *Interpretation of St. Mark's Gospel.* Columbus, Ohio: Wartburg Press, 1946.

Lenski, R.C.H. *Interpretation of St. Luke's Gospel.* Columbus, Ohio: Wartburg Press, 1946.

Lenski, R.C.H. *Interpretation of St. John's Gospel.* Columbus, Ohio: Wartburg Press, 1942.

Pamphilus, Eusebius. *The Ecclesiastical History of Eusebius Pamphilus.* Trans. Isaac Boyle. Grand Rapids: Baker Book House, 1969.

Robertson, A.T. *Harmony of Gospels.* Nashville, Tennessee: Broadman Press, 1922.

The Narrated Bible. Narr. F. LaGard Smith. Eugene, Oregon: Harvest House Publishers, 1984.